Dr. Manuel Pastor is a professor of sociology and American studies and ethnicity at the University of Southern California, where he also serves as director of the Program for Environmental and Regional Equity and co-director of USC's Center for the Study of Immigrant Integration. Dr. Pastor has received Guggenheim and Fulbright fellowships as well as the 2012 Wally Marks Changemaker of the Year award from the Liberty Hill Foundation in Los Angeles. He currently holds the Turpanjian Chair in Civil Society and Social Change at USC and lives in Los Angeles.

D1301592

STATE OF RESISTANCE

What California's Dizzying Descent and Remarkable Resurgence Mean for America's Future

MANUEL PASTOR

THE
NEW
PRESS

NEW YORK
LONDON

Requests for permission to reproduce selections from this book should be mailed to: Permissions Department, The New Press, 120 Wall Street, 31st floor, New York, NY 10005.

First published in the United States by The New Press, New York, 2018
This paperback edition published by The New Press, 2019
Distributed by Two Rivers Distribution

ISBN 978-1-62097-329-5 (hc)
ISBN 978-1-62097-557-2 (pb)
ISBN 978-1-62097-330-1 (e-book)
CIP data is available

The New Press publishes books that promote and enrich public discussion and understanding of the issues vital to our democracy and to a more equitable world. These books are made possible by the enthusiasm of our readers; the support of a committed group of donors, large and small; the collaboration of our many partners in the independent media and the not-for-profit sector; booksellers, who often hand-sell New Press books; librarians; and above all by our authors.

www.thenewpress.com

Composition by dix!
This book was set in Garamond Premier Pro

Printed in the United States of America

10 9 8 7 6 5 4 3 2 1

To my parents, Manuel and Alba Gil Pastor

CONTENTS

STATE OF RESISTANCE

1

AMERICA FAST-FORWARD

The 2016 election of Donald Trump brought a sense of triumph to some but a sense of shock to others. Questions were quickly raised that looked both backward and forward: What went awry with the polling? Did last-minute interventions by the FBI make a difference? Who might be first of the many groups to be targeted by the new administration and just how bad might it get? With fears rising and declarations of #NotMyPresident beginning to roil social media, failed Democratic candidate Hillary Clinton stepped before a podium the next day and gracefully conceded. Expressing her faith in the electoral process, she offered hope that Trump would be "a successful president for all Americans."[1]

The reaction from California was markedly different. On the same day that Clinton accepted the results came a dramatic statement from the heads of the California State Senate and California State Assembly, Kevin de León and Anthony Rendon, respectively. Expressing shock at the electoral turn of events and promising to challenge federal attempts to turn back progress on the environment, civil rights, and immigration, the two leaders concluded by writing that "we will not be dragged back into the past. We will lead the resistance to any effort that would shred our social fabric or our Constitution. California was not a part of this nation when its history began, but we are clearly now the keeper of its future."[2]

It was a rather remarkable declaration, not simply because a state so quickly and emphatically announced its rejection of the nation's choice for president but also because it was California doing it. After all, this was the state that had foreshadowed the rhetoric Trump adopted with its own 1994 embrace of Proposition 187, a ballot measure designed to strip "illegal immigrants" and their families of access to nearly all social services, including education for undocumented children. Indeed, in some ways, the United States in 2016 was going through its own Prop 187 moment: a Republican politician, behind his Democratic competitor in the polls, successfully stirred up support for his candidacy by bashing immigrants, particularly Mexicans.

What changed? How did the Golden State complete an arc from anti-immigrant fervor to a seeming embrace of all Californians? How did it shift from the capital of car culture and suburban sprawl to a leadership position in combating climate change? What was the path from leading the nation in mass incarceration to becoming "the first state to 'de-felonize' all drug use"?[3] What led California, a place where income inequality worsened faster and earlier than in the rest of the nation, to become one of the first states in the nation to adopt a $15 an hour minimum wage? And what does all this mean for the rest of the country and for the American future?

California Matters

Understanding both what happened and what will happen in California—and rooting this story in larger structural forces and long histories of civic change, not just political personalities—is certainly critical to the future of the Golden State. California may have moved from the crisis of division to a tentative state of repair, but "tentative" is the appropriate modifier: the state remains plagued by regional divisions, racial disparities, environmental challenges, and a desperate need to reboot the middle and shore up the bottom of the labor market. Addressing these issues will require creative policies as well as a new social compact that reflects the values, needs, and aspirations of all Californians. But while getting the state narrative right is an important part of that process, charting California's past, present, and future is also important for the United States as a whole. Because as much as those in the Midwest, the South, New England, and indeed any other part of the country may hate to hear it, the demographic, economic, and social trends reveal a simple truth: California is America fast-forward.

A state once known for its own California Dream, complete with abundant sunshine, plentiful jobs, and sprawling single-family homes, California is also the state where America seemed to first unmoor and unravel. Part of this was a dramatic and sometimes disorienting demographic change: California's ethnic makeup shifted dramatically between 1980 and 2000, with the non-Hispanic white share of the population falling from 67 percent to 47 percent. In the context of rapid Latino and Asian American/Pacific Islander growth—along with a profound process of deindustrialization that seemed to shake the foundations of the state's working and middle classes—an anti-immigrant fervor surged, finally culminating in the 1994 passage of Proposition 187.

Racialized conflicts were not limited to tensions about the newest Californians. With industrial employment shrinking, many turned to the relief that could be provided by drugs. Crack cocaine—a drug that soothed economic anxiety in that era in the same way that opiates do today—fueled the rise of militarized gangs that were, in turn, met by even more militarized police. In the late 1980s, Los Angeles police, years before the infamous 1992 beating of Black motorist Rodney King, were the proud owners of their own tank to batter down drug dens. Harassment was the order of the day; in one incident in 1988, nearly ninety officers broke open two apartment buildings, sprayed graffiti, detained nearly forty residents, and rendered nearly two dozen homeless without ever charging anyone with a crime.[4] Against this backdrop of police brutality, California's biggest city, Los Angeles, exploded into civil unrest in 1992, providing an early glimpse of the anger that would later drive protests in places like Ferguson and Baltimore and help to activate #BlackLivesMatter. With the streets in full disarray, the California public reacted with fear, passing laws that treated juveniles as adults, permanently locked up repeat offenders, and propelled explosive growth in the prison system.[5]

On the economic side, the Golden State saw yawning income gaps and stuttering growth. California moved from the middle of the inequality pack in 1969—when ranked against the rest of America's states—to a spot near the top of unequals today.[6] The reasons were complex and many, but in a foreshadowing of today's politics, many wanted to point the finger of blame at what seemed to be an obvious and socially vulnerable external factor: the influx of immigrants. But other structural forces were at play. During the recession period of the early 1990s, nearly half of the nation's net job loss occurred in California.[7] And while often unrecognized for its previous industrial might, California saw jobs in manufacturing of durable goods like cars, planes, and heavy equipment disappear almost as fast—by just under 20 percent—between 1990 and 1994 as they did in the 2007–10 recession period in auto-heavy Michigan.[8] As in the currently ailing Midwest, this slippage in manufacturing meant that traditional routes to the middle class were being obstructed—even as an emerging "new economy" in California swelled the ranks of professionals and the über-wealthy on one end, and the legions of working poor (frequently but not entirely immigrants) on the other.

Meanwhile, the social and political compacts that had once sustained the Golden State turned sour. This was a state made famous by its massive investments in infrastructure, including bringing water to an arid Southland and crisscrossing the landscape with superhighways that could move goods to market and people to employment. The investments were not only in physical capital: the 1960 Master Plan for Higher Education sought to guarantee that any capable California resident could obtain post-secondary instruction nearly cost-free and also helped to firm up a set of public research universities with significant positive spill-overs to industry. All of this reflected a sort of multigenerational commitment to the future; the Master Plan, for example, was adopted to accommodate a baby boom generation that was soon to graduate from high school and a set of businesses that wanted to stay constantly ahead of the technological curve.

Fast-forward a few decades and things were changing. Suburbanization had spread, feeding into a sort of social separation that led many Californians to see programs to benefit the poor as line items on their paychecks and not down payments on a better future. Increasing militancy in minority communities, including the rise of the Black Panther Party in Northern California and a vibrant Chicano movement in Southern California, fed into the fear that too many would want in on the compact that had made the state great—and such fears were stoked by a vibrant right-wing movement that cast strategies like fair housing as an attack on "property rights." Into the mix came Proposition 13, a 1978 measure that reversed property tax increases and then permanently limited their rate of increase, presaging a national tax-cutting fever that would be pushed along by former California Republican governor Ronald Reagan as he campaigned for the presidency. Education spending, which is one of the surest markers of an older generation investing in a younger generation, steadily slipped when measured against other states, and tuition began to skyrocket in the system of higher education. Mounting state debt, budgeting gimmicks to stave off a reckoning, and legislative deadlocks over revenues and expenditures became standard operating procedure as the state struggled to balance its books and sustain its future.

Fragmentation and political polarization became the order of the day. Rush Limbaugh began his talk radio career in Sacramento, and Republican governor Pete Wilson, once considered a political moderate based on his record as mayor of San Diego, decided to base his 1994 reelection campaign on drumming up concerns about undocumented immigrants. His main vehicle was Proposition 187, and both he and the ballot measure triumphed— suggesting that there might be political gold in the hills of suspicion and discord. Into the opening came what political scientist Daniel HoSang has called "racial propositions"—a series of ballot measures in the 1990s that sought to ban affirmative action, end bilingual education, and stiffen prison sentences for both juveniles and adults, disproportionately impacting men and boys of color.[9]

As the 2000s began, analysts as well as political and business leaders were bemoaning the state of the state, with one influential columnist heralding the new century with a book about California provocatively titled *Paradise Lost*.[10] In a sort of nearly complete trivialization of civic life, early in the ensuing decade, California voters recalled a governor they had just reelected, Democrat Gray Davis, and replaced him with a movie star action hero, Republican Arnold Schwarzenegger. By 2010, two keen observers of the state, Joe Mathews and Mark Paul, penned a pessimistic volume appropriately called *California Crackup*.[11]

Sound familiar? It should.

Consider that the United States will be a so-called majority-minority country before 2045. Indeed, the nation's demographic shift between 2000 and 2050 is a sort of slow-motion and nearly exact repeat of California's ethnic change between 1980 and 2000 (see Figure 1.1).[12] Concerns about the changing—and browning—face of the nation have contributed to the charged debates about immigration that helped to contribute to the Trump triumph, despite the fact that immigration into the country has stabilized, unauthorized immigration has almost entirely stalled, and the main factor leading to population growth and diversity in our future is the increase in native-born children.

Consider that American income inequality is nearly at an all-time high, driven by the shrewd manipulations of the top 1 percent

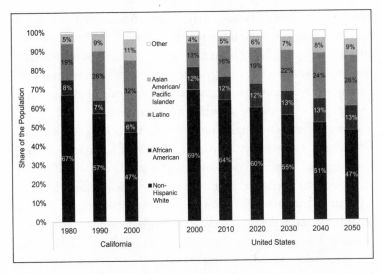

FIGURE 1.1: Actual and projected demographic change in California, 1980–2000, and the United States, 2000–2050.

as well as by a steadily rising rift between those just below the top—highly educated and technically savvy professionals—and those whose lack of education leaves them at the bottom of the labor market. Meanwhile, as has already happened in California, large swaths of the manufacturing system that helped working-class people become middle-class seem to be dressed in permanent mothballs. In echoes of the crack crisis that ravaged hard-hit Black communities in the 1980s and 1990s, part of the result has been an epidemic of drug use, in this case, the widespread use of opioids, particularly among those white workers who have been sidelined by the economy. The impacts have been profound: deaths from drug overdoses are now the leading cause of injury death in the United States.[13]

Consider further that the polarization and paralysis that plagued California seem to have become an accepted part of our political system. States and counties now tend to be firmly red or blue, and media outlets now "narrowcast" to a viewership that prefers its facts aligned and often rearranged to suit preconceived perspectives. With a Republican grip on the White House as well as the Senate and the House of Representatives, Congress may soon emerge from a season of indecision to an embrace of ideology. Deciding to not decide—or bending all decisions so that they reflect just one viewpoint—might not be a problem if little was at stake. But it's just the reverse, as there is a series of key questions confronting the nation: How do we cope with demographic change in a way that invites accommodation and not conflict? How do we address the sharp rise in income inequality and create a firmer basis for sustained job growth? How do we address big, complex issues such as persistent educational disparities, racialized policing practices, and impending climate change?

An answer may come from California, a state where there was a fall from grace and where there is now a rise from the ashes. For if California is America fast-forward in terms of pointing to the decline, perhaps the turn in state fortunes may help us get a handle on the national challenges ahead. After all, a funny thing happened on the way to the state's long-presumed disaster: California stopped skidding and began to turn around. Its deficits shifted to surpluses, its economy began to boast growth rates above those of the nation, and its voters raised taxes on themselves several times in order to heal the budget woes.[14] Public policy is finally turning to the issues of income distribution, with the state extending an income tax increase on the wealthy, raising its minimum wage in dramatic fashion, and shifting public school spending to students most in need.

California's discomfort about undocumented immigrants has likewise given way to a realization that this population is actually long settled in the state, with far more than half having been in the country for ten years or longer. Even before the rise of Trump, the state had largely ceased cooperating with federal immigration authorities on most police matters and had extended driving privileges to the undocumented and health insurance to their children—a triumph of common sense over the previous symbolic politics of denial. Meanwhile, the state has led on addressing climate change, the ultimate symbol of a multigenerational commitment, including putting in place strict targets to reduce greenhouse gas emissions and a cap-and-trade system in which emitters not able to meet the targets essentially pay others to do so. This has been accompanied by a commitment to invest at least a fourth of the revenues from that system in communities that are environmentally overexposed and socially vulnerable, a nod to the possibility of going green *and* growing just.

Moreover, those who declared a sort of generational warfare through Prop 13—the measure that rolled back assessments and limited tax increases on those who already owned homes and shifted the burden onto those still to buy—are now waving the white flag or, perhaps more accurately, being defeated at the polls. After decades of budgetary straitjackets created by Prop 13, including supermajority requirements for raising taxes that gave conservative Republican lawmakers a kind of veto power over state spending, voters have started loosening Prop 13's ties. New rules allow the budget to be passed by a simple majority, helping to limit the power of recalcitrant conservative legislators; meanwhile, voters approved temporarily raising taxes on the wealthy in 2012 and then extended those taxes for an additional twelve years in 2016. And since the real secret of Prop 13 is that, like many right-wing populist measures, its biggest beneficiaries were the wealthy and corporations, hard-nosed campaigns are under way to make public that fact and update the way that commercial and industrial real estate are assessed.

It's not all roses; there are clear risks ahead and a bevy of naysayers. Among the most prominent has been Joel Kotkin, an important urbanist who has argued that what has evolved in contemporary California is a sort of new liberal gentry whose wild-eyed environmentalism will complete the collapse of manufacturing, derail the possibility of suburban expansion, and dash the aspirations of millions.[15] For Kotkin, Texas and its less regulated and more sprawling economic and residential landscape represents the future; the triumph of "progressive" politics and policies in California will not lead to a restoration of its version of the American Dream but will rather trigger its final denouement.

Such pessimism is belied by key facts, trends, and possibilities; what we have now are the seeds of a new state in the making. The risks are real—the neglect of inland California, the damaging displacement caused by gentrification on the coast, and the slack middle of the labor market are all causes for concern (for a map of California, see Figure 1.2). But there will always be such battles when change is ongoing, and fretting about challenges can obscure the key questions ahead for both California and America. Among these: What happened to bring the state to its senses? Where does it need to go next to consolidate gains and create opportunity? And what does all this mean for a nation still seemingly convulsed by the issues and tensions that wracked the Golden State just a few decades ago?

Why Now?

For conservatives, California is often thought of as a cautionary tale, what can happen if you have too much diversity, too many hot tubs, and too many voters leaning in on the liberal end of the political spectrum. But if you play the tale all the way out—from its midcentury success to the decline suffered at the end of the last century to the resurgence stirring now—it may be not as much a warning as a sign of hope that the current national craziness will end—although not without inflicting substantial pain along the way. After all, the national spasms resulting from demographic

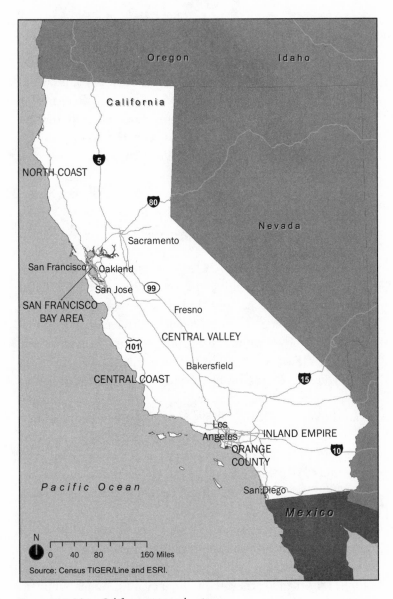

FIGURE 1.2: Major California cities and regions.

change, rising inequality, and political polarization may be causing headaches and mood swings now, but the view from the other
side of the cycle is not all that bad: California's economy is on the
mend (although more for some than for others), discourse is sur-
prisingly civil, and there are still too many hot tubs. Recognizing
that immigrants settle in, that economic shocks sort out, that environmental action does not sink jobs, and that raising taxes on
the wealthy does not stunt growth is key to assuaging national
anxieties about the challenges ahead.

This is particularly important because one of the key factors
behind California's stabilization is likely to take time for the nation: the slowed pace of demographic change. In California, the
share of foreign born is on the decline, and the state's largest metro
area—Los Angeles—is the only large U.S. metro that did not see
an increase in Hispanic children between 2000 and 2010.[16] Perhaps most significant has been the shift in what might be termed
a "racial generation gap"—the difference between an older population that is mostly white and a youth population that is mostly
kids of color. Such a gap can be both measured and tracked over
time: Figure 1.3 charts this by showing the percentage of seniors
who are white and the percentage of youths who are white between the years 1970 and 2015.[17] Note that the widening difference between the two lines—the racial generation gap—occurred
in the years of California's maximal political turmoil (from 1970
to the mid-1990s). Since then, the gap has stabilized and has begun to decline—and with that has come a diminishment in racialized state politics as well.

Why is it important to think about the age chasm? Research
suggests that the racial generation gap can lead to social distance
between generations—with the old not seeing themselves in the
young—that then lowers voter willingness to consider public investments, including in public education.[18] That certainly seems to
fit the California pattern—both the long period of disinvestment

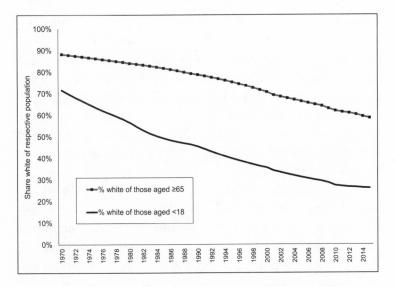

Share white of respective population

- ■ % white of those aged ≥65
- —% white of those aged <18

FIGURE 1.3: Racial generation gap in California, 1970–2015.

sparked by Prop 13 and now the sudden turn to thinking we may just be in it all together. But simply hoping that disgruntled white voters will just naturally age out or wise up is not exactly a fix. Instead, we must be honest about and address the generational disconnect in order to create bridges to a new social contract.[19] And we need to do that quickly: California's decades of conflict need not be half a century of slow-paced agony for the rest of the country. A dash of rules change, a bit of attitude change, and a clear commitment to common ground can help others avoid wasted energy spent on ultimately futile political conflicts.

Of course, to get there, we have to understand what is really behind California's comeback. One popular account focuses on the return of Democrat Jerry Brown, a former governor who presided over the beginnings of the decline and is now presiding over the beginnings of the renaissance. The emphasis on a key individual feeds into a common and tempting American misperception: that a singular hero can symbolize and actually explain the drama. It is true that Brown brought a certain fiscal probity as well as a fierce commitment to addressing climate change; moreover, his shift from spacey to sage, from saboteur to savior, makes for a neat redemption story. But such a tale is incomplete and misleading, not only because it leaves out the broader forces that drive history but also because it ignores the multiple actors who have also played their roles, especially those associated with California's sophisticated social movements.

What were these broader forces? Demography played a role—a higher share of people of color helped to tilt the state left—but demography was not necessarily destiny. As Roger Kim, former executive director of the Asian Pacific Environmental Network, notes, "Yes, demographic change can work in our favor but you have to do the hard work of investing in the infrastructure to make it so. . . . California doesn't look like this by chance; there was an incredible amount of work that went in."[20] Actually mobilizing that population required campaigns to naturalize immigrants threatened by California's anti-immigrant mood swing as well as broader efforts to develop new leadership and generate enthusiasm among infrequent voters who might be upset about the racialized attacks on affirmative action, the dramatic increase in incarceration, and the widening divides by income.

The economy played a role as well. Deindustrialization helped to create a large mass of the working poor, but this actually triggered public sympathies and facilitated city and county campaigns for a "living wage." The shift from older industries to high tech gave rise to business leaders generally more liberal in their leanings, more open in their attitudes, and more likely to see a role for government in, say, addressing climate change or promoting green industries. Emerging research helped to facilitate a growing civic consensus that high levels of inequality were actually corrosive to economic stability as well as democratic governance.[21] And the combination of demographic, economic, and political trends produced support for a more concerted effort to address the state's opportunity gaps: in 2013, California passed something called the Local Control Funding Formula, an effort to ensure that more educational resources flowed to the poorest children in the state's public school systems, and in 2016, California was also among the first states to adopt a plan to raise its minimum wage to $15 an hour.

California is also beginning to reinvest in twenty-first-century infrastructure, including efforts to connect the state via high-speed rail, to shepherd in an era of mass transit in urban Los Angeles, and to rework the state's busy ports to reduce their impact on climate and air pollution. California's larger cities, once the arenas of economic distress and civil unrest, are staging a comeback as a new "creative class" seeks to agglomerate near urban amenities; in a sort of "be careful what you wish for" moment, city planners and advocates for low-income residents who once worried about disinvestment and neighborhood decline now find themselves struggling against the displacement caused by gentrification.

Shifts in the political rules of the game have been essential as well. In 2008, the drawing of electoral districts for state and national offices was removed from the hands of the legislature and is now done by a citizen commission; in 2010, the state's budgeting rules were changed so that an expenditure plan can pass with a simple majority rather than a two-thirds supermajority, a rule that gave small blocks of conservative legislators maximum leverage; and in 2012, the regulations governing term limits for state officeholders were changed such that California's legislative leaders are not constantly thinking of their next electoral move and have more capacity and time to strategize and govern.

All these demographic, economic, and political trends help explain the turnaround, but another key part of the California comeback—one left aside by most writers and analysts—has been the role of social movements in shifting the underlying political calculus. As noted earlier, organizers did not assume that demography itself would bring change; movement builders were intentional about amplifying the voice of the new majority. The state has become a hotbed of movements for decent wages, immigrant rights, racial equity, and environmental justice. So rather than what we saw in D.C. through the administration of Barack Obama—in which a moderately progressive president found himself unable to accomplish his agenda as the grassroots excitement of his presidential campaign fizzled and the red-hot heat of Tea Party activism shifted the dynamic—change in California was propelled by a buzzing band of organizers who pushed for a more inclusive and more sustainable state.

Indeed, the state's ability to achieve fiscal balance with new taxes on the wealthy was actually an idea prompted by movement activists who dragged the political establishment left—and utilized a new form of "integrated voter engagement" that combined community organizing with voter mobilization to flex the political muscle that made it happen. A more pro-immigrant set of state policies evolved partly because of concerted lobbying by immigrant rights activists, with their victory partly symbolized when Kevin de León, a former organizer who cut his teeth protesting Proposition 187, became president pro tem of the senate. And recent successes in pushing state ballot propositions to reduce sentences and shrink the prison population were secured by advocates who had the guts to ask voters for support in a nonpresidential election, believing (rightly) that they could motivate new and occasional voters to the polls—that is, craft a younger and more minority electorate—even without the usual presidential lure at the top of the ticket.

Omitting movements from the picture—and focusing just on a septuagenarian governor or even the economic and political rules of the game—will leave you with a story that is one step short. Policy change does not always start in the halls of state or local legislatures but rather in the streets, workplaces, and voting booths, where power is contested. Movements are not everything—the shifting preferences of the business class and ways in which politicians respond to changing incentives are also key. But understanding the strategic choices of California's organizers is critical to understanding the evolution of the state and can also help others in the United States understand the need for and nature of grassroots work in an era of reaction. In short, while Americans are normally tempted to think that what matters is the right person—that Obama could magically save us from our own divisions or that Trump alone can make the difference between decline and recovery—it is really the right collective capacities and alliances that are needed to drive change and make it stick.

Understanding the need for continued mobilization and policy change is also key to future progress in the Golden State. Californians are a bit like the person who finds sobriety after a long period of addiction: amends are important but just a starting point to undoing all the damage caused along the way. Saying you are sorry that you starved the state in order to lower taxes does not restore the education that was denied a generation. Feeling sheepish about ignoring racial disparity and banning affirmative action does not address the frightening gaps in college completion for Latinos and African Americans. Being shamefaced about excessive sentencing, overincarceration, and rampant prison construction has little impact unless you now choose to exhibit a commitment to effective reentry programs. And expressing embarrassment about our overreliance on autos is more convincing if you also double down on efforts to address greenhouse gas emissions.

The state will therefore need to both lead the nation and heal itself. Politicians and corporate leaders will need to speak with and work with labor organizers addressing inadequate pay and a shrinking middle class, environmental advocates pressing to hold the line on air quality, and undocumented immigrants who cannot vote but who nonetheless can and do lobby elected officials. It is in the rebalancing of forces that a new and more sustainable state can be crafted—and this will be important for America not only because California can model what the nation can become but also because it may wind up being one of the last lines of defense for the majority of Americans who did not vote for a President Trump.

Addressing the federal government's abandonment of leadership in confronting climate change, Governor Brown vowed in December 2016 that "if Trump turns off the satellites, California will launch its own damn satellite." [22] Meanwhile, many of the state's high-tech coders, engineers, and executives have vowed to not contribute to the building of a Muslim registry or to any efforts that could lead to mass deportation. [23] And while the pro–"law and order" speechifying of Donald Trump has led many in the Black community to worry about the unleashing of state violence in their neighborhoods, California cities continue to try to make progress on improving relationships between communities and police.

So California is in a state of resistance—but the task ahead will be not just to defend but also to develop and deploy. The state can illustrate what the nation could gain if it drops the anti-immigrant sentiment, confronts the reality of climate change, and works together to address income inequality; because of this, the Golden State needs to get it right. California will also need to spread the message in ways both symbolic and concrete, including working to export good policy today as much as it exported bad policy in the past, and sharing some of the evolving models of integrated voter engagement that have better aligned movements and politicians.

Telling the Story

State of Resistance seeks to illuminate the California story, ensure that it is told correctly and completely, and draw lessons for what is ahead. In order to do that, I organize our tale in terms of an arc that charts the rise, fall, and rise of the Golden State. I could begin almost anywhere in the state's history—from the indigenous residents, or the Mexican arrivals, or the gold rush miners and financiers, or the railroad lines that connected the state to the rest of America. My start is more relevant to understanding the lessons for the contemporary period: after setting a bit of a historical stage, I focus on the California of the 1950s and early 1960s, a place known for its discrimination and inequality to be sure, but also one that could rightly boast of being a platform for opportunity.

I argue that the state's strong and interwoven base—a vibrant economy, a growing housing stock, thriving educational institutions, and seemingly well-functioning political systems—was rooted in a social compact that saw the need to welcome new arrivals and invest in future generations. It all broke down as economic growth faltered and communities of color tried to get a more meaningful piece of the action—essentially, racism got the better of the state and led it to shortchange its own future. But neither the descent nor the resurgence were due to chance: I point to a vibrant set of right-wing social movements for the former and progressive social movements for the latter, and argue that each acted effectively on a stage that had been set by larger structural forces.

Of course, the real world is frequently a bit messier than the historical arcs or analytical frameworks that seek to massage it into digestible and understandable parts. Economic and fiscal issues both affect and are affected by the political rules of the game; demographic changes set the context for political alliances, especially whom they will include and how much work will be required to sustain them; and business leaders are frequently not on the same page as workers and communities about where a state or a nation should head. Yet the central point is that the real secret to California's once and future success was exactly its agreement on a social compact in which the public and private sectors worked to create paths upward for both those who were in the state and those who were to come.

Restoring that sense of common ground is critical for California's tomorrow. State politics have indeed shifted: traditional environmentalists have now bought into the importance of climate justice, at least some of the state's billionaires are concerned about inequality, and so-called minority activists are bringing into fuller engagement those swing constituencies of color that determine elections. But if the state wants a progressive and inclusive future, it will also need to define a clearer set of public policies. It will need to fix a housing crisis that is displacing the working class from their communities in urban centers in California. It will need to go beyond celebrating its new embrace of immigrants— and fortify an educational system that will allow the children of immigrants to thrive. It will need to make further progress on de-incarceration and police-community relations and commit to a broader agenda to advance the state's Black communities. And it will need to firmly move beyond car culture and work to strengthen climate policies designed to protect the planet and shore up vulnerable populations.

Whether the Golden State gets this right matters not only for Californians but for the nation as a whole. California's negative politics have often spilled over, including tax cuts that became part of the contemporary Republican mantra as well as anti-immigrant politics that poisoned places like Arizona and Alabama. America now looks like California at its lowest point: wracked by racial tension, anxious about its economic future, and willing to follow leaders with simplistic solutions. The country needs resistance, to be sure, but it also needs a vision of what America can become.

In that context, California needs not just to hold the line against reactionary forces but also to make progress on its own challenges, share forward-looking policies, insist on the primacy of movement organizing, and hope that other states are willing to listen. The Golden State went through its winter of discontent—and the nation seems poised for its own dark season. Having often led America in business and technology, demography and fashion, culture and contention, California now has the opportunity—and responsibility—to lead with examples of new coalitions and innovative policies for justice, opportunity, and a shared and sustainable future.

2

FROM DREAM TO DRAG

In 1996, UCLA professor David Hayes-Bautista co-authored an op-ed in the *Los Angeles Times* with a rather compelling and somewhat frightening premise. What, he asked, could a state possibly do to make progress when it found itself host to a "population group that had a 25 percent poverty rate, a 50 percent chance of not completing high school, barely 9 percent of whom were college graduates and over half of whom arrived in California only recently?"[1] For most readers in the 1990s, the immediate evocation was of a California awash in Mexican and Central American arrivals, a state looking backward at its best years and looking forward to inevitable decline. The echoes today are clear: the appeal of "Build the Wall" in the last presidential election was based partly on a notion that the numbers are too large and the immigrants too different to be successfully integrated.

As it turns out, the underskilled and recently amassed population Hayes-Bautista was describing was not the Latino masses of the 1990s but the Anglo migrants present in California in 1950. Many had streamed in across state borders to flee economic dislocation in the Great Plains as a combination of the Great Depression and the Dust Bowl created an influx of desperate, willing-to-work white migrants in California, much like the Mexican debt crisis and the Central American civil wars would do for Latinos generations later. The result was a state hosting a population that was undereducated and seemingly underequipped for a modern economy. Yet just a few decades later, California's economy was booming, education levels were rising, and a mass expansion of public education and suburbia had taken a heterogeneous mix of newcomers and transformed them into an eager and committed group of homeowners.

How did the state move from what many worried was the potential abyss of the postwar epoch—so many migrants and so few resources—to a broad swath of the public living out the California Dream? It might seem convenient to tell a story based on hard work, strong culture, and the magic of the market—that is, a vision in which the newcomers are their own heroes and their own reason for success—but such a tale would be misleading. For what instead seems to have allowed so many to achieve their individual dreams was not just their own efforts but also a broader collective commitment to public investments that made industry, higher education, and suburbia happen.

Indeed, California in the 1950s and 1960s was precisely the sort of demonstration project for an active government that many conservatives seem to fear at a national level. It was a golden era for the Golden State, driven by a bipartisan commitment to good governance, public investment, and the expansion of educational opportunity. Not all was perfect and certainly not all was inclusive: the state remained wracked by racial divisions, including active housing discrimination and sharp gaps in education access. Indeed, before the 1954 *Brown v. Board of Education* decision that desegregated schools nationwide, *Mendez v. Westminster* in 1947 successfully challenged the separation of Mexican American students in Orange County. But despite the racial gaps, California was the place to be, even for minority groups that joined the wave of migrants during World War II. By 1962, it was the nation's most populous state, a position it continues to hold today.[2]

By the 1970s, however, the state seemed frayed: wracked by social and political conflict and beset by anxiety about the transformations, particularly demographic, that had seemed so central to its welcoming character. While the economy continued to grow, hints of industrial weakness were appearing and a suburban-based tax revolt essentially began the defunding of the very government that had bred success.[3] By the 1990s, the full scale of the crisis would become apparent: dream turned to drag and then to dysfunction. While some of this was due to bad decisions by political elites—particularly about how to promote or resist integration and how to ease growing fiscal pressures—beneath it all was a troubled populace fueling a right-wing social movement that changed the politics of the social compact that had characterized the Golden State's golden era.

America feels, of course, at a similar crossroads. Against a backdrop of economic uncertainty and changing demographics, conservatives have staged a long march to national political influence. While their talk is frequently dressed up in the language of opportunity, it often feels like their main point is to lift up the drawbridge just as new people are arriving: they want a federal government that made mass homeownership and higher education possible for a generation of baby boomers and their parents to instead slash revenues and services for newcomers being born, crossing our borders, or trying to break free of structural discrimination. Understanding how the Golden State ripped itself apart— how its own residents allowed their racism and economic pain to promote shortsighted policy—will be key to challenging that perspective in years to come.

The Rise of California

California has always been a magnet for migrants filled with hope and ambition. From the gold rush of the late 1840s and early 1850s to the "booster" period associated with the great transcontinental railroads, the real estate frenzy and nascent suburbanization of the early twentieth century, and the economic explosion of wartime production in the 1940s, California was widely known by the middle of the last century as the place to come and remake yourself. Indeed, Hollywood captured this dreaming mentality and exported it to a world eager to consume the fantasy.

California's commitment to infrastructure was the platform required for such reinvention. For example, creating reliable supplies of water was key to turning arid lands into agriculture paradises *and* fueling urban growth. By 1901, engineers had already diverted the Colorado River to flood an area named the Salton Sink, leading to its renaming as the Imperial Valley and its subsequent rise as a major agricultural producer, particularly of winter vegetables.[4] By 1913, the infamous William Mulholland had engineered the completion of an aqueduct that took water from the Owens Valley and diverted it to quench the thirst of a growing Los Angeles—facilitating suburban growth in the San Fernando Valley, triggering the city's annexation of this area, and implicating developers and city officials in a murky web of interconnections that would later give rise to the noir film *Chinatown*.[5]

In keeping with the spirit of bending nature to political will, the City of Los Angeles annexed the sleepy harbor of San Pedro and transformed it into a port complex that is now the leading entry point in the United States in terms of volume and value of imports. Partly as a result of these huge public investments, the economic and population dynamism once associated with San Francisco—which benefited mightily as a financial center for the gold rush—drifted south to Los Angeles through the early part of the twentieth century. Industries beyond the usual real estate, agriculture, and entertainment specialties associated with the Southland boomed: by the end of the 1920s, Los Angeles lagged behind only Akron, Ohio, in tire production and Detroit, Michigan, in auto production, an outcome driven by high local demand in L.A.—where cars were king—but also made possible only by an extraordinary system of rail transport that delivered the inputs for final vehicle assembly.[6]

Infrastructure was seen as so essential—so much a part of

fortifying the state's economic DNA—that investment in its expansion continued even during the economically strained years of
the Great Depression. The Arroyo Seco Parkway, the Los Angeles–
to–Pasadena roadway that was the precursor to the modern freeway, was completed in 1940. The iconic Golden Gate Bridge was
built between 1933 and 1937, with the Bay Bridge that spans
Oakland to San Francisco completed in 1936. The Boulder Dam,
now known as Hoover Dam, was completed in 1935, leading to
a flow of energy and water that would help to position Southern
California as an ideal site for defense manufacturing during the
war. The national economy may have been slow, but state spending
on infrastructure for the future was brisk.

While the Great Depression might not have delayed the expansion of the state's physical infrastructure, it did lead to other
changes, including a significant demographic shift and the evolution of a viciously right-wing streak in California politics. Interestingly, the state saw a decline in the share of the population that
was Mexican, mostly because concerns about immigrant competition for employment led to a campaign for mass deportation that
wound up snagging not just the foreign-born but also native-born
U.S. citizens.[7] Nonetheless, California saw a wave of another sort
of migrants: poor whites fleeing drought and economic slowdown
in Texas, Arkansas, and Oklahoma, with many flooding the agricultural labor markets of the Central Valley, as vividly depicted
in Steinbeck's *Grapes of Wrath*.[8] The state's preexisting white
population, mostly of Midwest stock, tended to look down at the
newcomers as unwashed masses not truly capable of integration,
a sentiment that would be echoed later in the 1980s and 1990s
for Latin American arrivals, and is currently claimed about immigrants and refugees across the nation.

With the new low-skill arrivals following the harvest, often
taking the place of departed Mexicans or competing with those
who remained, agricultural wages plummeted, falling by nearly
half between 1930 and 1933.[9] Living conditions were poor,

characterized by grueling work, poor nutrition, child labor, and substandard housing.[10] Farmers banded together to suppress the labor strikes that inequality provoked, with one key battle occurring in the San Joaquin Valley in 1933 when roughly eighteen thousand cotton pickers went on strike and were met with grower-organized vigilante violence. Federal labor authorities, worried about the ripple effects on both production and social peace, intervened to settle the conflict and began developing a series of migrant camps to at least address the housing side of the desperation in the fields.[11]

As Kathryn Olmstead notes in *Right Out of California: The 1930s and the Big Business Roots of Modern Conservatism*, this series of conflicts in agriculture facilitated the evolution of a particularly virulent and nativist right-wing element in California politics. California had long had its conservative streak; while there was a strong labor presence in the Bay Area, exemplified by the militancy of the International Longshoremen's Association, headed by storied labor leader Harry Bridges, Los Angeles in the early twentieth century was better known for the anti-labor attitudes and actions of its business elite and their media mouthpiece, the *Los Angeles Times*.[12] But the struggle of the 1930s had all the elements for making a modern version of conservatism that might be recognizable today: growers were enraged by the federal government's attempt to limit their right to exploit workers; alarmed by the racial mixing occurring under the banner of labor organizing; firmly convinced that all claims for justice were the result of communist provocation; and willing to dress up this toxic stew in the language of local control and traditional values.[13]

The Second World War brought pain and dislocation to the state and the country, including to mainland Japanese American families that were removed from their homes and incarcerated in far-off locales. At the same time, the war generated tremendous economic growth in California. With water and power at the ready, ports positioned to send products, and a labor force that could be tapped from the state's agricultural industry as well as attracted from the rest of the country, defense manufacturing took off. Shipyards churned out military vessels at breakneck pace and airplane production soared, with 60 percent of federal wartime spending on manufactured goods in California devoted to aircraft production.[14] The resulting labor gaps in agriculture were filled by a "bracero" program, established in 1942, which brought in Mexican guest workers, and the remaining shortages in the manufacturing labor force were plugged by a combination of women moving into nontraditional employment and African Americans escaping the Jim Crow South for new industrial employment.[15]

Between 1940 and 1944, total nonfarm employment in California increased by more than 61 percent, over twice the pace of job growth in the rest of the United States.[16] Perhaps unsurprisingly, this led to a further influx of residents into the state in the 1940s: between 1940 and 1950, a period that captured both the wartime lure and an immediate postwar in-migration, particularly of veterans seeking a better life, California's population swelled by more than 53 percent, more than any other state in the Union.[17] While California's share of the national population was on a steady uptick throughout virtually all of the twentieth century, the increase in that share was particularly sharp in the 1940s and then the 1950s, with both decades offering a nearly 2-percentage-point increase in the share of all Americans choosing California as their home (see Figure 2.1).[18] With the wartime boom and its postwar aftermath, the phrase "Go west, young man" had acquired new meaning: achieving the American Dream increasingly began to mean making it in the Golden State.

Incorporating these new migrants and residents was a key challenge, but as Harvard historian Matthew Hersch noted, it was met by "commitments by federal [and] state leaders and private businesses to expand local housing, education, utility, and transportation infrastructures."[19] A key state figure leading the way was Governor Earl Warren, a Republican who was elected in 1942

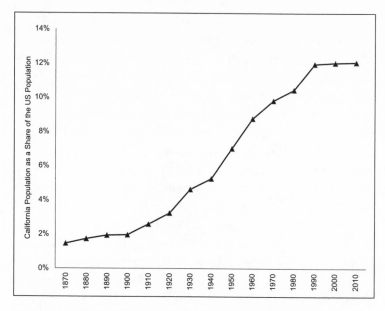

FIGURE 2.1: California population as a share of U.S. population, 1870–2010.

just as California was to experience its defense-driven population boom.[20] Reflecting the state politics of the time, he was resolutely bipartisan, nearly triumphing in the Democratic as well as the Republican primary in 1942 (California's system allowed for cross-filing).[21] The bipartisan support may now seem just a bit quaint in retrospect—and it certainly differs from today's national cacophonous reality and from the partisan trench warfare that would evolve later in California's history. But both the multiparty support and the cross-filing rules that made it possible were a product of the state's political culture, itself partly due to Progressive-era reforms, in which great value was attached to those trying to find the middle ground.

The reign of Earl Warren, from 1943 to 1953—the longest consecutive run of any California governor—certainly typified this straight-up-the-middle approach, and his administration paralleled and propelled the rise of California. Once again, the commitment to infrastructure was key. Even as his term began, he promoted Charles Purcell, the chief engineer behind the Bay Bridge, to the role of state public works director and asked him to develop a master plan for a new state highway system, one that would eventually intersect with the emerging interstate system and set the stage for postwar development. Meanwhile, the economy was pushed along by defense spending, not just during World War II but also as America slipped into a cold war with the Soviet Union and a hot war on the Korean peninsula.

Over the 1950s, national defense spending rose by 246 percent, with one-quarter of all defense contracts going to California, well above its 7 percent share of the national population as that decade began.[22] The aviation industry, now producing missiles as well as planes, thrived, and the new influx of workers—as well as veterans either returning after the war or attracted by the sunny climes of California—helped to drive an immense expansion of suburbia. An emerging system of roads and highways, funded by the state and then helped along in the late 1950s by the National Interstate and Defense Highways Act, literally paved the way for the new sprawl. But it wasn't just enhanced mobility that made suburbs possible: there was also a combination of federal incentives, including government-guaranteed loans and tax breaks on mortgage interest, that contributed to the new spatial arrangements.[23]

This nascent metropolitan landscape was inscribed on and extended a preexisting system of "industrial suburbs" such as South Gate in Southern California and San Leandro in Northern California.[24] South Gate was paradigmatic: crafted early in the twentieth century and perfected in the aftermath of the war, it offered small but workable homes for those employed in mass manufacturing.[25] Adjacent to employment but with lawns that evoked visions of a pastoral life, South Gate and its soon-to-be imitators were accompanied by more upscale suburbs intended to house the more highly educated professionals laboring in the defense industry. They were often side by side—in Southern California, for example, aerospace engineers lived in Manhattan Beach while aviation assembly workers resided in nearby Lawndale. Both the upscale and midscale suburbs were united, however, by their common commitment to excluding African Americans and other people of color from the good life that whites sought and the suburbs seemed to embody.

Warren presided over this early ascendancy of the postwar state, and in the words of the dean of California historians, Kevin Starr, he "served the aspirations of its burgeoning middle class."[26] He was, however, plucked away from the governorship to become chief justice of the Supreme Court in 1953 and was succeeded by Goodwin Knight, a moderate Republican who continued the thrust on infrastructure, including the creation of a single Department of Water Resources and the further development of California's freeway system. While he was easily reelected to his own full term in 1954, Knight turned out to be a bit of a historical blip: much of what he carried out had been put in place or given momentum by Warren, and he seemed to more or less leave the state as he inherited it. Caught up by internecine battles within his own Republican Party, he was "persuaded" to forgo reelection as governor in 1958 and instead ran for an open Senate seat—which he lost.

The California Compact

The next California governor of real consequence was Democrat Edmund G. "Pat" Brown. Previously the state's attorney general, Brown hit the gubernatorial ground running, proposing bans in racial discrimination in hiring, seeking to expand medical care for the poor, and pushing for a state minimum wage, a measure that ran into a buzz saw of opposition from right-wing forces in agriculture.[27] Still, Brown managed to sign more than a thousand bills in his first legislative session, including aid to schools and state-funded health care for poor and disabled people, safety regulations, standards for air quality and pollution, increases in unemployment insurance, improvements in workers' compensation, and pay raises for state workers—all funded by the largest California tax increase in a quarter century.[28]

Most important: Brown sought to take the earlier investments in physical infrastructure and supplement them with investments in public education. Building on the California Water Plan (1957) and The California Freeway System (1958), both of which facilitated suburbanization and economic growth, Brown pursued a Master Plan for Higher Education (1960). The basic idea of the Master Plan was to combine and coordinate three systems: the University of California, which would continue to focus on research and postgraduate education; the California State Colleges (now called the California State University) system, which would largely provide BAs and be less selective; and the California Community Colleges system, which would be open to nearly all, providing a pipeline to the other parts of the triad as well as offering vocational and paraprofessional training, and eventually playing an important role in workforce development.

What the adoption of the Master Plan codified was the belief that the real way to sustain California's growth over time was not just by investing in roads, waterways, and ports—the current focus of many infrastructure proposals in contemporary Washington— but also by investing in people. Over the course of his governorship, Brown went beyond words and doubled state spending on the university system and tripled it on the state college system, lifting California's college attendance rates well above the national average at the time.[29] By the early 1960s, "half of California's high school graduates were going to college, compared to an average of about one-third in the rest of the nation."[30] By 1970, California was the second-most educated state in the United States, based on the percentage of working-age adults having completed at least two years of college, perhaps the most appropriate benchmark given California's emphasis on the community college system as part of the educational strategy.[31]

Even as California improved its physical infrastructure and human capital, it sought to address the challenges wrought by success. With California accounting for nearly 20 percent of net job creation in the United States between 1950 and 1963, the state faced pressures to provide both public services and private housing.[32] While handling sharp increases in population and employment may seem like a rather pleasant problem to tackle, particularly in light of the nation's recent experience with job shortfalls and shrinking revenues in the wake of the Great Recession, it presented its own problems, particularly with regard to needed revenues. One way in which costs were contained: not everyone was included implicitly or explicitly in the emerging California system of public investment, economic opportunity, and educational access.

This was typical of postwar America. As Ira Katznelson has argued in his provocatively titled volume, *When Affirmative Action Was White*, many of the benefits of the New Deal, including Social Security, federal loan guarantees, and higher education, were largely confined to whites.[33] Whites were also disproportionately represented in the "good" jobs—offered by major corporations and regulated by strong unions—that characterized the sort of "golden age" of U.S. capitalism between 1945 and the 1970s.[34] Race was, in fact, central to managing growth; the economic system could not accommodate all comers and so exclusion was part of the recipe.

California's suburbs, for example, were highly segregated even as they were being rewarded with new schools, new roads, and even federal and state largess.[35] One illustrative example was Lakewood in Southern California, a development that sprung up in the early 1950s and mirrored the more famous Levittown in its assembly-style mass production of homes. Lakewood was financed in ways that were "symptomatic of postwar conditions.

The federal government provided 100 percent financing ($100 million in construction loans and mortgage guarantees) for construction under Section 213 of the National Housing Act, an obscure provision that allowed the federal government directly to subsidize cooperative housing ventures. Once the homes were sold, however, the cooperatives dissolved, and the banks owned the property."[36] The residents left in place, having benefited from governmental assistance, were almost entirely white.

This was, of course, part of a long-standing legacy for the "industrial suburbs"; in the 1930 and 1940 censuses, the city of South Gate in Los Angeles County had only two Black residents out of more than 25,000, with the local property association explicitly endorsing racially restrictive covenants as a way to preserve property values.[37] While racially restrictive covenants were formally ruled illegal by the Supreme Court in 1948, racially restrictive practices remained commonplace in both California and the nation. For example, the Los Angeles Real Estate Board refused to sell homes to Black families in white neighborhoods, or to admit Black members—which, in effect, stripped or at least limited many Black veterans from benefiting from the wealth-building potential of the postwar GI Bill.[38] The racial dividing line was occasionally reinforced by violence: in Southern California's San Fernando Valley, the suburban paradise made possible by the Owens Valley water grab, white homeowners waged campaigns intimidating and harassing people of color, including vandalizing their homes and posting a sign that stated "Black Cancer here. Don't let it spread!"[39]

In Northern California, Daniel HoSang notes that "according to one estimate, of the 350,000 new homes constructed in Northern California between 1946 and 1960 with FHA support, less than 100 went to Black homebuyers."[40] Suburbs like San Leandro, immediately abutting multicultural Oakland, managed to combine a legacy of federal loans almost entirely available only to whites, actual restrictive covenants, and good old-fashioned discriminatory practices to maintain racial exclusivity.[41] In a sweeping and impressive 2003 volume, *American Babylon*, Robert Self weaves together the story of Oakland and San Leandro, noting the social and employment problems left lingering in the former while the latter was celebrated by the *Wall Street Journal* as both a beacon for new industry and "successful because 'it hasn't been forced to absorb a heavy influx of minority groups and unskilled workers.'"[42]

Such widespread residential segregation was bound to be challenged, particularly given the civil rights activism of the 1960s as well as a minority population that was small but growing, particularly in some key locations in the state. The minority vote was of special interest to Democratic Party operatives looking to cement their hold on state political power after decades of Republican rule, particularly as a set of decisions and rule changes in the 1950s—including the elimination of the cross-filing that had allowed Warren to run as a Republican *and* a Democrat—encouraged parties to take a more partisan approach.[43] Figure 2.2 illustrates the shifting political opportunity structure by showing the overall trends in the demography of the state between 1900 and 1970.[44] Up until 1940, the state was overwhelmingly white, but after the wartime increase in the Black population and especially after 1950, the share of California's population made up of Blacks, Latinos, and Asian Americans and Pacific Islanders was slowly on the rise.

By the early 1960s, the Civil Rights Movement was making progress nationwide, the political calculus of California Democrats had shifted, and the pressure was on to open up housing opportunity throughout the state. In 1963, William Byron Rumford, a Black pharmacist turned member of the state assembly, managed to shepherd through a California Fair Housing Act that sought to eliminate discrimination in private as well as public housing. It passed in late September and was signed a month later by Governor Brown.[45] But the victory was relatively short-lived:

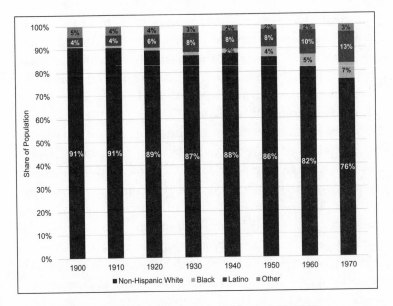

FIGURE 2.2: Long-term demographic change in California, 1900–1970.

the racial and political fears that had been stoked by the state's agricultural right wing in the 1930s were now infecting the state as a whole, and the California Real Estate Association quickly cooked up Proposition 14, a ballot measure intended to strike down Rumford's reform and reinstate the right to discriminate, all in the name of respecting "property rights."

The property rights rhetoric echoed the southern defense of Jim Crow and foreshadowed the contemporary framing of the Tea Party—and it managed to win the day. In the 1964 election, voters overwhelmingly supported Proposition 14 and seemingly embraced the idea that the postwar infrastructure being built by the state of California was not really intended for all Californians.[46] Indeed, in reviewing the "No on 14" campaign advertisements, author Kurt Schuparra concludes, "The message was clear: the Rumford Act [which 14 tried to reverse] threatened the lily-white suburban life that had seemingly become part and parcel of the American Dream."[47] In short, the spoils that had been acquired from a system designed to privilege white Americans and their hard-won homes were to be preserved for exactly that demographic: the suburb, separate from the chaos and mixing of the city, was sacred, it was now under threat by inclusion, and so it needed to be protected at all costs.

This was, of course, part of a broader national pattern of challenging residential segregation, but it was also one of the first salvos in a sort of racial, generational, and spatial (city versus suburb) warfare that would come to dominate California politics for years to come. The triumph of the discriminatory will was, at least in this particular instance, short-lived: in 1966, the California Supreme Court struck down Proposition 14 in a sort of "Are you kidding?" ruling in which it pointed out that voters could decide many things, but they were not really free to violate the equal protection clauses of the U.S. Constitution. The defeat infuriated conservative voters, who often celebrated the U.S. Constitution but thought that a few of its key protections were also best forgotten. In the same year as the ruling, they helped to unseat Pat Brown, partly because he had expressed his relief that the proposition had been struck down by the court; in his place, they elected Republican Ronald Reagan, who insisted that the court decision benefited "'one segment of our population' while restricting 'one of our most basic and cherished rights,' the ability to sell property to anyone."[48]

As a result of his defense of policies like these, Reagan earned himself accusations of being a "bigot," a charge he deeply resented—and then later shored up when he ran for the presidency in 1980 and declared his support for "states' rights" at a fairground near Philadelphia, Mississippi, where three young civil rights workers had been infamously killed in 1964. Adept at "dog whistle" politics, Reagan stroked racist resentments with a charming smile—and then expressed shock when people of color and political observers saw the coded appeal for what it really was. So, too, Donald Trump—who announced his presidential campaign by labeling Mexicans "rapists" and later declared that he was the "least racist person that you have ever met."[49] Of course, Trump has little of Reagan's charm, and his rhetoric seems shouted with a bullhorn, not whispered in a dog whistle. Still, the sort of bubbling racial tensions that fed the Trump phenomenon—the sense that privilege is slipping away in uncertain times—also fueled the Reagan election and the policy changes that were soon to come.

The Compact Cracks

It was not just race: by the mid-1960s, many Californians felt that the promise and possibility of California were beginning to unravel. For example, students attending the university system of which Brown was so proud seemed to be in full revolt: in the fall of 1964, the Free Speech Movement was launched at UC Berkeley to protest a decision to more tightly enforce restrictions on political activities on campus property. Policy-wise, the movement was successful: the university did eventually loosen its regulations, leading to the cacophony of political voices that are now evident to anyone walking in contemporary Sproul Plaza, where the protests largely occurred. But that happened only after students occupied a building, were arrested en masse, and offered ordinary Californians an early glimpse of the campus revolts that would come to characterize America for the next decade, particularly as the Vietnam War heated up.[50]

Still, race was a crucial part of the state's shifting politics. The Watts rebellion of 1965—initially triggered by perceived police brutality—was the largest civil disturbance up until that time, resulting in thirty-four deaths and more than a thousand injuries as well as more than $40 million in property damage (a figure that would amount to more than $300 million if we account for inflation and adjust to 2016 dollars).[51] A subsequent report analyzing the causes of the "riots," commissioned by Governor Brown and coordinated by John McCone, a former head of the Central Intelligence Agency, stirred controversy because it suggested that those hitting the streets were almost entirely uneducated, unemployed, and delinquent individuals.[52] Activists countered that many who did not riot nonetheless shared the same anger—and both the report authors and the critics agreed that there was a need to address fundamental causes like the lack of jobs, low-quality housing, and poor education.[53]

Both the anger and the economic distress affecting Black communities were not confined to Los Angeles. In Oakland, for example, homes that had been purchased by returning Black soldiers were condemned, seized via eminent domain, and redeveloped as part of the concern over "blighted" neighborhoods abutting central business districts.[54] The employment resulting from this "urban renewal"—in which residences were supposed to give way to industry and commerce—was far less than had been promised.[55] Partly as a result of the job shortfall and partly as a reaction to Watts, Oakland officials adopted a strategy—captured in a 1968 book whose ironic title, *Oakland's Not for Burning*, was not meant as irony—centered on federally sponsored training for jobs at the city's port complex. Unfortunately, efforts to really reach the poorest workers for port or other employment were not always successful.[56]

Back in Southern California, the 1965 Watts riots accelerated suburbanization in the form of white flight. The area now known as South Los Angeles, which once included a significant number of white homeowners, became 80 percent African American by 1970. Nearby suburbs, including Compton, which had been overwhelming white in 1950 and then well integrated by the early 1960s, saw a mass exodus of white homeowners.[57] Since many of these suburbs had been, like Lakewood, incorporated as cities without a strong fiscal base—who needed their own resources when the federal government was subsidizing freeways and suburbs and the state was building schools?—the new and often poorer population was a recipe for eventual fiscal stress.[58] While all this would have lasting impacts on the contours of the state, the immediate effect was on California politics.

The combination of demographic change, social protest, and geographic shifts helped to fuel a growing conservative reaction. In Orange County, one suburban beachhead for the right, and one of the fastest-growing counties in the United States in the 1950s, due in large part to military spending, the role of federal largess was largely ignored by residents, who instead helped the county become a key platform for the anti-communist conspiratorial musings of the far-right John Birch Society.[59] The sense that government was too big and taxes were too high may have had ideological roots, but it also seemed to stem from the fact that more and different people wanted to reap the benefits from government expenditures. As one analyst put it, "for Orange County's white middle class, minorities were essentially out of sight and out of mind, but, due to federal and state policies, not out of their wallets."[60]

White racial anxiety was further inflamed by growing militancy in minority communities. Such militancy was part of a national trend, reflected in the turn from civil rights to Black Power as frustrations grew with the slow pace of change. But, as was and is often the case, California was a bit ahead of the national times. Partly in reaction to police brutality against African Americans, the Black Panther Party for Self-Defense was founded in Oakland in late 1966; a well-documented part of the organization's activities involved tailing the police in Oakland in order to deter police violence, with members' weapons of choice being not the contemporary cell phone camera but, well, actual weapons. By mid-1967, a group of Black Panther Party members walked into the state legislature armed with rifles to protest a proposal to strip the rights of Californians to openly bear arms.[61] The imagery of African Americans undaunted by state power was shocking—and

Governor Reagan quickly signed off on state legislation banning open carry of loaded weapons, showing that the conservative commitment to Second Amendment rights was limited to a particular kind of gun owner.[62] It's a sentiment recently echoed in the lack of reaction by the National Rifle Association to the 2016 police shooting of Black gun owner and motorist Philando Castile.[63]

Of course, the Black Panther Party was about more than arms—and that may have been one of the reasons it was so threatening. Aside from tackling the issue of police abuse, its members created a political platform calling for full employment and decent housing, launched one of the earliest testing efforts for sickle cell anemia, and established a well-known and oft-admired free breakfast program for schoolchildren, which is now a standard practice in many urban schools.[64] But for Reagan and much of the public, what stuck was the imagery of armed Black men standing off against the police, impressions reinforced when party members, such as co-founder Huey Newton, either engaged in violent skirmishes with police or found themselves targets of police violence.[65]

Meanwhile, California's Latino population was also becoming more politicized. Some of the earliest efforts to organize the state's largely Mexican and Mexican American population after the Second World War had focused on rural areas and on issues of segregation in terms of education, housing, and access to public infrastructure, such as community swimming facilities.[66] In 1947, the Community Service Organization (CSO) emerged in East Los Angeles, founded by Edward Roybal and guided by Fred Ross of the Industrial Areas Foundation, who would later go on to "discover" and recruit a young organizer named Cesar Chavez. Consisting of businessmen, unionists, workers, and veterans, the CSO focused on voter registration drives in East L.A., education reform, and police brutality.[67] The CSO also forged ties with the International Ladies' Garment Workers' Union and United Steelworkers, offering inklings of the Latino-labor alliance that would eventually become a linchpin of social movement organizing in California.[68]

But while the CSO's focus on voter registration drives helped to elect Edward Roybal to the L.A. City Council in 1949—where he subsequently went on to become the first Latino congressman elected in the nation since the nineteenth century—by the middle of the 1960s, many younger Latinos viewed CSO organizing as too conventional, too polite, and too limited in its impacts.[69] This echoed the Black Power critique of the broader Civil Rights Movement and also resembles how in the current era, DREAMers— young undocumented immigrants who came to the United States at an early age—launched their own direct action campaigns seemingly at odds with the mainstream immigrant rights movement (though more recently the two have become increasingly integrated).[70] By the spring of 1968, Mexican American students staged a walkout from the three major high schools in East Los Angeles, demanding a better education and challenging the bigotry of teachers.[71] Two years later, the 1970 National Chicano Moratorium, protesting both the U.S. war in Vietnam and the disproportionate death of Mexican Americans in that war, staged a mass rally of 25,000 to 30,000 people in L.A.[72] Police violence against the protestors was met with resistance; four hundred people were arrested, forty officers were injured, and three individuals were killed, including a prominent Chicano journalist, Ruben Salazar.[73]

It might be tempting to think that events important to Latinos in Los Angeles might not fully spill over to the state or the nation. But it's important to remember that nearly 20 percent of all Mexican-origin Latinos in the United States lived in Los Angeles County in 1970, making this a location of enormous symbolic importance to the broader Mexican American community.[74] It was also important for California: the rise of ethnic militancy, including of an increasingly restive and organized young Asian American community, coupled with the wave of protests against the Vietnam War and campus actions on numerous fronts, gave a slightly older and much whiter California population a fear that the ways of society so dear to them were falling apart.[75]

Much as with the Trump phenomenon of 2016, the sense of unease—of discomfort with a society in which once-quiet voices of color were speaking more boldly about their rights and their future—drove a reactionary grassroots mobilization against school busing, against student demonstrations, against challenges to police authority, and very much against the expansion of state government. Reagan gave disaffected white suburbanites a voice at the top, particularly in the symbolic ways he embraced the individual's right to protect his or her segregated housing and articulated a firm commitment to law and order. But while "a major legacy of the conservative movement of the 1960s can be found in the diminution and rejection of governmental authority to remedy race-related social inequities," being known for resisting integration left a somewhat uneasy taste in the mouth.[76] So California conservatives needed to find a more palatable issue—one that might have the same effect of resisting accommodation to a changing California but do so in a more racially ambiguous way. The perfect foil: a campaign to lower taxes.

California Crumbling

Launching a tax revolt was, however, not the first thing on Governor Reagan's agenda. He might have been welcomed as a sort of conservative savior for the old California, but his immediate first task involved shoring up state finances. Showing an instinct to trim what the right considered a bloated government, the Reagan administration tried in its first year to reduce spending by 10 percent but found itself both stymied politically and concerned about the impacts of such big cuts. Showing characteristic pragmatism—Reagan was often more ideological in tone than in

practice, a fact frequently forgotten by his sycophants—he proposed the largest tax increase in the state's history, amounting
to about a third of General Fund spending; indeed, his program
incorporated an increase in income tax rates on the wealthy that
actually made the tax structure more progressive than it had been
under Pat Brown.[77] Moreover, despite Reagan's constant chiding
of the University of California and its liberal and libertine incli-
nations, higher education state spending increased by 136 percent
over the course of his two terms, outpacing the increase in overall
state spending.[78]

What became more prominent were symbolic moves to shore
up the support of anxious conservatives, something for which
there may be national echoes under the Trump administration.
For example, Reagan's electoral promise to "clean up that mess
in Berkeley"—that is, to tame the unruly students—was fulfilled
in May of 1969 by ordering the California Highway Patrol, accompanied by Berkeley police officers, to flush out three thousand
protestors who were seeking to defend People's Park, a university-
owned plot of land that local residents had converted to an unauthorized community park.[79] The clash led to the death of an
onlooking student, roughly a thousand arrests, and the invasion
of Berkeley by nearly 2,200 National Guard troops.[80] This tough
approach to students was of a piece with the national, particularly
Republican, shift toward an embrace of "law and order" as a trope
to gain the support of older voters concerned about the seeming
dissolution of a world that had once seemed ordered, disciplined,
and firm.

Another part of that Republican turn—prominently part of
the 1968 presidential campaign of Richard Nixon in which he
sought to lure southern white voters away from a Democratic
Party that had come to support civil rights on a national level—
was the embrace of what Daniel HoSang calls "political white-
ness": essentially echoing platitudes about equal opportunity but
raising concerns about an ever-expanding state government that

could make equal opportunity real. Reagan did not support yet another effort to overturn the Rumford Act, the ban against segregation in housing, but that was only because he knew that it was a loser in the legislature.[81] However, he insinuated that state aid might be helping undeserving minority constituents, and California voters got—and acted on—the racial message: in 1972, they voted to ban school busing for the purposes of integration and to reverse other state policies meant to promote school desegregation.[82] Like the earlier attempt to resurrect housing segregation through popular demand, this ballot proposition was eventually rejected by the courts in another "Are you kidding?" moment.[83]

Fueling the overall anxiety in the state was an increase in unemployment in the United States and California; Figure 2.3 shows the pattern of unemployment between 1962 and 1978.[84] Unemployment at both the national and state levels dipped during the height of the 1960s boom, a sort of golden era for employment fueled in part by military spending for the Vietnam War. However, joblessness began a sharp increase from 1969 forward. A slight recovery in which unemployment dipped in the early 1970s was quickly followed by a sharp increase in 1975. While manufacturing in California continued to grow in the 1970s, after more or less plateauing between 1967 and 1972, signs of deindustrialization were starting to show in the rest of the country.[85] Fears that the jobs lost were not just a casualty of the business cycle but were at risk of never coming back were palpable in a worried electorate—a sort of early foreshadowing of the economic stress that would drive national politics more than a quarter century later.

Indeed, that fear of permanent displacement certainly exists today, particularly after decades of manufacturing loss have piled up in places like the Midwest. In the late 1970s, generalized concerns about higher than average unemployment were exacerbated by a peculiar phenomenon: inflation, usually dampened by weak labor markets, was also on the uptick. While national inflation averaged

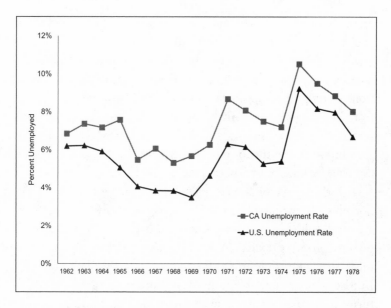

FIGURE 2.3: Percentage unemployment, California and the United States, 1962–1978.

2.4 percent between 1962 and 1968, a period in which unemployment was low, inflation averaged nearly 7 percent between 1969 and 1978, even as unemployment was hitting new and higher plateaus.[86] And in California, the worst part of what would later be termed "stagflation"—the combination of slow growth and rising prices—was that job loss was going hand in hand with a dramatic increase in home values.

That might, at first glance, sound like an odd concern: normally, surges in housing values would seem to be a good thing for homeowners. But apparently, there can be too much of a good thing, particularly if it affects the tax take on stalled incomes. In the 1960s, California homeowners had become accustomed to housing inflation on the order of 2 to 3 percent a year; by the mid-1970s, it was occasionally 2 to 3 percent a month.[87] Between 1970 and 1980, the median value of a house in California rose by more than 250 percent, about 50 percent faster than in the United

States as a whole; interestingly, median rents rose less rapidly and at about the same pace as in the United States as a whole.[88] Many factors conspired to make this happen—a growing suburban resistance to overdevelopment and emerging environmental restrictions likely pushed up home costs while the shift over the 1960s from building single-family homes to building multifamily units restrained rent pressures.[89] But while faster price rises did mean growing wealth in the form of housing equity, they also impacted assessments and thus property taxes.

The rising tax bills were particularly problematic for older homeowners, who tended to be on fixed or nearly fixed incomes. As early as his first campaign, Reagan had raised the specter of possible property tax relief for the elderly—a politically appealing idea, since who could be for forcing seniors from their homes?[90] But Reagan was not able to make significant progress on tax reform: he secured an increase in the exemption for homeowners in 1972 that was considered a signal achievement but soon offered scant relief as housing prices skyrocketed.[91] The challenges around the property tax structure thus lingered and soon fell into the lap of Jerry Brown, the son of Pat Brown, who took office in 1975.

Democrat Jerry Brown, who would return to the seat in 2010, seemed to encapsulate the times—and not just because he was the youngest governor in more than a century and would achieve a seeming hipness by dating folk rock superstar Linda Ronstadt. Frugal by nature, convinced that the economy was hitting its limits, and strikingly flexible (indeed, opportunistic) in many of his political positions, Brown tended to veer right, then left, and then all over in a way that made his ideological predilections hard to pin down.[92] His first term as governor had a lot of imagery associated with it, some of which highlighted his tightfisted ways: he famously chose to live in a cheap apartment near the capitol rather than in the governor's mansion—which was, in any case, undergoing renovation—and gave up Reagan's preferred ride, an armored Cadillac, in favor of a state-issued Plymouth Satellite.[93]

But the most important part of Brown's famous frugality was not his modest dwelling or substandard vehicle but his unwillingness to increase state spending even as inflation pushed taxpayers into higher income tax brackets and amped up revenues to the state government.[94] While hiking spending levels would have created some political problems, particularly with conservative voters already chafing at the size of state government, it would have at least built a set of constituencies resistant to changing the tax intake. Instead, Brown let the cash accumulate: whereas the state's General Fund ended with a $900 million surplus in fiscal 1975–76, the surplus was more than four times as large heading into the 1978–79 fiscal year.[95] In this context, a tax cut, particularly given the pressures facing homeowners, seemed hardly likely to damage the state, and this fueled momentum for property tax reform.[96]

The other factor driving the desire to curtail property taxes was a series of California Supreme Court decisions in 1971 and 1976 that had disconnected local spending on schools from local property taxes.[97] The legal reasoning was sound: an accident of geography—whether you were in a rich community or a poor community, which actually was not an "accident" given California's racialized housing history—could have sharp impacts on taxable resources and thus prevent access to equal education. In 1977, the legislature took up the challenge of geographic equity by passing a law that would provide aid to poorer districts, partly through providing direct state resources, partly by redistributing property tax from higher income areas, and partly by capping revenue collection in wealthier districts. But while this sounded fair, it also served to transform the relationship between the property tax collected and the perceived amenities received. Previously, elderly homeowners without children were sometimes

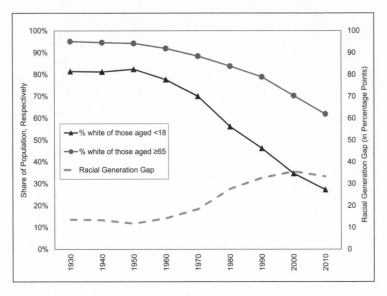

FIGURE 2.4: Racial generation gap in California, 1930–2010.

resentful of spending money on education; added to that mix now were middle- and upper-middle-class families that had moved to high-performing districts, accepted high taxes as part of the cost of educating "their" children, and now found out that a portion of their contribution was headed elsewhere.[98]

It did not help that the children of the state were now starting to look fairly different from the taxpayers and particularly the seniors with high voting propensities.[99] Figure 2.4 offers a long-term look at what we earlier termed the "racial generation gap," that is, the difference between the share of seniors (age sixty-five years and older) who were white and the share of those under the age of eighteen who were white in the state of California.[100] Note that in the period between 1930 and 1960—when the commitment to building economic and social infrastructure was strong—the old looked demographically very much like the young. Somewhere in the middle of the 1960s, this shifted dramatically, as evidenced by the line measuring the generation gap (the dashed line indicating the difference between the two share measures); the gap stabilized in the 2000s and then began to decline, likely having a stabilizing political impact.

But the racial generation gap was anything but stable in the 1970s, and the heated racialized rhetoric reflected that. The main architect of tax-cutting Prop 13, Howard Jarvis, wrote after it passed that immigrants "just come over here to get on the taxpayers' gravy train," making clear that some of the impulses about cutting taxes were about preventing the "other"—especially the foreigner—from tapping into the infrastructure investments that had made California great.[101] This negative reaction was unsurprising: California was in the midst of a big "immigrant shock," partly as a result of the way that the 1965 Immigration and Nationality Act ended country quotas that had previously worked against arrivals from Asia and Latin America.[102] While it was not foreordained that this opening to more of the world would have a special impact on California, proximity to Mexico and the Pacific Rim played a role: in 1960, the state held about 13 percent of the foreign born in the United States, just a bit above the 10 percent share it had held a decade before. By 1980, however, California held more than 25 percent of all U.S. immigrants—and by 1990, it hosted nearly one-third of all immigrants living in the United States.[103] Indeed, California—with only 10 percent of the nation's population in 1980—absorbed just over half of the nation's increase in the foreign born over the decade that followed.[104]

While this "immigrant shock" would soon feed into a more targeted anti-immigrant fervor, the immediate shot across the bow was Prop 13 and its attempt to symbolically pull up the drawbridge just as new guests were arriving. Indeed, exit polls showed that eight in ten seniors, exactly the generation whose kids had most benefited from an earlier series of public investments, supported the measure in the eventual elections.[105] Pushing along the campaign for Prop 13's tax cuts was Howard Jarvis, a gadfly who had run unsuccessfully for a series of state and local races and was the executive director for the Los Angeles Apartment Owners' Association. A superb organizer—glib, charismatic, and focused—he and anti-tax advocate Paul Gann managed to drive a 1977 effort to collect enough signatures to put on the 1978 ballot a proposition that would reshape California's politics for decades.[106]

The Wrecking Ball

Prop 13 had many moving parts, some of which seemed to go under the radar. The big appeal to the public was the promise to roll back assessments to 1975 property values (unless the property had been sold since then), to limit the property tax to 1 percent of assessed value, and to cap future increases to no more than 2 percent a year.[107] But the proposition also required a two-thirds approval by voters for local increases in "special" taxes, effectively hamstringing municipalities seeking to invest in themselves. Adding to that was a requirement that a two-thirds vote was needed in both the state assembly and the state senate to raise revenue in any way, a feature that meant that a minority party—which, in the California case, turned out to be Republicans—had a stranglehold over fiscal policy.[108]

And this was on top of a mess of complexities and supermajority requirements already built into California's fiscal system that had, in fact, headed off any preemptive approach to avoiding Prop 13. In the year before the vote, numerous alternatives were proposed, including what is called a "split roll," in which commercial and industrial properties might be taxed at a higher rate, another way of providing relief to the average homeowner. But the state had a two-thirds requirement for any budgetary measure, one of just a few states in the United States with such a restriction, and it was not until early 1978 that a legislative alternative bill to

Prop 13 was passed. It was put on the ballot as a competitor; it, too, promised to lower residential property taxes, although by an average of 32 to 35 percent rather than the whopping 57 percent promised by Prop 13.[109]

By that point, distrust was high and the die was cast: despite warnings that Prop 13 could shipwreck local and state finances—which apparently the state legislature had been prepared to do in more temperate fashion with its own alternative—the lure of massive tax cuts was just too tempting for an electorate experiencing economic anxiety. And while some accounts downplay the racial element of the Prop 13 appeal, Joe Mathews and Mark Paul point out in their aptly titled *California Crackup* that the grassroots proponents of Prop 13 were the very same people who "picketed and marched against busing students to desegregate schools."[110]

It was in this complex stew of economic distress and racial anxiety that Prop 13 passed in June 1978 with nearly two-thirds of the vote. Nearly immediately, the promised tax cuts materialized. While the image of who was to be protected was elderly pensioners seeking to live out their well-deserved final years in their comfy suburban home, the big winners were larger companies with massive property holdings; according to one estimate, homeowners received less than a quarter of the savings, whereas an analysis over a slightly longer time frame (five years) suggests that homeowners saw a bit over a third of the gains.[111] Subsequent analysis also made clear what should have been an obvious point: those with more wealth and so larger homes would gather the lion's share of the residential benefits.[112] But even though the bulk of the gains went elsewhere, the relief for ordinary homeowners was palpable and much appreciated.

Moreover, state policy makers reacted in such a way that the tax cuts initially seemed to cause relatively little pain, feeding into a myth that much of government spending was wasteful or duplicative. Not all the hurt was avoided—the first summer of Prop 13 brought the cancelation of most summer school programs as well

as the closing of some libraries. But, frightened about the consequences of cutting local services and education spending, the state
engineered a complicated series of moves that involved budget
freezes and expenditure cuts that nearly doubled the available state
surplus, creating a $4.2 billion emergency relief package for local
governments that quickly made up for about 60 percent of the aggregate shortfalls.[113] With the state filling in part of the spending gaps, particularly in education and county-level social service
spending, authority and decision making moved to the capitol.[114]
Ironically, Prop 13—a measure pushed by anti-state forces—had
effectively given the state government more influence and power.

While the quick reaction in the state capital of Sacramento
might have limited the damage, it also contributed to a bit of
magical thinking that was later transferred, with dangerous
consequences, to the national scene: taxes could be cut, services
could be maintained, and California could blithely continue to
go forward, none the worse for wear and tear. This masked the
long-term erosion of finances to come, including the need to jack
up fees to attend California's once proud—and inexpensive—set
of colleges and universities as well as the inevitable cuts in social
services and state infrastructure that would be prompted by the
drip, drip, drip of revenue shortfalls. The effects rippled outward
as well: in 1979, more than twenty other states passed some form
of property tax limitations, while others dabbled in reductions in
state income tax.[115] The wrecking ball that had been taken to the
state was soon to be battering the nation.

Jerry Brown, who had campaigned against Proposition 13,
quickly relabeled himself a "born-again tax cutter."[116] One might
wonder why he did that and why he was so vigorous in his efforts
to shield the state from its worst effects—particularly when other
politicians were suggesting that allowing cuts to take place would
be just the recipe to shock California voters into realizing the
harm they had caused. It's easy to say that he was a political cha-
meleon, that he was gunning to run for the presidency (which he

had done in 1976 and would go on to do again in 1980 and 1992), and that his infamous "flexibility" was simply being demonstrated yet again. Yet there is a much simpler explanation: Brown was responding to a legitimate set of social actors that had made a demand and changed the political environment.

For whatever one thinks of Jarvis, Gann, and the tax cuts they inspired, they were part of a broader wave that was, in the words of sociologist Isaac Martin, "a social movement: a sustained, collective, and unconventional challenge to authority."[117] It is too easy to think of social movements as a term confined to the left—that is, the Black struggle against racism and state violence, the farmworker fights to shift the balance of power in the fields, or the valiant efforts for LGBTQ equality that would emerge in future years. But movements, as we have seen with the rise of the evangelical right and, more recently, the Tea Party and even Trump, can be authentic, grassroots, *and* very much right-wing.[118]

Martin notes that California tax cutters constituted a social movement not to broaden rights but rather to retain a particular sort of privilege: the ability to be taxed not on the actual value of your property but on the historic value of your property.[119] This was a policy move destined to favor seniors and long-rooted Californians: it is what some call a "welcome, stranger" tax, in which newcomers are contributing a greater share of the property tax, although it might also be labeled "stay away, stranger," in that it seeks to enact a discouraging entry fee. This was very much antithetical to the open approach to newcomers that had characterized California in its heyday: a state willing to invest in infrastructure for those who had not yet arrived.[120]

Indeed, it is this shift embodied in Prop 13 that more or less symbolizes the closing of the state and its adoption of a social compact confined to those already in—or, better put, in some time ago. Such a declaration of generational warfare was echoed in the Trump campaign, in which every effort was made to reassure elders that Social Security and Medicare would not be touched while spending on everyone else would be ravaged.[121] That campaign was also accompanied by a pretty literal adoption of the "stay away, stranger" approach in its xenophobic appeal to deport immigrants, deny entry to refugees, and build a border wall.

But the point here is that what shifted property tax policy in California was a set of movement actors, aggrieved individuals who were willing to work beyond traditional legislative procedures, take matters into their own hands, and shift the public debate and subsequently public policy. Also important, these were activists largely based in suburban locales and very much dedicated to the protection of the suburban ideal. This was reflected in the voting: for example, in the East Bay, in the city of Oakland, 52 percent of the voters rejected Proposition 13, whereas 72 percent of voters in adjoining San Leandro voted in favor of the measure.[122] Seeking to hang on to their little piece of the American Dream, suburban homeowners sought to protect themselves from tax hikes that would force them from their homes.

Understanding this dimension—and its parallels to the earlier fight to preserve housing segregation with Proposition 14—is important to glimpsing the underlying racial, generational, and class tensions at play: basically, you won from Proposition 13 if you had been the beneficiary of a real estate market that had historically privileged whites and so given you early access to homeownership. With the rollback to 1975, as time went on, homeowners who stayed put would gain even more—their property values and equity would go up while their taxes would not (or at least not in pace with the housing value increase). Meanwhile, new arrivals to the market—those African Americans, Latinos, and Asian Americans/Pacific Islanders hitting the cusp of family formation—would pay full freight. On the flip side, the spending cuts that this new tax system would induce would likely impact most those urban communities that had the most social needs, tended to rent, and were disproportionately people of color.[123]

Of course, recognizing the movement base for Prop 13 does not mean that a bunch of scrappy activists did it alone: while the re-sentment of high property taxes was an issue that was widely and deeply felt, Prop 13 would not have won without allies with the financial and political means to run a campaign that could win.[124] In short, like the Tea Party activists who followed years later, these actors were aware of their own interests and not simply manipu-lated by others; on the other hand, their victory was made possible by more moneyed interests who were to gain from the reshuffling of property taxes, particularly commercial and industrial property owners.[125]

The wrecking ball taken to California's finances would soon go national. Former governor Ronald Reagan rode the low-tax anti-government political wave and ran for and won the presidency in 1980. His first big move to resuscitate the economy: the Economic Recovery Tax Act of 1981, a bill that lowered marginal income tax rates, especially for the rich.[126] It was a move eventually tempered with a tax increase to repair the damage to federal finances—again, that hint of Reagan pragmatism—but it set in motion a seemingly permanent fiscal crisis in Washington, D.C., as well. Meanwhile, California, once so proud of setting the national pace in terms of dynamic industries, investments in both physical and human capital, and a can-do attitude of welcoming and accommo-dating new arrivals, was closing in and shutting off—and just get-ting primed to be rocked by a series of more explicitly racialized conflicts that would characterize the 1990s.

Looking Back

From the vantage point of the mid-1930s, it would have been hard to predict California's success. The state was continuing to attract new arrivals but mostly because they were fleeing Dust Bowl di-sasters. The fields of the Central Valley, host to an agriculture in-dustry that was key to the state's economy at the time, had become the site of economic desperation and social conflict. An industrial sector, particularly in automobiles and related suppliers, had been created but was, like the rest of America, being battered by a national depression. The state was churning through a series of one-term governors, none considered remarkable for their leadership and each going down to defeat when seeking a second term.[127]

From what seemed like very little eventually came a lot. Starting in 1943, the state was blessed with a series of multiterm governors, some of whom, particularly Earl Warren and Pat Brown, were very much emblematic of their times. Each recognized the need for a strong public sector: California thrived from defense spending, which would later help drive both manufacturing and electronics spin-offs; benefited from basic infrastructure investments that created a platform, including complex and interlocking water and highway systems, for business activity; gained from the Master Plan for Higher Education that generated a workforce capable of participating effectively in the economy that was to emerge; and benefited from a set of land-use, transit, and tax policies that allowed for—indeed encouraged—a healthy housing stock in the form of postwar suburban development.

In short, the California Dream, while it may have been individually realized in the small homes, private yards, and secure cul-de-sacs dotting the state's residential landscape, was very much made possible by public policy. And behind that public policy consensus was something even a bit deeper: a social compact that even included those who were not yet here. California had seemingly made the commitment to see newcomers to the state as future residents and not invaders, to therefore provide homes, schools, and opportunity to all who were willing to come and work, and to achieve this by forging the sort of cross-party dialogues that would generate lasting middle-ground consensus.

Not all was well with California's version of the New Deal. For one thing, the ambitious expansion of California's road system and the state's commitment to suburban sprawl had brought choking smog, particularly in Southern California. The problem had many specific roots, including the nature of meteorological conditions that trapped pollution in the L.A. Basin, but it fundamentally stemmed from the attitude of an earlier generation of Californians: they basically sought to tame the planet, diverting water, creating ports, and establishing cities in what had once been deserts. In the 1960s, an emerging generation of committed activists, scientists, and policy makers questioned whether this was the right approach to the environment, and environmental attitudes and policies began to change.[128]

But while there were the inklings of a turnaround on environmental issues in the 1960s, the challenges of racism were increasingly clear. California might have been thriving, but many racial minorities were locked out of the best housing, the most desirable schools, and the most remunerative occupations. Frustrated by inaction, political awareness and militancy in Black and Latino communities was also on the upswing—and the traditional residential firewall of racial segregation that had allowed California to contain that anger in ghettos and barrios was being struck down. The state's voters tried to resurrect their own version of apartheid by passing a ballot that relegalized housing discrimination; a bewildered state supreme court pointed out that majority rule was not meant to suppress minority rights. Along with chaos on the college campuses, the struggle of communities of color to get in on the California Dream created a rising sense that government, at least insofar as it extended benefits to new groups, needed to be curtailed.

Meanwhile, the economy began to falter in new and different ways: unemployment was rising but so was inflation. Homeowners, once so proud of rising property values, were now concerned about whether they could meet the tax hikes soon to follow. Their concerns were exacerbated by the fact that the people most likely to gain services from new revenues were increasingly unlikely to look like them. It was a perfect stew of racial anxiety and economic drift—not unlike that in the contemporary United States—and it spawned a tax revolt that engulfed first California and then the nation. Interestingly, this was not really led by traditional politicians: as governor, Ronald Reagan had attempted a modest property tax reform that proved too little, too late, whereas Jerry Brown was against tax cuts before he was for them.

Indeed, political figures were responding to a groundswell of resentment being channeled by a series of right-wing social movements. These built on an organizational and ideological base, particularly a strong strain of right-leaning activism that caught on in the Central Valley of the 1930s. The new fertile ground for anti-government organizing turned out to be the suburbs, a striking contradiction since the suburbs themselves had been created by federal and state commitments to cheap loans and free roads.[129] But with consistency considered the hobgoblin of little minds, right-wing forces fought to cripple the state by reworking the property tax system in a way that would favor older and more established Californians. Business interests also stood to gain from stirring the pot of tax reform—and it is perhaps unsurprising that the face of the Prop 13 movement was Howard Jarvis, a lobbyist for apartment owners. But it was a real and authentic movement nonetheless—and that meant that it would eventually take a countermovement to begin to reverse the fiscal damage wrought by tax cutting.

But this is getting ahead of ourselves in the history. Much like an alcoholic before recovery, the state had not quite hit rock bottom. Right-wing social movements had managed to take apart the commitment to public infrastructure—and to one another—that had made the state work. They had managed to export a toxic mix to the nation in the form of rolling tax revolts and the Reagan presidency. But there was more to come, as conservatives pivoted from an implicitly racial attack on government to a more explicit set of racial propositions designed to threaten and immiserate the emerging "new majority" of people of color. If you think it all sounds way too contemporary—economic anxiety and fears of demographic change combine to produce the shredding of the social safety net—you are not mistaken. And the parallels become even more frightening and illustrative as we move to the next phase in California's dizzy descent.

3

THINGS FALL APART

The 2003 recall of Democratic governor Gray Davis and the circus of 135 candidates running to replace him put the sad state of California politics on a national stage. As America watched, the campaign careened like a bumper-car ride over a mere ten weeks—the recall rules required that an election be held within eighty days, and smelling blood, Davis's own lieutenant governor both verified the tight timeline and jumped in as a candidate. Meanwhile, former body builder and action-movie actor Arnold Schwarzenegger, a Republican, announced his candidacy on *The Tonight Show*, presenting himself as an out-of-the-box figure who could save the state from dysfunction, fiscal crisis, and partisan warfare—sound familiar? Combining outlandish promises with a style of campaigning that borrowed liberally from the world of entertainment (again, sound familiar?), he promised to roll back a recent increase in registration fees for vehicles—and signaled his commitment to this at rallies by dropping a wrecking ball to smash an old car.

How did California move from the glory days of serious politicians like Earl Warren and Pat Brown to the full trivialization of state politics embodied by the 2003 campaign? It is a long and sordid tale through the eras governed by Republican George Deukmejian, Republican Pete Wilson, and Democrat Gray Davis, driven partly by the white backlash hinted at in voters' constant efforts to restore housing and school segregation and crystalized by the passage of Proposition 13. Through the 1990s, the state's voters embraced the racial order more directly, voting to toss un-documented children out of schools and require local officials to report their parents, to ban affirmative action and bilingual edu-cation, and to get tough on crime in a way that increased the state prison population, largely African American and Latino, seven-fold between 1978, the year Proposition 13 passed, and 2000.[1]

But it wasn't just racialized fears of disorder at play: dramatic shifts in the state's economy, particularly the loss of good manu-facturing jobs, added to the stress and uncertainty that had been triggered by the stagflation of the 1970s. The early 1990s were particularly devastating as California experienced nearly one-half of the nation's net job loss between 1990 and 1992, and around 40 percent of the longer-term national decline in manufacturing employment between 1990 and 1994.[2] As the state was pulling apart by race, class, and generation, it was also beginning to sepa-rate more dramatically by geography, with Northern California hosting the dynamic industries of the future, Southern California inundated by new and less-skilled immigrants, and rural Califor-nia seemingly left out of the prosperity picture.

By the turn of the millennium—when California voters re-called a governor they had just reelected and took a chance on a movie star whose career seemed to be slipping—polarization and paralysis were the order of the day. As Joe Mathews and Mark Paul wrote in their 2010 book *California Crackup: How Reform Broke the Golden State and How We Can Fix It*, California was in deep crisis with no clear exit strategy—a broken state that many did not think was fixable.[3] It was, in short, a bit like the America of today: cacophonous debates intended to stir emotions, not inspire solutions; decision-making rules deliberately designed to prevent decision making; and a simmering racial resentment driving and justifying a failure to invest in the future.

However, bubbling beneath the swirl of toxic politics was an emerging movement response to the rightist impulses that had birthed Prop 13 and so much more. Anthony Thigpenn, a onetime member of the Black Panther Party, one of the many organizers fighting back in the 1990s, and also one of the main architects of the coupling of community organizing and voter mobilization in the 2000s and 2010s, has noted that "every year there was some, mainly negative, fight that we had to fight because of the right wing's ability to qualify statewide ballot measures. Whether it was an attack on unions, attack on teachers, Prop 187, English only, all this was happening between 1996 and 2001."[4] The resistance came from the protesters who waved Mexican flags to protest anti-immigrant propositions, from the coalitions that opposed the attacks on affirmative action and bilingual education, and from the nascent institutions that sought to work at municipal and regional levels to assert the interests of the working poor. It is that set of flowers peeking their head above the disinvestment rubble that helped to set the stage for what would be a shift in state politics—and understanding their origins is critical to determining where both California and America need to go and, more important, how they will get there.

Slip, Slipping, Slipped?

In the 1980s, the main drivers that had once supported the California economy and provided for middle-class mobility began to falter: manufacturing slipped, state finances worsened, and income inequality began to tick up. By the time the 1990s arrived, a weakened underlying economy was bashed by cutbacks in federal defense procurement, provoking a deep economic recession from 1990 to 1994. Unlike the period of World War II or the postwar boom—when the state government stepped up to the emerging challenges by preparing for the growth pressures that were soon to come—this time the state seemed to lack an effective public response and proved largely unable to forge a new infrastructure for success. California instead—much like the United

States now—turned in on itself to cast blame on what were that era's new arrivals, a wave of immigrants being pushed northward by economic and civil distress in Mexico and Central America.[5]

That the state's economy and politics would collapse so completely was not so clear at the beginning of the 1980s. Certainly, any observer looking over the emergency patches plugging the fiscal leak created by Proposition 13 could have predicted that there were troubles ahead. For example, hoping to maintain education spending, state voters passed Proposition 98 in 1988, a measure that mandated a minimum of state dollars to be spent on education. Originally criticized by conservatives as too rigid, the measure nonetheless appealed to their suburban base because it provided funding for smaller class sizes in schools. But it was one of many fixes that seemed to just make other things worse: with Prop 13 hamstringing revenue and Prop 98 requiring that a share of that constrained budget be spent for schools, both social service programs for lower-income Californians and longer-term infrastructure investments were frequently left in the lurch.

Prop 13 had another negative impact, one that eventually interacted with larger economic changes. With property taxes a less significant share of local revenues, municipal governments increasingly turned to retail sales taxes. In that fiscal scenario, shopping malls and auto dealerships were preferred to factories or homes since both of the latter land uses would not see much new revenue given the constraints on property assessments.[6] This tended to exacerbate the undersupply of housing and promote suburban sprawl; away from city centers, land was more readily available to build spread-out stores and field vast parking lots for eager customers. Meanwhile the bias toward sales taxes worked against the generation of high-quality jobs in industrial facilities even as it favored the growth of part-time and lower-wage employment in retail.[7]

This set of incentives could not have been worse given a series of other pressures on the California economy. In general, deindustrialization hit California a bit later than it did the rest of the country—the collapse of traditional industries and spectacular plant closures in the Midwest in the 1980s led the way.[8] But California did not escape some of that early damage: in 1978, California had six auto assembly plants, but by 1982, only one of them, a GM facility in Van Nuys, was still operating.[9] Moreover, Black California was impacted earlier than most, partly because of the concentration of African American workers in older plants and older industries that were eclipsed by both foreign and domestic competitors.[10]

Still, up until the 1990s, the worst of the impacts of deindustrialization on employment levels were masked, at least in the aggregate figures, because of California's specialization in high-tech and defense industries—as well as growth in low-wage manufacturing, which added employment but generally at lower wages.[11] While "high-tech" now conjures up images of coders and search engines, in the 1980s, the sector was less about software and much more about computer assembly and chip manufacturing. By 1982, information technology accounted for 27 percent of state value added in manufacturing, while the sector's share of production workers stood at 32 percent.[12] Over the next ten years, the share of workers fell even as the share of value added rose dramatically, suggesting the higher productivity of that set of industries. Meanwhile, resource-dependent industries like oil refining and fruit and vegetable canning declined, with a simultaneous shift of economic centrality from the rural Central Valley to Silicon Valley and its Bay Area environs.

The defense-spending prop for the California economy was kicked away with the end of the Cold War. With the threat of conflict diminished, defense spending began to stall in the late 1980s and military bases starting closing in 1990.[13] Negative impacts should have been expected: the U.S. Department of Defense and, to a lesser yet still significant extent, the National Aeronautics and Space Administration were important contractors for high-tech industrial firms in California, and especially for Los Angeles County. Moreover, aerospace industry firms, such as General Dynamics, Northrop, Lockheed, and McDonnell Douglas, accounted for 28 percent of manufacturing employment (and 5 percent of total employment) in Los Angeles County in 1991.

By 1993, California's unemployment rate had risen to 10 percent, nearly 3 percentage points higher than the 7.2 percent rate in the rest of the country.[14] The pain was not evenly distributed: according to census data, non-Hispanic whites saw a fall of about 32 percent in manufacturing employment between 1990 and 2000, whereas African Americans saw a fall of about 43 percent in manufacturing jobs over the same period. The fall in job quantity was accompanied by a decrease in job quality, something that we can see if we break out manufacturing by what are called durables and nondurables—basically, products that last longer, like autos and planes, and those that do not, like clothing and processed food. Jobs in durable manufacturing generally pay more—and so it was significant that for African Americans, the decline in the better-paid durable sector was on the order of 50 percent versus a more modest 22 percent decline in nondurables.[15]

Adding to the wage pressures wrought by the structural shifts away from and also within manufacturing was a decline in unionization. The unionization trends in California are shown in Figure 3.1. Private sector unionization rates fell by nearly half between 1983 and 2000, a trend on pace with the nation but alarming nonetheless.[16] The unionization drop-off was even worse in manufacturing—from 21 to 7 percent over the same period, partly reflecting the recomposition between more highly paid durables, where labor had a toehold, and the less-organized and less-well-paid sector of nondurables.

But the chart reveals another important trend: even as private sector unions were slipping into crisis, public sector unionization actually rose, with the share of public sector workers who were unionized increasing from 43 percent in 1983 to slightly over half

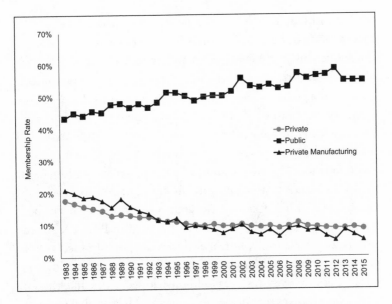

FIGURE 3.1: Private and public sector union membership, 1983–2015.

by 2000. The decline of private sector unionization in tandem with the rise of public sector unions had an important political effect: long before Republican governor Scott Walker of Wisconsin took advantage of this trend to attack public sector unions in his own state in 2011, it had become easy for workers once protected by a union and once believing themselves to be in solidarity with other unionized workers to instead view themselves as taxpayers being burdened by public sector union workers who were much better positioned to hold on to their wages and benefits.

This was all the more the case in California because union influence in state government actually rose in the wake of Proposition 13—probably not at all what proponent Howard Jarvis and his allies had in mind.[17] By starving local governments and school systems and making them ever-more reliant on redistribution from the state, the new fiscal arrangements meant that those seeking to protect public sector labor rights and benefits needed to lobby mostly in a single location—the capital city of Sacramento—rather than in multiple locations across the state. But while this made it easier for public sector unions to secure high wages for their members, not every success in the state capital was interpreted with sympathy by the rest of the hard-pressed working class; rather, it was perceived by many Californians as simply adding to a government that was distant, expensive, and out of touch.[18]

Proposition 13 had yet another perhaps surprising impact: it helped to induce a bankruptcy in one of the state's most conservative locales, Orange County. The county had been one of the bedrocks of the "fiscal populism" that gave birth to Prop 13, but the results were hard to live with: with state support strained and local voters positively allergic to new taxes, the county treasurer instead chose to invest reserves in high-yield securities, like the sort of risky derivatives that helped to shipwreck the national economy in 2008. By 1994, the county was raising 12 percent of its revenue from interest income on these securities, well above the 3 percent average for the state—and it was projecting that it would obtain a startling third of its revenues from interest income in 1995.[19]

It sounded too good to be true—and it was. Orange County was forced to declare bankruptcy when interest rates did not fall in line with the treasurer's predictions. One San Francisco–based financial adviser to local government suggested that "you can pin this almost 100 percent on Proposition 13," a declaration that might have caused some to doubt the wisdom of combining low taxes and casino capitalism.[20] But this was Orange County: voters refused to raise taxes and instead county government eventually raided other agencies to pay back bondholders. And in another act of conservative consistency: the fact that the combination of Prop 13 restraints and free-market investment strategies had produced disaster was gleefully ignored in favor of yet more complaints about an overreaching government.

Meanwhile, the state's economy began to experience an important geographic shift in terms of activity and momentum. While less dependent on military spending than Southern California, Northern California had not been exempt from the economic strains. Between 1984 and 1991, even before the recession gained full force, employment growth in Silicon Valley was less than 1 percent a year, half the rate for the United States as a whole; manufacturing employment in Silicon Valley (putting together computers and integrated chips, among other things) actually slipped by nearly 1 percent a year over that same period.[21] But one difference between Silicon Valley and Southern California as each experienced economic pressure in the early 1990s was that the former had active business leaders who recognized that they were in the midst of deep structural change and sought to mobilize a response. The result was something called Joint Venture Silicon Valley, the first of a series of regional collaboratives that would struggle in the 1990s, most prominently in Northern California, to find a new path forward.

Still, there was no clear path for a once-proud state that seemed to be coming apart in terms of race, politics, and economic fortunes. California had ranked twenty-fifth of the fifty states in income inequality in 1969—smack dab in the middle. By 1989, California had moved up to fourteenth in the state inequality rankings, and by the time the 1990s were done, it was the sixth-most unequal state in the Union.[22] So while the Clinton years (1993–2001) were soon to bring a period of national economic expansion, California in the early 1990s was a land of shedding jobs, eroding unions, and downsized hopes—a familiar phenomenon outside of California today. This was a far cry from the beacon of opportunity that had called so many to the Golden State in the 1940s and 1950s—and the economic desperation that resulted was soon to manifest in a particularly vicious sort of racial politics.

Scapegoats and Scoundrels

As the economy slipped, immigrants, the poor, and people of color soon became convenient scapegoats for the state's woes. In the white suburban communities of Los Angeles, Orange, and San Diego Counties, the same strain of conservatives that had produced the tax revolt of the 1970s was pivoting to a campaign to "save our state" from the growing immigrant presence.[23] The attacks happened both through specific policy proposals and through the negative portrayal in the public debate of the poor, of people on public assistance, of immigrants, and of people of color. But the reason that the image of a growing minority population as a drain on the state resonated so strongly had to do with context and history.

One factor: California was indeed experiencing an immigrant "shock." Forty percent of the increase in the U.S. foreign-born population in the 1970s occurred in California, a startling figure until you realize that in the subsequent decade of the 1980s, it was even higher: in those ten years, slightly more than half of the entire uptick in the U.S. foreign-born population occurred in the Golden State. Another way of looking at this: between 1970 and 1990, the share of the foreign born in California jumped from just under 9 percent to nearly 22 percent; over the same period in the rest of the United States, the share of the foreign born barely budged, rising from 4.3 percent to 6.1 percent.[24] In essence, the rest of the country was shielded from the demographic wave as California absorbed the bulk of the flows resulting from the economic dislocations and civil wars plaguing America's southern neighbors. In that light, it is little wonder that anti-immigrant politics made a special debut in California, foreshadowing what would happen to the rest of America in the 2000s and 2010s.

But why did anti-immigrant politics gain such traction in the 1990s—a period in which California was taking only 21 percent of the national increase in the foreign born—even though it was the 1980s when the bulk of the immigrants began to arrive en masse?[25] Like the current storm in U.S. politics, it was partly because while the 1980s were tough, with wages stagnating and the seeds of deindustrialization beginning to sprout, the true economic devastation hit with force in the early 1990s as the national recession and federal cutbacks in defense spending rocked the Golden State. But the ease of scapegoating in that circumstance was also because the racial die for California politics had already been cast, making the 1990s particularly fertile for such xenophobic appeals.

For example, when Democratic governor Jerry Brown left office in 1983, he was succeeded by a conservative Republican, California attorney general George Deukmejian.[26] Deukmejian had the good fortune to run in 1982 against Los Angeles mayor Tom Bradley—or perhaps better put, he had the good fortune to be white. Bradley, the first Black mayor of a large predominantly white city, was widely considered a favorite, and polling data suggested that he would coast to victory.[27] But when the votes were cast, he had lost, giving rise in political science literature to something called the "Bradley effect," that is, the discrepancy between what voters will say to a pollster because they don't want to be perceived as discriminatory—and what they will do when the curtain is drawn in a voting booth.[28]

That Deukmejian was elected in this context—and reelected by an overwhelming majority in a second run against Bradley—speaks volumes about the racial politics bubbling beneath the surface in the 1980s. And it wasn't just about who won and lost: the structure of government was itself becoming less effective and less accessible to the "new majority."[29] As Peter Schrag convincingly argues in *Paradise Lost*, voters in the state effectively took control of governance by essentially stripping the legislature of its ability to raise revenues and then taking matters into their own hands with an explosion of ballot initiatives.[30] Nearly the same number of initiatives were passed in the eighteen years between 1978 and 1996 as in the sixty-seven years between 1911 and 1978.[31] It's part of the reason why this book has to bounce from proposition to proposition to tell the state's political story, but the underlying strategy was simple: lock down the tax code and then consolidate decision making in the hands of an older, white majority more likely to vote in off-year elections.

California's racial divide and broken social consensus were further symbolized by the Los Angeles civil unrest of 1992. Triggered by the shocking verdict in the trial of four police officers accused of beating a Black driver named Rodney King—a sort of early demonstration of the way the system is rigged in favor of police even when their actions are filmed—the resulting days of rioting cost more than fifty lives and caused nearly $1 billion worth of property damage (more than $1.5 billion in today's dollars). While this eventually turned out to be a significant turning point for social movement organizing on the left—mostly because the civil unrest vividly illustrated the rage that could be channeled to better ends if only community-based organizations could become more effective—it was also a shock to the average Angeleno and Californian. In Los Angeles, for example, the immediate political reaction was the 1993 election of a Republican mayor, Richard Riordan, who proclaimed that he was "tough enough to turn L.A. around," a sort of prime law-and-order example of "dog whistle politics."[32]

It was in this racially charged atmosphere that Republican Pete Wilson, a former San Diego mayor who was generally considered a moderate by the standards of the GOP, was elected and began his term as governor in 1991. It seemed like a bit of a short straw: as he arrived, the economy skidded, the state budget was strained, and he responded with a series of fiscal measures, including a plaintive call on the federal government to repay California for providing services to immigrants.[33] Democratic senator Dianne Feinstein helped to make immigration a mainstream issue in the public debate, particularly with a June 1993 op-ed in the *Los Angeles Times* in which she came out publicly with a hard stand against "illegal residents" and a call for tougher border enforcement and proposals to cut what she claimed were nearly $2 billion in additional state-assumed fiscal costs from education and other services.[34]

It was in this context that former U.S. Immigration and Naturalization Service official and lobbyist for the Federation for American Immigration Reform Alan Nelson teamed up with Harold Ezell to draft the language that would eventually become Proposition 187, an effort to strip undocumented immigrants of access to virtually all state public benefits.[35] Wilson initially did not heed Nelson and Ezell's more restrictionist gambit and instead focused between 1991 and 1993 on lobbying Washington, D.C., for the more than $200 million that he claimed the federal government owed the state for services provided to "illegal aliens." Arguing that the real issue was the need for welfare reform, he threw his weight behind Proposition 165, the Government Accountability and Taxpayer Protection Act, on the 1992 ballot.[36] If passed, it would have reduced welfare spending and given the governor more powers over the budget. Instead, it failed, with 53 percent of voters casting ballots against it, partly because of a smart move by public employee unions and their allies to place a competing initiative aimed at raising taxes on the rich; that measure also failed, but it managed to act as a diversion and draw away corporate donations and business energy from the governor's effort.[37]

With his direct approach to the budget undone, the economy still struggling, and a reelection campaign on the horizon, Wilson had to figure out another appeal to the voters. It was back to immigrants, although this time more directly: he threw his weight behind what would become Proposition 187 (Illegal Aliens Ineligible for Public Benefits), persuading the state Republican Party to donate $200,000 for a flailing signature-gathering effort to qualify the measure drafted by Nelson and Ezell for the ballot.[38]

Wilson then took the message to heart, including developing a famous campaign ad showing a grainy black-and-white video of Mexican immigrants running across the border accompanied by an ominous voice-over proclaiming that "they keep coming."[39] It worked: once as much as 23 points behind his election challenger, Democrat Kathleen Brown (yup, Pat's daughter and Jerry's sister), Wilson captured 55 percent of the votes and Proposition 187 passed with 59 percent of the vote in 1994.[40] It also provided wind to the GOP sails: Republicans won five additional statewide contests and gained nine more seats in the state assembly.[41]

Part of the reason for the Prop 187 victory and its coattails: while the state was nearly majority-minority, with whites making up only 53 percent of the population in 1994, the electorate was still 80 percent white.[42] But while the victory for Prop 187 was heralded by anti-immigrant activists, it proved to be Pyrrhic. Proposition 187 sought to ban undocumented immigrants from public social services, nonemergency health care, and public education, and to require various state and local agencies to report anyone suspected of being in the state without legal documentation status to the state attorney general and immigration authorities—but it had a significant underlying problem: it was largely unconstitutional.[43]

As a result, virtually every part of the law was overturned in the courts, although Wilson and the GOP got to keep their seats, at least for a while. This short-term thinking—toss out "red meat" policies to an enraged and racially antagonistic electorate and leave the worrying about constitutionality to a later date—was certainly mimicked by the original "travel ban" promoted by the incoming Trump administration in early 2017. What is the more interesting question—and perhaps hopeful parallel—is what took place to make sure the hold of Wilson and the GOP on the state reins of power was indeed just "for a while." It was a turning point for California activists—and one hopes the same for the national resistance building since the 2016 elections. In the words of Maria

Elena Durazo, an important L.A.-based labor leader who would go on to be secretary-treasurer of the Los Angeles County Federation of Labor from 2006 to 2014, "Prop. 187 was a big factor in reminding us that we had to do something on the electoral level that was different, and it helped to radicalize the immigrant community in a broad, broad way. Way beyond the labor movement, way beyond the workers we were organizing in the unions. In a very huge way, they radicalized."[44]

The tension between these more radicalized elements of resistance and mainstream Democratic leaders certainly has contemporary parallels in debates about how to contend and contest in the era of Trump—as well as in the 2016 election itself. Should voters be provided alternatives that are bold and different—or is the best approach to play to an imagined moderate middle? In the Prop 187 case, the main traditional opposition perspective came in the form of Taxpayers Against 187, a group of labor unions, civil rights organizations, and Democratic allies who contended, in the words of the official ballot argument against the proposition, that "illegal Immigration is a REAL problem, but Proposition 187 is NOT A REAL SOLUTION."[45] With that logic in mind, they suggested that kicking undocumented kids out of school and undocumented adults out of nonemergency health services was likely to cause an increase in crime and communicable disease and actually raise social costs.[46] It was certainly meant to catch the then-middle of the electorate, but it was also a rather odd approach for the long haul: rather than humanizing the undocumented and stressing what immigrants could add, it painted the population as a sort of pestilence that would cause less damage if it was quarantined in existing institutions than if it was set to roam free among the population.

But if some thought that the best strategy was to basically play on the same fears that triggered the initiative in the first place, a different approach was being developed in the streets and neighborhoods of urban California. The grassroots effort was particularly important in Los Angeles County, which in 1990 held more than 46 percent of the recently arrived foreign born in California. Nearby Orange and San Diego Counties hosted another 16 percent of all the state's recently arrived, a concentration that explains why the politics both for and against immigration was particularly heated in these locales.[47] Southern California's grassroots activists essentially concluded that Prop 187 was likely to win and believed that a tactic of contributing to the demonization of immigrants to defeat it was not only politically distasteful but actually worked against a longer-term goal of mobilizing these new communities to defend themselves against attack.[48]

Disagreements over strategy erupted sharply in the wake of a march in October 1994 that ended with nearly one hundred thousand protestors at L.A.'s city hall, with many waving Mexican flags; for the more moderate taxpayers-style opposition, this was exactly the wrong image to impart and they denounced the approach both in public and in private.[49] For the progressive activists, the march instead signaled a proud declaration that immigrants had a right to be different and yet still a part of California society—that integration meant something different from assimilation and that human rights actually were attached to humans, not just citizens. Among the lead organizers of that march: Kevin de León, who would go on to become the president pro tem of the state senate in 2014 and one of the co-authors of the forceful California rebuttal to Trump that opens this book.[50]

As activist groups debriefed and reflected after the election results, several key lessons were drawn. For the activists, the fact that more radical organizers in San Francisco had been able to turn that city and county against Proposition 187 suggested the benefits of focusing on the communities most impacted by negative policies rather than avoiding the race issues that might cause discomfort for middle-class whites.[51] On the other hand, that was San Francisco—and progressive activists had to admit that they were often ill-suited to compete in the electoral arena in less liberal areas of the state, partly because of the political terrain but also because they had often developed their groups through either direct advocacy or direct service delivery rather than through voter mobilization.[52] Winning would require both organizing a "new majority" to lift up its own issues *and* developing a professionalized approach to elections—a combination that would help to turn the state around nearly two decades later.

The Hits Keep Coming

Unfortunately, two decades is quite a long time—and in the meantime, the new organizers would get plenty of unpleasant opportunities to test their theories, enhance their voter strategies, and practice purely oppositional politics. For as it turns out, Prop 187 proved to be just the first blow in a series of what Daniel HoSang has eloquently termed "racial propositions"—that is, initiatives put on the ballot to capitalize on the white fear and resentment of immigrants and people of color prominent across the state in the 1980s and 1990s.[53]

Indeed, the onslaught that started in 1994 may have been signaled by Prop 187, but it was not confined to simply an anti-immigrant zeitgeist. With Republican governors George Deukmejian and Pete Wilson promising to get "tough on crime," and against a backdrop of the 1992 civil unrest in Los Angeles, many voters were looking for a fix to restore order.[54] It came in the form of a three-strikes initiative, Proposition 184, that did much more than the label implied: not only did it mandate that the state sentence a defendant to twenty-five years to life for a third felony conviction, but it also raised sentencing requirements for a second felony and did not require that the "third strike" felony actually be of a violent nature.[55] Worried about political consequences of appearing to be coddling criminals, the state Democratic Party was "unusually mute on this measure"; while some individual

Democrats were vocal in their opposition, most prominent political figures, such as Senator Dianne Feinstein, were either in support or chose to keep quiet about the possible risks of overincarceration.[56] Against a backdrop of economic stress and demographic change—and with violent crime trending upward in the early 1990s—Prop 184 won with a resounding 72 percent of the vote.[57]

The impacts on the state prison population can be seen in Figure 3.2, in which California's prison population is charted against the sum of all other state prison populations in the rest of the United States.[58] As can be seen, the increase in the prison population actually predated the three-strikes approach, but it continued at an accelerated pace thereafter; while the newly incarcerated three strikers added to the buildup, including one man sentenced to twenty-five years to life for snatching a slice of pizza from some youngsters, it was part of a general "lock 'em up" pattern already under way in the Golden State.[59] The expanding system was expensive: state spending from the General Fund on "corrections" increased by more than twentyfold between 1978–79 and 2007–8, rising from about 20 percent of state spending on higher education to about 85 percent of spending on higher education.[60] And while the figure also makes clear that California began to turn the corner on a rising state prison population in the late 2000s, this was mostly driven by court orders mandating a reduction in overcrowding as well as the need to shed costs in a fiscal crisis, including moving some inmates from the state system to county jails.[61]

What is not there in the graph is the demographic composition of who got caught up in the law-and-order hysteria: in 1995, the prison population was more than 70 percent people of color, more or less evenly split between African Americans and Latinos, even though the adult population in that year in California was about 43 percent people of color.[62] The distorted color of justice was not surprising: while the flagship killings that prompted the three-strikes proposal—the murders of Polly Klaas in 1993 and

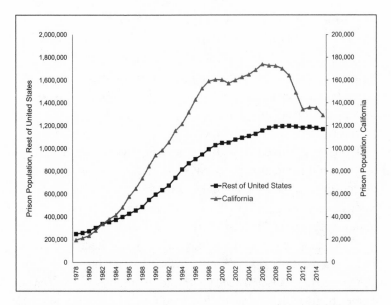

FIGURE 3.2: State prison population, California and the rest of the United States, 1978–2014.

Kimber Reynolds in 1992—were both done by whites (no Willie Horton lurking in this inflammatory background), it seemed clear that voters had a pretty good idea of who they were hoping to lock up for life.

The anti-crime, pro-punishment tone was reflected later in another proposition that bookended the decade. This idea, behind what became Proposition 21—basically treating juveniles as adults when accused of certain crimes—was initially put forward in 1998 by then governor Pete Wilson. Wilson seems to have thought that just like Prop 187 and Prop 184 greased his path to gubernatorial reelection, this assault on teens would help pave his path to the 2000 Republican presidential nomination; as it turns out, his proposal did make it to the 2000 California primary ballot, but Wilson himself did not.[63] It mirrored related measures throughout the country, all prompted by a view that violent crime among youths was on a dramatic increase.[64] And in keeping with the spirit of the times, Proposition 21 did not propose to prevent crime by amplifying youth services, improving education, and guaranteeing jobs. Instead, it sought to strip away protections for juvenile arrestees and make it easier for them to be tried as adults, again with racial imagery about "superpredators" making clear who it was that was being targeted.[65]

Of course, targeting youths also had another impact: helping to mobilize youths themselves to defend their own interests. According to Yuki Kidokoro, formerly of an environmental justice organizing group called Communities for a Better Environment, Prop 21 "helped catalyze a growing youth movement in California. It happened to coincide around the 2000 Democratic Convention in Los Angeles which led to a big convergence of movements, especially the youth movement; because of that, it helped to create leaders who understood themselves to be part of a broader movement."[66]

But while there were glimmers of hope in new organizing beginning to gain some momentum, the basic story of the 1990s was simple: the racialized hits just kept coming. In 1996, for example, Proposition 209 was placed on the ballot. Also known as the California Civil Rights Initiative (CCRI), it aimed to ban affirmative action by prohibiting so-called discrimination or preferential treatment by state and other public entities, including in university admissions.[67] While opposition to affirmative action had acquired a bipartisan sheen after being endorsed at the national level by the Democratic Leadership Conference, a group chaired by then Arkansas governor and future Democratic president Bill Clinton, Wilson clearly saw the fight as a way to signal his movement toward the increasingly conservative base of the national Republican Party.[68] It also conveniently made explicit the divisions between "blue collar labor constituencies and the civil rights and minority wings of the Democratic Party"—a tension that continues to this day.[69]

The initial pre-proposition salvo in the affirmative action battle came in the summer of 1995, when Pete Wilson and Ward Connerly, an African American member of the University of California's Board of Regents, proposed that the UC system ban the use of "race, religion, sex, color, ethnicity, or national origin" in university admissions and employment.[70] The resolution was passed 14–10 by the UC Board of Regents. Tasting blood, Wilson and Ward then led a campaign to get Proposition 209 on the ballot by gathering 1.1 million signatures.[71] As with Prop 187, tension as to how to respond erupted between traditional Democratic leadership and more grassroots organizers. Feeling boxed in, leadership proposed something that would not be quite as racially tinged— but just racially tinged enough to get mainstream support. The Equal Opportunity without Quotas measure was their compromise: it sought to end quotas and would have stopped "the hiring of 'unqualified applicants' and levied fines against anyone found to have improperly benefited from an affirmative action program." However, that measure was shelved when it was determined that it would have ended the support to school programs created during the desegregation pushes in the 1970s and 1980s.[72]

With no alternative measure to promote, many mainstream Democrats argued that CCRI could instead be defeated by stressing the ways in which affirmative action benefited white women. By contrast, Jan Adams—a community organizer at the Applied Research Center in Oakland who had been engaged with the grassroots efforts challenging Proposition 187—argued that Proposition 209 could be defeated by educating and mobilizing "Black, Latino, Asian American and progressive white voters" as well as limiting the "margin of support among white voters for the initiative to no more than 55 percent."[73] This shift in strategic organizing was catalyzed in the form of Californians for Justice, an effort that managed to collect eight hundred thousand signatures, recruit eight thousand volunteers, and train two thousand people.[74]

This attempt to mobilize an "emerging majority" also forti-
fied local efforts like Action for Grassroots Empowerment and
Neighborhood Development Alternatives (AGENDA) in South
L.A.; as AGENDA's founding director, Anthony Thigpenn, com-
mented, "We built first an organization focused on grassroots
leadership development and power building, then a very broad
electoral coalition in South L.A., something called the South L.A.
Affirmative Action Project. From there we then built an even
broader coalition in L.A. County as part of the anti-209 statewide
coalition. That was AGENDA's first experience in doing serious
systematic electoral work."[75] But it would not be the last, as the
lessons learned from doing serious electoral work—and coupling
that systematically with community organizing—would go on to
inform an integrated voter engagement strategy that would have
a fundamental effect on the state as it moved into the twenty-first
century.

Unfortunately, the work had not matured and the new century
had not arrived: neither the mainstream nor the grassroots efforts
were enough to turn the tide and Proposition 209 was approved
by nearly 55 percent of the vote.[76] On the other hand, exit polls
indicated that the measure was rejected by 74 percent of African
American voters, 76 percent of Latino voters, and 61 percent of
Asian American voters.[77] Reading the electoral entrails suggested
some interesting possibilities. First, the Black-Brown alliance was
not necessarily expected; although Latino opposition to 209 was
partially because of constant reminders that Pete Wilson supported the ban, this seemed to bode well for the future of multiracial organizing in California. Second, the Asian American/
Pacific Islander sympathy for affirmative action, particularly given
the way that some argued that that population would benefit from
more "objective" criteria, was early evidence of what turns out to
be a steady drift leftward by Asian American and Pacific Islander
voters.[78]

In a striking parallel, just over twenty years later, the Trump administration has set its sights on the same affirmative action policy battle nationally—and as in the Golden State, what seems politically appealing now may be likely to further drive people of color away from the Republican Party. Meanwhile, back in California, the effort to ban affirmative action was followed up two years later with Proposition 227, a measure designed to restrict bilingual education just as the state's number of limited English proficient (LEP) students had jumped to 1.4 million, the most LEP students in the country.[79] The proponents of Prop 227, which was billed as "English for the Children," argued that bilingual education was holding students back and mainly served a sort of bilingual education establishment consisting of teachers and other professionals—exactly the sort of slam against supposedly self-reproducing bureaucracy that is a favorite of right-wing ideologues.[80] The main financiers of the measure articulated a high-minded rhetoric about educational opportunity—indeed, the lead sponsor, businessman Ron Unz, had opposed Prop 187 and was deeply concerned about being portrayed as a racist. But for many voters supporting Prop 227, the attempt to drive a stake through bilingualism resonated with their fear that Latinos were resisting assimilation and that California was slipping away back to its once-Mexican roots.

As with earlier propositions, mainstream political consultants suggested that the way to swing voters was by emphasizing unforeseen consequences—like the scary prospect of mixing older Latino students with younger non-Latino students because they would share the same level of English ability. Meanwhile, the progressive position was itself under challenge, partly because some Latino parents really did want their children to be mainstreamed into English. Labor unions, which could have assisted the anti-227 coalition, were distracted by another ballot initiative aimed at limiting the power of unions to support political causes.[81] As a result, the measure passed with 61 percent of the vote.[82] Yet the racial divides were stark: according to a *Los Angeles Times* exit poll, two-thirds of white voters, nearly 60 percent of Asian American voters, nearly half of African American voters, but less than 40 percent of Latino voters supported Prop 227.[83]

In short, it was hard not to see the 1990s as a rather brutal series of blows aimed at what was soon to become the state's new majority. The state began the 1990s with a deep recession that tended to impact communities of color even more sharply than others and that was followed by a series of ballot propositions seeking to restore an earlier California, one with fewer immigrants and more English, fewer civil rights and more "public safety." Added to the sense of attack was a national-level welfare reform in 1996 that imposed work requirements and a lifetime cap on assistance, and also introduced regulations that limited access to support even for legal immigrants.[84] For Californians of color, the economy was slipping, the political noose was tightening, and the safety net was being shredded.

While the 1990s series of racially motivated propositions were often given electoral life by calculating politicians, including a governor cravenly seeking reelection and then the presidency, the deeper driving force was the same right-wing populist movement that had resisted residential integration and tried to lift up the fiscal drawbridge with Proposition 13. To fight the drift to the right, traditional Democratic leaders and institutions tried to counter with reasoned but backward-looking appeals: yes, immigrants are bad, but better that we keep them contained in schools; yes, juveniles are prone to crime, but we'll save money by locking them up for shorter periods of time. Meanwhile, another group of organizers was beginning to realize that the only way to counter a legitimate, if unattractive, social movement on the right was with another movement on the left, one with an authentic base, a clear and positive vision, and an actual strategy for winning and taking power.

Those debates continue to play out on a national level today, with more mainstream actors suggesting that there may be possibilities to work with a political figure who also manipulated racial anxiety to secure the presidency, and more progressive forces arguing that what is really needed is a movement that can resolutely resist conservative overreach and chart a grassroots path back to power. In California in those days at the crossroads—and in the nation today—it would take some time for that movement of resistance to develop, mature, and achieve electoral strength and policy influence. In the meanwhile, more blows to the body politic were to come, including to the rest of America.

Exporting Austerity and Fear

It was bad enough that California was being dragged right just as the state needed to find a more inclusive footing for its inevitably more diverse future. But it was also the case that the Golden State was increasingly becoming a platform for trying out bad ideas before shipping them to other states as quickly as possible.

The first in the series of negative exports came in the form of a generalized revulsion against taxes. After Proposition 13 passed in 1978, other states quickly became emboldened to enact similar change. Within six months, seventeen states had placed restrictive tax measures on their ballots, with all but five being approved. Eventually, twenty-five states enacted legislation that tied spending to economic growth, something clearly aimed at constraining the expansion of state governments.[85] Perhaps the most surprising copycat legislation came in Massachusetts, a supposedly liberal bastion. "Proposition 2½"—dubbed this in part because it imposed a 2.5 percent limit on taxes as a percentage of assessed property value and put a similar 2.5 percent limit on annual increases in property assessments—was literally written with the help of Howard Jarvis.[86] And as in California, the resulting revenue gaps eventually came to hurt education and other key spending.[87]

While the state-by-state tax revolt rollout had its own complex dynamics, particularly given variations in the rules governing state and local finance, there was one rather straight through line from Prop 13 to national politics: the rise of Ronald Reagan, a Republican. Reagan "described Proposition 13 as a rebellion against 'costly, overpowering government' and urged Republicans to adopt Proposition 13 as their mascot in the 1980 presidential race."[88] He himself did so by embracing tax cuts as a major tool for stirring economic growth, a far cry from the fiscal probity he had demonstrated by raising taxes when first becoming governor of California.[89]

The national tax-cutting fervor was facilitated by a bit of magical thinking promulgated by the Prop 13 experience: because California had immediately made up for local spending shortfalls by dipping into reserves, it created the illusion that government could be cut with few consequences. When Reagan took the presidency in 1981, he persuaded senators and representatives to buy into the fantasy: in July of that year, Congress passed the single largest income tax cut ever enacted, with Reagan arguing that this would boost growth so much that it would pay for itself with increased revenues.[90] It did not really work out that way—the deficit doubled under Reagan—and it took the presidency of Bill Clinton, in a sort of foreshadowing of Jerry Brown's fiscal sobriety in California, to finally move the government back to a fiscal surplus, a phenomenon not seen since 1960.[91]

That was just in time to hand the economy off to another supply-side fantasist, George W. Bush, whose 2001 and 2003 tax cuts—sold as middle-class relief but aimed largely at the wealthiest Americans—managed to double the national debt and derail the economy. Another Democrat, in this case Barack Obama, cleaned up the mess—just in time for President Donald Trump to propose sketchy tax plans also aimed at benefiting the biggest corporations and wealthiest Americans, also promising rapid growth, and also far more likely to blow up the deficit.[92] In short, the tax-cutting fervor at a national level has generally hurt fiscal balance and often impeded the ability to invest in the future. California and Proposition 13 had basically been dry runs for economic destruction—first in the largest state, then in America as a whole.[93]

California's toxic exports were not limited to fiscal strategies: the passage of Proposition 209, the constitutional amendment to ban affirmative action, touched off a broader movement led by former University of California regent Ward Connerly to spread this brand of racial denial (or rather, racism denial) far and wide.[94] In the immediate aftermath of the passage of Prop 209, Connerly founded the American Civil Rights Institute (ACRI) to support local organizers trying to place similar ballot propositions in more than twenty states.[95] The most immediate manifestation of his efforts was the passage of a similar affirmative action ban in the state of Washington in 1998, with an even clearer replication occurring in Michigan in 2006 when the ACRI funded local forces and helped to secure a 16-point electoral margin against the use of "racial preferences."[96]

The point is simply that what started in California did not stay in California. Proposition 227, which basically banned bilingual education in 1998, quickly led to other movements to enact similar legislation in Arizona, Colorado, and Massachusetts.[97] Meanwhile, the three-strikes idea took off after early passage in Washington and California. Spurred by "tough on crime" rhetoric—and fueled by worries about personal and economic insecurity, with today's echoes being fear of terrorism and job loss—the basic idea of mandatory sentences for third-felony convictions was extended to more than twenty states, with most passing in the mid-1990s.[98] And completing the picture, the granddaddy of all racialized bad ideas, Proposition 187, also had legs—although like the affirmative action debate, this took a bit of time to mature and infect the rest of the national body politic.

When it did, it was a doozy. As other states eventually experienced the sort of growth in their immigrant populations that had discombobulated California, there was a wave of highly restrictionist measures in response. States like Colorado, Idaho, Oklahoma, and Virginia began to try to limit access to public benefits to a growing population of undocumented residents.[99] Meanwhile in 2010, Arizona set a new low point for anti-immigrant legislation with Senate Bill 1070, an effort that not only attempted to cut off undocumented immigrants from work but also made it a state misdemeanor to be in the country illegally. It capped that off by authorizing local authorities to enforce the law by checking a person's status based on "reasonable suspicion," a standard that opponents suggested amounted to an invitation for racial profiling.

Copycat efforts soon cropped up in Alabama and Georgia, often resisted by business interests worried about losing their workforce.[100] Strikingly, those movements did not only have their philosophical roots in the Golden State; they seemed to have their real roots there as well. In Alabama, for example, the head of a federation of Republican women pushing restrictionism had actually been a councilwoman and mayor in an L.A. suburb during the turmoil that produced Prop 187.[101] Of course, the most significant impact came in the form of the Trump phenomenon: bashing immigrants for political favor became a path to the American presidency.

Standing back from the rubble caused by hate, it may be easy for Californians to point the contemporary finger at the xenophobia wracking other states, particularly now that a slew of pro-immigrant politicians and policies have changed California's own political terrain. But as historian Julie M. Weise reminds us, "Californians should resist the temptation to congratulate themselves on their state's open-mindedness. When it comes to insulting immigrants and building walls to keep them out, Californians were pioneers"—indeed, not just pioneers but often eager purveyors of the anti-tax, anti-opportunity, and anti-immigrant franchise.[102] And while this history of exporting the bad can leave a rightful mark of shame, it also suggests a new and important role and responsibility for California: sharing the movement-building efforts since the 1990s that have helped to turn the state around.

One Last Gasp

But that admonition gets ahead of the story, partly because as the twenty-first century dawned, California was still cresting to full implosion. The 1990s had indeed been a harrowing time: wave after wave of right-leaning proposals battered a state undergoing rapid demographic change, shocked by recession, and looking to get its social and economic footing. But just when Californians needed a period of stabilization—to assess the damage they were causing to their government, economy, and sense of social solidarity—came a sort of last gasp that laid bare the dysfunction now cloaking the Golden State.

As the 1990s were nearing their close, Gray Davis—a Democratic lieutenant governor whose stolid personality was well captured by his first name—decided to enter the 1998 race for governor. The good news for him: the Republicans decided to nominate Dan Lungren, a state attorney general who had none of the moderate credentials that had allowed Pete Wilson to mask what was in effect an extreme agenda. Lungren was instead the real deal: labeled the "ideological soul mate" of Newt Gingrich when serving in Congress, he was an ardent supporter of three strikes and, as the state's attorney general, had proposed trying teens as adults as early as 1993.[103] Given the conservative victories of the 1990s, Lungren seemed to have a chance—but apparently, California voters liked their governors to start in the middle of the political road and then be dragged rightward by the reckless votes of the populace itself. In any case, while "Lungren emphasized his crime-fighting record, Davis talked about improving education and the need for inclusive politics in this wildly diverse state. As a result, Davis staked out the vital middle ground and won handily" with an extraordinary 20-percentage-point margin.[104]

The good news for newly elected governor Davis was that he had won; the bad news was that he had to govern. Among the challenges he quickly faced was an electricity crisis brought on in part by a bill passed unanimously by both the state assembly and the state senate in 1996 that had deregulated the state's electricity industry.[105] Akin to the national financial deregulation signed by President Bill Clinton in 1999—which would help to trigger the financial meltdown of the later 2000s—the theory was that unbridled competition in the energy sphere would allow consumers to enjoy low prices and stable supplies. Instead, it worked a lot more like the subprime loans and financial derivatives that would nearly destroy the nation's financial system in 2008: it resulted in both economic crisis and political scandal.

With the freedom to let the market dictate outcomes, whole-sale prices quintupled between the summer of 1999 and the summer of 2000, even as blackouts rolled through the state.[106] The state's two main investor-owned utilities became insolvent; one was forced to declare bankruptcy, and California's consumers and businesses were estimated to have paid $40 billion in additional energy costs.[107] Profiting from market manipulation were traders associated with Enron, who had managed to create the appearance of shortages and congestion on the grid in order to drive up prices.[108] Meanwhile, the electricity crisis did little to enhance Davis's reputation as a skilled manager, particularly as California sought to address the blackout issue by locking itself into high-cost contracts to purchase electricity.

Added to the economic and political strain was what came to be known as the "dot-bomb" recession, a national downturn that had its roots in the sharp decline in the California high-technology industry.[109] Here, too, the inherent instability of markets played a role: with tremendous interest in the burgeoning Internet, the tech-heavy NASDAQ stock market exploded in value, with its bellwether index peaking in March 2000, quickly collapsing through the next year, and finally bottoming out in October 2002 after the exchange had wiped out around $5 trillion in market valuation.[110] The impact on the national economy was actually relatively modest: a national recession started in March 2001 and ended a scant eight months later. The overall impact on California was also relatively modest, but the regional variations were striking: Santa Clara County, the heart of Silicon Valley, lost more than 8 percent in employment between January 2001 and April 2002, while Orange County and San Diego County actually saw employment go up over that same period—and Los Angeles County posted a net decrease in jobs only after April 2002, when the effects on aviation and tourism from the terrorist attacks on September 11, 2001, rippled their way across that local economy.[111]

The tech collapse had impacts beyond a sharp hit to "professional and business services"—a rubric that covered a lot of the new software companies.[112] First, it shook the confidence of Silicon Valley: after seeing itself as the wave of the future and the exemplar of the "new economy," it had managed to tank just like the older aerospace and manufacturing sectors. Second, the downturn had a negative impact on state finances, particularly since California had a relatively progressive state income tax, a feature that may have warmed the liberal heart but one that also made revenues particularly sensitive to this sort of high-end downturn. Indeed, by the summer of 2002, state lawmakers were facing a nearly $24 billion deficit, a challenge they remedied through cuts and borrowing.[113]

Despite the sea of disasters confronting him, in 2002, Davis lucked out again as he faced a conservative Republican contender, businessman Bill Simon. He managed to win with a 5 percent margin—but, tellingly, did not even achieve a majority.[114] Moreover, turnout was low—which, in turn, lowered the necessary number of signatures for a recall. With the threshold diminished

and the elections signaling that Davis was vulnerable, anti-tax activists launched a recall effort in early 2003, frustrated by Davis's
maneuvers to balance the state budget. They were quickly aided
in their battle when Davis's administration reversed a tax cut on
car licensing fees and, overnight, tripled registration costs for most
Californians. Hell hath no fury like a California driver scorned—
and so the race was on.

The election to come actually had two parts: voters were to vote
on whether to recall Davis and, if that passed, on who his successor
would be.[115] Jumping into the race to succeed Davis were Arnold
Schwarzenegger, Arianna Huffington, and 133 others, including a
porn star who did not secure the governorship but did manage to
make her way to *Celebrity Rehab* in 2008.[116] It was a sort of circus
that seemed guaranteed to produce the most skilled clown as the
winner—and Arnold Schwarzenegger, who eventually turned out
to be more serious and level-headed than his campaign would have
suggested, triumphed through a tremendous sense of showman-
ship that worked well in a short election window.

He assumed the governor's seat and immediately lived up to
his most spectacular promise, eliminating the increase in the car
registration fee. That quickly blew a $4 billion gap in the state
budget, and he then sought to work with Democratic legislators to
balance the budget.[117] However, bipartisanship broke down when
he called lawmakers "girlie-men" for not agreeing to his demands.
Misreading his 2003 victory for a mandate, he then launched a
2005 special election effort to pass a series of propositions, including limits on state spending, union power, lawmaker power
to draw districts, and teacher tenure. It was a conservative wish
list, to be sure, but it had a fatal flaw: the electorate had become
less than enchanted with the right-wing approach, and all his
propositions went down in defeat.[118]

A chagrined Terminator soon turned to combating global
warming rather than progressive constituencies and the state

pivoted toward a sort of tortured stability: budgets were still a
challenge to deliver on time, mostly because a determined Republican minority kept holding back their votes, and the economy, at
least until 2008, continued to grow even as wages for most continued to fall. Waiting in the wings, picking up small victory after small victory, were a series of progressive groups detailed in
Chapter 5, with savvy organizers slowly learning to get it right
in terms of local policy and working their way toward a strategy
for state politics. Their decade was coming, helped in part by a
series of economic and political changes that reset the stage for
struggle.

From Chaos Comes . . . ?

By 2009, Schwarzenegger had been in power for six years. The
budget he had promised to repair was skidding into red ink; the
economy he had promised to fix was being devastated by a housing meltdown; and the bipartisanship he had promised to revive
was nowhere in sight. With an unemployment rate that was on
its way to doubling between 2007 and 2010 and a Republican minority in the state legislature blocking any form of revenue relief,
it was no surprise that Kevin Starr, the preeminent historian of
California and the state librarian from 1994 to 2004, pronounced
that "California is on the verge of becoming the first failed state
in America."[119]

Other observers jumped into the analytical fray, with some
seeking to blame overregulation, liberal politics, and greedy public sector workers.[120] That was no surprise: when crisis is at hand,
everyone finds their favorite traditional scapegoat, often without
a lot of analytical support. But the signs of state dysfunction had
been there since 1978. With Prop 13, California had declared war
on its own future, tying up its fiscal system with tax limits that

starved needed public investment, discouraged quality employment, and furthered social disconnection. The voters had reacted to newcomers not with a conscious decision to build infrastructure, the hallmark of an earlier era, but instead with a desire to strip services, protect white privilege, and force new arrivals to give up their home languages. Reasonable worries about crime and security had generated not public support for job programs and improved education but rather a desire to lock up youths, expand the prison population, and, for many who were caught up in the system, throw away the key and their lives.

With the state adrift, California voters eventually foreshadowed what was to come to the nation in 2016: they elected a celebrity with a big ego and no experience to run the shop. Schwarzenegger came ready to change business as usual, promising to revamp state government and make the sort of conservative reforms that would finally tame spending and overregulation in Sacramento. But something was shifting beneath his feet that the Governator did not fully appreciate: the conservative social movement that launched Proposition 13 and the slew of more directly racist add-on proposals was slipping as the demography was changing and new progressive movements were on the rise.

These progressive movements were not just challenging the right but also pushing against traditional Democratic politics. Their view was that a "new majority" for California was possible, one that would reject racist appeals and restore the commitment to public infrastructure. They were generally based in more urban areas in coastal California, a weakness they would soon strive to address. They would be helped along by environmentalists looking for new allies—and warily considered by a business class that was slowly realizing that quality of life, strong human capital, and steady infrastructure were also key to their economic success. And while not all of this was perfectly clear at the time—change is always murky in the making—the new organizing, the

new economy, and the new environmentalism were opening possibilities for a political, economic, and social recovery. Whether
they can do the same for the nation as it works its way through
the current moment is a topic we come back to at the end of this
volume—but first, let's tell their story here in California.

4

SETTING THE STAGE

In April 2016, *Newsweek* featured a cover emblazoned with a photo of California Democratic governor Jerry Brown. Splashed across his forehead was a title that read "Altered State," a turn of phrase that harkened back to the psychedelia often associated with the state. Celebrated in the story within was a confluence of many good things: a booming state economy, a functioning political system, a newfound fiscal balance, vanguard leadership on climate change, and a widespread and not at all grudging acceptance of the ethnic diversity that had once caused the state to splinter across racial lines. It was a rather rosy picture, raising all sorts of questions about the change: how did a state considered to be nearly ungovernable and hopelessly adrift just a decade before now find itself being touted as such a success story? Lurking just beneath the main title and gubernatorial photo was *Newsweek*'s explanation of the transformation in an unsubtle subtitled nutshell: "How Jerry Brown Quietly Saved California."

It's a convenient tale, one in which a politician once lampooned as "Governor Moonbeam" returns decades later, in 2011, sobered by his time out of office, chagrinned by the damage he helped to cause in his first pass at the job, imbued with wisdom picked up by his famous stint with Mother Teresa, and ready to focus his time-honored penny-pinching ways on a state budget gone awry. Like many such stories, there are elements of truth—Brown was gone for a long time and he did hang out in India. But a simple tale of singular triumph can obscure a more fundamental fact:

California didn't get into the ditch just through a few poor policy choices, and it would not have been able to dig itself out without a series of important economic and political changes—and a set of social movements that were able to take advantage of those shifts.

Indeed, some of the same forces that were driving the economy toward inequality and social stress in the 1990s and early 2000s were also creating the basis for an eventual turnaround, at least in terms of policy. In particular, the widening income divide highlighted the significance of working poverty, generating both new political sympathies and new political actors. Persistent and painful income differentials by race helped lead the state past a fruitless debate of class versus race, one that seems to continue to plague contemporary Democrats reading the tea leaves from the 2016 presidential electoral loss. Meanwhile, the emerging power of high tech shifted the economic dynamism and wealth of the state to the Bay Area, giving business politics a more liberal—or at least less reactionary—cast. All three phenomena, along with a growing recognition of the regionalization of the California economy, conspired to produce a tentative acceptance of the notion that economic policy makers should pay attention to equity as well as growth.

Another element scrambling the state's "political economy" was a growing interest by high tech investors in clean energy and the green economy, a sector that needed government support and government intervention in the form of, for example, renewable energy requirements. The commitment to addressing climate change also reinforced pressures to reconfigure the traditional city-suburb landscape through compact development, itself a response to a growing class of professional and technical—and younger—workers that tended to value diversity and the urban ethos. While it took some time and is actually still nascent, this trend tended to strengthen cities and weaken far-flung suburbs, impacting the geographic bases for progressive and right-wing social movements alike. Along with demographic change, this growing urbanization eventually helped to produce a shock even in long-red parts of the state: Orange County—historic host to some of the most conservative movements in the nation—went blue in the 2016 presidential election.

Another part of the evolving stage: key political reforms that recognized that California's populist embrace of low taxes, strict term limits, and supermajority requirements on budgeting had become a recipe for ineffective government. Untangling the political constraints through a series of ballot measures would be key—even though the path was circuitous and the original impulses did not always emerge from the progressive side. But the evolution of new rules for budgeting, redistricting, and electoral primaries, along with all the other factors mentioned earlier, helped to set the platform for what would really bring about a new California: the evolution of progressive forces with a plan to gain power and a voice in state elections and decision making. California's transformation is thus a story in two parts—the shifting opportunity structure and the ways in which leaders and activists stepped up—and so the tale spreads across two chapters, with this one focusing on the changing terrain on which a new sort of organizing would take place.

Surfing the New Economy

The national economic debate these days is often concerned with the insecurity and polarization being wrought by a constantly churning economy. Some, for example, worry about the impact of trade on employment and wages, while others put the blame for labor market deterioration on immigrant competition.[1] Some stress the disequalizing impact of technology and education in job markets that value both current skills and the ability to learn.[2] Others point to the ways employment and job patterns vary by region, with some parts of the country left behind while others are thriving.[3] And there are those who point the finger mostly at the top 1 percent—that is, at the very top of the income distribution—and argue that it is their ability to concentrate capital and finance that has squeezed the rest of us.[4]

If there was a place where all these varying economic trends and pressures showed up in a sort of preview of "coming attractions," it was California. Deindustrialization came one step later in California than it did in the rest of the country, but when it arrived, it hit with a vengeance. Figure 4.1 offers a breakdown of monthly employment levels for certain key sectors between 1990 and 2016, and it depicts much of the changing story.[5] Note the steady decline in durable goods employment, that sector of manufacturing that produces longer-lasting goods such as motor vehicles, electrical equipment, and machinery and also tends to pay higher wages; after the steep fall in the early 1990s, driven in part by defense cutbacks, employment recovered briefly but then steadily fell through the 2000s, with another hard whack to the sector coming in 2007 with the start of the Great Recession. Nondurables manufacturing—of products like processed food and clothing—could not make up the difference and indeed steadily declined after about 2000.[6] What arrived to take up the slack was construction, with the housing boom of the late 1990s and the first half of the 2000s giving a significant boost to jobs in that sector—until the financial and housing crash of 2007–8 induced a cutback such that construction jobs fell by nearly 45 percent between August 2006 and the low point in March 2011.

The shifting economic structure helps to explain the widening divide that came to drive social tension and dominate political discourse. Manufacturing and construction have generally been sectors providing relatively well-paid employment more available to those with fewer skills and less education. Yet even as these sectors were being dinged, others were on the upswing, particularly highly remunerated jobs in high-tech services, including software publishing, Internet services, and business support. This recovery

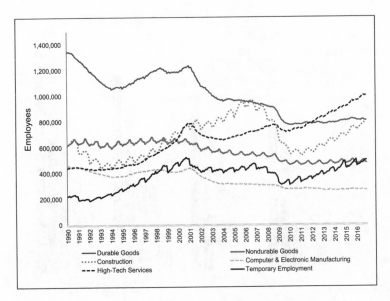

FIGURE 4.1: California employment in key sectors of the economy, 1990–2016.

of "tech" came as the actual manufacturing of computers and electronic components left California: shuttered were the factories in Silicon Valley that had been a key part of providing the sort of middle-class lifestyle that made the San Jose metro such an important platform for family economic progress.[7] In their place and exactly in that locale rose the service or knowledge portion of the industry; as Figure 4.1 shows, statewide employment in this sector more than doubled between the early 1990s and 2016 and, in fact, became a more significant source of employment than durable manufacturing in the 2010s. And in a preview of the contemporary "gig" economy, another sector managed to more than double its job count since the early 1990s: temporary employment, with all the insecurity and instability that sector brings to its workers.[8]

Given the patterns in the industrial structure—particularly a decline in the sort of durable manufacturing that provided a steady income for those with lesser skills and a rise in the high-skill

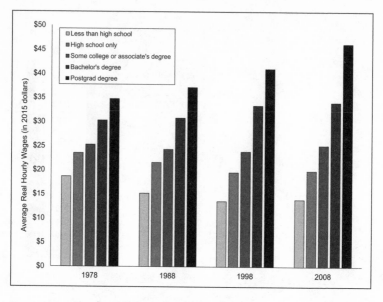

FIGURE 4.2: Average real hourly wages (in 2015 dollars) by educational level in California for workers age twenty-five to sixty-four, 1978–2008.

knowledge economy—it is little wonder that education began to matter more than ever for economic success. Figure 4.2 shows the behavior of real hourly wages for various education levels shown for successive ten-year periods in California; combining the decades in this way allows a glimpse of the wage distribution just ahead of various recessions (of the early 1980s, 1990s, and 2000s, and, of course, the Great Recession).[9] What is seen is basically what has been happening more recently to the United States as a whole: the bottom fell out for the less educated, with decline on the order of 25 percent for those with less than a high school degree and 16 percent for those with just a high school degree. Meanwhile, those with a BA saw their real hourly wage go up by 12 percent while those with a professional or postgraduate degree saw their real wages go up by 33 percent over the period depicted. The increasing relationship between wages and education was

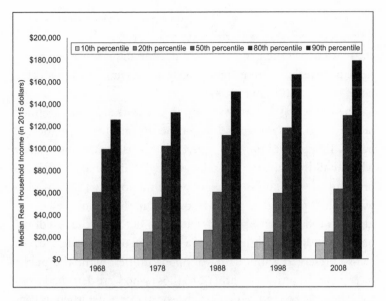

FIGURE 4.3: Change in the California median real household income (in 2015 dollars), 1968–2008.

good news for those who were slotted for the university but bad news for those boxed out because of inadequate public schools and the racially driven attack on affirmative action. The impact on the overall distribution of household income was profound; Figure 4.3 shows the pattern and traces the evolution over a longer period of time given that data on household income are available as far back as the 1960s. Note that the middle of the distribution more or less held its own since our starting point in 1968— although since this is household income and not wages, part of the way families maintained their living standards was by having more family members working longer hours for less money. On the other hand, those at the bottom of the distribution saw slippage in their fortunes while those at the top saw steady gains in the shifting California economy; for example, the household at the ninetieth percentile—meaning 10 percent of households are better off while 90 percent of households are worse off—saw a 42 percent real gain over the forty-year period, whereas those at the tenth percentile saw a 6 percent decline and those at the twentieth percentile, a group more likely to be among the working poor, suffered an 11 percent fall.[10]

The result was a sharp increase in the working poor. Defined here as working year-round, full-time, in families with income below 185 percent of the poverty level—the threshold below which children in such a family are eligible for free or reduced-price lunches in public schools—working poverty in California was about 2 percentage points below that in the rest of the United States in 1980 but rose to 2 percentage points above the rest of the nation by 2000.[11] While this was a clear sign of economic distress, it also presented a unique set of opportunities: while the public often tends to be unsympathetic to those who were detached from the labor market and relying on the social safety net, there is generally more empathy for those "deserving poor" who are working hard and still not making it.[12] Organizers sought to build upon these sympathies: in the same era in which welfare "reform"—that is, welfare cutbacks—gained ground at the national level under President Bill Clinton, local municipalities in California and elsewhere began supporting a series of living wage laws designed to ensure that local government spending would not go to enterprises paying wages below a reasonable level.[13]

Meanwhile, at the top of the income distribution, it was, shall we say, the best of times. A 1991 report from California's Franchise Tax Board reported that adjusted gross income for the top 1 percent had increased by more than 75 percent between 1980 and 1988—although the report also offered the somewhat comforting news that the bottom quintile of the distribution had seen nearly a 10 percent gain while the middle quintiles more or less held their own.[14] But that pattern of a wider divide with gains nonetheless across the spectrum—a comforting outcome for those who imagine a rising tide of wealth will lift all boats—was in the 1980s, the decade before deindustrialization packed its main California wallop. Between 1994 and 2013, average adjusted gross income rose by more than 80 percent for the top 1 percent even as the bottom fifth saw adjusted gross income fall by around 8 percent.[15]

Growing inequality also had a geographic dimension. The general decline of manufacturing in Southern California, especially of the higher-paying jobs in durable manufacturing (e.g., cars not clothes), impacted livelihoods in that part of the state even as the rise of high-tech services gave a new burst to the main hosts of the emerging information industries, the Bay Area in general and Silicon Valley in particular.[16] As Figure 4.4 shows, between 1985 and 2015, median household income slipped in the Central Valley—which includes the Fresno and Bakersfield metro areas—as well as in what is often called the "Inland Empire," that is, Riverside and San Bernardino Counties. Los Angeles and Orange County more or less stayed steady while San Diego saw an uptick, partly because through the 1990s and 2000s, that region was becoming a locale for biotech as well as for some software firms. However, the real story is the way in which median household income rose dramatically in the San Jose and Bay Area metros—Northern California began to run away from the rest of the state in terms of income and economic activity.[17]

The new economic geography was also reflected in the fortunes of the top 1 percent. The California Budget and Policy Center reports that the income of the top 1 percent grew by nearly 250 percent between 1989 and 2013 in San Jose / Silicon Valley and by more than 200 percent in the immediately adjoining two-county San Francisco–San Mateo region; given the near doubling of incomes for the superwealthy on the peninsula, the mere 55 percent increase for their counterparts in Los Angeles actually seems tame by comparison.[18] And while it might have been great to be rich in Fresno—think how much better-off than others in nearby teeming poverty you could feel—income growth for the top 1 percent in that metro area was just under 25 percent for the same time

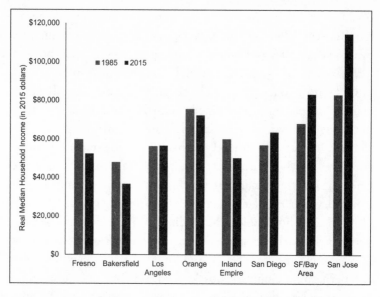

FIGURE 4.4: Real median household income in various California regions (in 2015 dollars), 1985–2015.

period. With über-wealth—and eventually Uber wealth—growing in the Bay Area, it was little wonder that that region's business class would come to dominate the state's policy and political discourse.

Yet another dimension of inequality: race and nativity. Figure 4.5 shows a four-year moving average for median household income by major ethnic groups for California for key years from 1990 to 2015.[19] While it is clear that the recession of the early 1990s battered African Americans and Latinos more than whites and Asian Americans/Pacific Islanders, what is striking is the persistence of the relative differentials over most of the period. There was, however, a sharp deterioration in Black household incomes in the 2000s; even though non-Hispanic white incomes also dipped a bit after the Great Recession, the ratio of Black to white median household income actually fell from 68 percent to 53 percent over

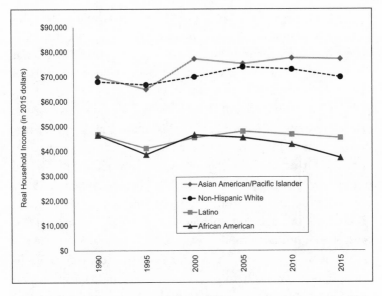

FIGURE 4.5: Four-year moving average of real household income (in 2015 dollars) by race/ethnicity in California, 1990–2015.

the period depicted, suggesting at least one reason why addressing Black economic fortunes has become so crucial to contemporary social justice advocates.

How much of the difference by ethnicity, particularly for Latinos, is due to differences in nativity and immigration? As it turns out, immigrant status seems to be important but not always determinative. Over the whole time period for which data were available, median household income for Asian and Pacific Islander immigrants was about 7 percent less than for native-born Asian Americans/Pacific Islanders, whereas median household income for immigrant Latinos was nearly 30 percentage points below the median income for U.S.-born Latinos. The more significant income hit taken by Latino immigrants is due to a variety of factors, including a higher likelihood of being undocumented, generally lower levels of education, and overconcentration in lower-paying

parts of the labor market.[20] Still, median household income for
U.S.-born Latinos averaged 23 percent lower than that for U.S.-
born whites over the time period depicted, suggesting that it was
difficult to pin the poorer economic outcomes of Latinos just on
mass immigration.[21]

In the current national debate, some claim that paying too
much attention to "identity politics," including racial disparities,
is a distraction from the central issue of restoring a strong economic base that can benefit everyone.[22] But as California shifted
from majority white to majority people of color in the late 1990s
to plurality Latino in 2014, the idea of ignoring persistent racial
differentials in wages and income was no longer viable, even for
those whose primary emphasis was on economic growth.[23] After
all, if this was the next California, raising the next generation in
grinding poverty was hardly a recipe for economic prosperity. So
while the state's initial response to the demographic shifts had
been a racialized freak-out that led to undermining immigrants,
underinvesting in education, and banning affirmative action, addressing the needs, aspirations, and possibilities of the emerging
"new majority" would require a new approach to both the economy and state politics.

As Goes the Political Economy . . .

Economists often track incomes and well-being in ways that make
it seem as though the main drivers of change are anonymous and
autonomous external forces, such as the rise of China, the growth
of technology, and the slow erasure of manufacturing employment. But while the economy is indeed a market phenomenon, it
is also a set of political choices—whether to lower taxes or invest
in infrastructure, whether to support the expansion of housing or
live with homelessness, whether to regulate financial instruments
or allow for risky speculation. Likewise, economic outcomes

themselves change who can wield influence and for what: industries on the rise may have more resources to exercise sway over public policy than those on the decline; the rise of working poverty can shift the usual political sympathies for policies like raising the minimum wage; and the evolution of a more urban economy can alter the balance of forces between a suburban right and a city-based left. The analysis of this two-way impact—policy on the economy *and* the economy on politics—is often called "political economy."

Among the most important drivers of a new political economy in California were the industrial shifts and geographic differentiation highlighted earlier, particularly between Northern, Southern, and inland California. In an intriguing volume, *The Rise and Fall of Urban Economies: Lessons from San Francisco and Los Angeles*, economic geographer Michael Storper and several colleagues try to understand why this happened, at least with regard to the divergence between North and South. In explaining the stark difference in the evolution of regional incomes, Storper and colleagues argue that both L.A. and the Bay Area hit the period of national deindustrialization well-endowed with aerospace and other sectors burgeoning with the potential for innovation. In their view, much of the Bay Area's relative success in the last several decades has to do with "the different ways the two economies reshaped their social and economic networks, the practices of their firms, and the overall ecology of organizations in their economies."[24]

This explanation likely makes too little of the initial industrial infrastructure—any region that started the 1970s with Hewlett-Packard and Fairchild Semiconductor, as did the Bay Area, was well positioned to succeed as computing costs fell, electronics expanded, and information technologies came into higher demand. But regardless of the reasons for the differentiation in economic activity over time, here we are more interested in the political economy consequences for the state as a whole—and one of the most important of these was the rising influence of Silicon Valley and Bay Area business leaders in key areas of the state's economic profile and political decision making.

Why was this significant? Silicon Valley has long embodied an interesting internal contradiction: its competitive risk takers are frequently connected, partly through venture capital firms and partly because of mobility between business enterprises, and often see themselves in a sort of collective ecosystem that allows for individual success.[25] Partly because of this, there has been a sense, now somewhat eroded by growing internationalization, of business responsibility for stewarding the region.[26] For example, the Silicon Valley Leadership Group, founded in 1978 by David Packard and originally named as the Santa Clara County Manufacturing Group, never saw its job as securing tax breaks or business favors; it left that task to local chambers of commerce, which then sought to fight over more mundane matters, like whether a living wage ordinance would have the unlikely effect of steering away business in the hottest innovation market in the world. Instead, the leadership group and a subsequent public-private partnership, Joint Venture Silicon Valley, sought to coalesce with other public and private actors to push for affordable housing, mass transit opportunities, green space, and other social and environmental infrastructure.

One of the reasons for the unusual business support for extensive social-serving infrastructure—notably of the type that had propelled the Golden State to its earlier success—was the idea that these were factors key to the quality of life that could attract and secure the loyalties of the high-skilled workers key to the new economy.[27] That approach, also taken up by another business grouping called the Bay Area Council, seems to have worked: although the Bay Area's sort of heavy-handed environmental and land-use planning are, in the fantasy world of conservatives, supposed to scare away business, the Bay Area and Silicon Valley were attracting about a third of the nation's venture capital in the mid-2000s. As of 2014, even as many Bay Area businesses embraced more interventionist strategies to fight climate change, the region's share of total national venture capital had risen to well over 40 percent; indeed, the venture capital per capita in the Bay Area is about twenty times higher than in the country as a whole.[28]

The rising influence of Bay Area business thinking was facilitated by the relative decline of other business groupings. In particular, Los Angeles business and civic sectors entered the 1980s and 1990s limping. The 1992 civil unrest played a role in scaring away investors, but the fact that such a conflagration even happened— and that there was such an ineffective response in both the immediate aftermath and the years to come—said a lot about the region's increasingly fragmented business and political class. This was a far cry from the past, in which a small and powerful group of corporate leaders called the Committee of 25 had managed in the 1950s and 1960s to run the city of Los Angeles from behind the scenes, toppling mayors and anointing new ones.[29] However, the industrial slippage of the 1980s and 1990s and the departure of larger companies from the region left Los Angeles with little centralized business power at all, a factor that actually helped to propel the rise of a community- and labor-based alternative.

That doesn't mean that L.A. had no economic strategy. As industry slipped, entertainment and tourism continued to keep the region humming, and tech has had its own recent evolution in Los Angeles.[30] L.A. business leaders have also been working to catch up with Bay Area action, pushing significant sales tax increases in 2008 and 2016 to expand the region's rail and bus lines as well as to address homelessness. Still, most of the region's strategic direction has, until recently, been a bit more lowbrow. For example, building on its port facilities, the region's main planning agency pushed hard on the development of the logistics industry, a sector of the economy that has tended to generate medium- to low-wage jobs even as it enveloped the region in truck exhaust and encouraged further residential and employment sprawl as companies expanded into the Inland Empire for modern warehouses.[31]

In any case, the sort of center of the new economy shifted northward and with that came a growing recognition of the need for business leaders to think more broadly about the social and environmental infrastructure that made their regions success-ful. The previously mentioned Joint Venture Silicon Valley was established in 1993 with the goal of resuscitating that regional economy. While from a present-day perch that goal might seem odd—really, the Silicon Valley in need of help?—defense cut-backs had hit the semiconductor industry hard. Looking for what would really move the economy forward over the long haul, busi-ness and other leaders gleaned that the real secrets were human capital, quality of life, and the degree of regional cooperation. The Joint Venture slogan—"Collaborate to Compete"—sort of said it all: Silicon Valley would make it in the world economy only if the public and private sectors worked together, if the region avoided excessive business-labor conflict, and if traditional civic leaders incorporated at least enough grassroots community voices to pro-vide political cover.[32]

Joint Venture's success led to interest on the part of funders and others who wanted to see whether a new approach could get past the various conflicts raging through the 1990s. This led to a repli-cation in the form of "regional collaborative initiatives" generally driven by business but with varying degrees of participation from social sectors and environmental advocates and planners.[33] These took many different forms—the San Diego Dialogue was quite different from the Lake Tahoe–based Sierra Business Council, and, naturally, there was no single effort in fragmented Los An-geles but instead a series of separate collaborations. Still, by 2003, there were twenty functioning initiatives, often coming together for conferences and collaborations sponsored by major California foundations.

The new business movement was heralded as a sort of bottom-up approach to restoring the old bipartisan consensus that once ruled California, in this case at the regional level, where economic and social actors could meet face-to-face. That is certainly over-stating both its goals and its impact, but the regional collabora-tives did tend to change the conversation by arguing that economy, equity, and the environment were three legs of a successful metro-politan stool.[34] The rhetorical and sometimes actual organizing space opened up by this shift created opportunities for groups like Urban Habitat, a Bay Area–based organization long focused on environmental justice, to push for "social equity" as part of a regional development strategy.[35] Meanwhile, environmentalists who had long been concerned about the loss of green space caused by sprawl took advantage of the opening to suggest that a more compact style of development might be more economically effi-cient as well as more sustainable; equity proponents joined in on this bandwagon, partly because they were concerned about how sprawl had stripped resources from cities.[36] From a state that had perfected suburbanization in its many varieties was emerging pressure from multiple sectors to experiment with what would be-come known as "smart growth."

Build It and They May Come

"Smart growth"—an amalgam of ideas that stressed how redirect-ing growth back to cities could lower infrastructure costs, reduce the carbon footprint, and create new opportunities for low-income communities—remained a hard sell, partly because there was so much already invested in California's sprawl machine. But it did make some ground both in California and in the nation, helping to push along or support existing efforts to revive older parts of California's cities as residential, retail, and business loca-tions. As the 1990s bled into the 2000s and then the 2010s, public and private investments helped moribund downtowns transform into regional attractions, replete with access to transit, walkable retail, and smaller infill units.

Pasadena in Southern California is a compelling example of this type of transformation. In the late 1980s and early 1990s the most vibrant downtown business was a pornographic bookstore—which, like a cockroach after a nuclear meltdown, is still there, just a bit more upscale. A nearby mall was enclosed in concrete, shut off from the street, and served by underground parking so commuters could avoid any contact with the urban masses; it was a sales tax engine for the city and a perfect exemplar of car culture, suburban separation, and the perverse land-use incentives wrought by Prop 13. But by 1994, denser housing was approved by a revised general plan and planning began for a rail transit line that a decade later would come straight into the heart of the city. In that context, "Old Pasadena" took off and street life thrived in the new urban funk. Meanwhile, the nearby mall, called Plaza Pasadena, went belly-up and developers eventually took down the walls, opened the shops to the street, and by 2001, had relabeled the new more pedestrian-friendly center Paseo Colorado.

The city of Los Angeles would soon follow, experiencing its own downtown reworking and renaissance as a center of retail and residence throughout the 2000s and now into the 2010s; it is little wonder that a writer for *GQ* enthused in 2014 that L.A. now hosted the nation's "coolest downtown" and that "America's Next Great City Is Inside L.A." [37] In the Bay Area, the suburban climes of Silicon Valley remained home to many of the high-tech campuses for companies like Google, Apple, and Facebook. But tellingly, even here urbanization became the order of the day: with many high-tech workers valuing the diversity and excitement of the city—think Google employees living in San Francisco and commuting to the Googleplex in Mountain View on a Google bus (with the overuse of the word "Google" suggesting the insularity of that ecosystem)—there were market as well as planning forces pushing along a new metropolitan configuration.

The slow shift away from the suburb and toward urbanity can be seen by comparing population growth in California's "prime cities"—that is, those that are anchors for major metropolitan areas, such as Los Angeles, Pasadena, Glendale, and Long Beach in Los Angeles County or San Francisco, Oakland, San Jose, Fremont, and Sunnyvale in the Bay Area—against the population growth in the rest of the state.[38] In the 1960s and 1970s, the decade-over-decade growth in the rest of the state was about 8 percentage points higher than decade-over-decade growth in the prime cities—and as late as the 2000s, the gap in favor of the rest of the state was still about 6 percentage points. With population growth outside of the biggest cities—that is, in suburbs as well as far-flung rural areas even farther away from the central core—historically exceeding population growth in the big cities, suburbanization was the norm. But if we take the most recent period for which reliable population data are available, 2010–15, and project outcomes for the current decade, it turns out that growth in the prime cities will outpace growth in the rest of the state by 2 percentage points—a remarkable turnaround and perhaps a sign of things to come.[39]

The city-leaning population shift has not been just a matter of changing tastes. The move to more compact development required new policies and practices, including new forms of lending and new zoning to encourage developments that were mixed-use and mixed income. Policy change, in turn, required rounding up unusual allies; for example, the Bay Area Alliance for Sustainable Development was formed in the late 1990s and early 2000s (later renamed the Bay Area Alliance for Sustainable Communities), bringing together business (in the form of the Bay Area Council), metropolitan planners (from the Association of Bay Area Governments), and equity proponents associated with a previously mentioned environmental justice group called Urban Habitat (which was busily putting together a broader group of advocates that would be called the Bay Area Social Equity Caucus). From 2000 to 2002, these groups worked on a "Smart Growth and Regional Livability Footprint" strategy for the Bay Area; this process helped to create a set of conversations between once-disparate regional actors, forging a new understanding of how to balance competing interests in determining land use and prioritizing public investments.[40]

And it wasn't just Northern California. In 2001, a group of researchers assembled at the University of Southern California (USC) put out a study with the provocatively titled: *Sprawl Hits the Wall*.[41] Their central thesis was that the old style of development typical of Southern California—and really, all of California—was no longer viable, partly because of environmental limits, partly because of economic costs, and partly because of the social disconnection it induced and the inequality it reinforced. Their broad recommendations sounded a bit rhetorical: grow smarter, grow greener, grow together, and grow more civic-minded. But among the conveners of the USC seminar was Antonio Villaraigosa, a former assembly speaker who would go on to run for mayor on exactly that platform.

Once elected in 2005, Villaraigosa helped push along programs to lower the city's greenhouse gas emissions through new building standards and to clean up the environmentally damaging impact of the logistics industry, particularly at the port complex that Los Angeles had so proudly willed into existence in the early part of the previous century. He also sought to facilitate a major behavioral change—to convince Angelenos to chill on their love affairs with automobiles and suburbs. Among his signal achievements was securing business, labor, and community support for Measure R, a county-level ballot initiative in 2008 that raised sales taxes to invest in mass transit—a measure that passed with a margin high enough to jump over the Prop 13 two-thirds threshold even against the backdrop of a deepening national and local recession. Along the way, Villaraigosa—a mayor who had himself been engaged in unions and social movements and whose field operation for the 2005 campaign was run by an experienced community activist, Anthony Thigpenn—insisted that business come to the table with promises of more jobs, higher wages, and openness to community concerns about environmental inequities.

Meanwhile, in the Central Valley, business attitudes may have been particularly entrenched—this was, as noted earlier, one of the geographic bases of the California right—but even there, the latter part of the 2000s and later the 2010s saw modest progress on issues of the built environment. Any forward action in Fresno was somewhat surprising: local activists working for economic and social incorporation have long tended to suggest that they're up against "DOA": developers, oil companies, and agricultural interests, all of whom depend on cheap land and cheap labor. That has often meant that any new strategy to move the economy to a high-road path or away from sprawl was also DOA—that is, dead on arrival.[42] But in 2005, a Brooking Institution report about Hurricane Katrina sought to explain how concentrated poverty had made New Orleans vulnerable to the storm; Fresno's cameo in the report was that it actually topped second-place New Orleans as the number one major city in terms of concentrated poverty.[43] This sort of parenthetical embarrassment led to a mayoral commitment—by a Republican mayor—to address the issue and eventually led to a remarkable effort—by another Republican mayor—to rework the city's general plan to promote more compact development in the downtown.[44]

All this reworking of the metropolitan form was given new impetus by the state's adoption of a strategy to confront climate change. Republican Arnold Schwarzenegger's path to the governor's seat was unusual—from action hero to swashbuckling candidate in a recall election—and he turned out to be different in another way as well: he bucked his party's commitment to climate denial and in June 2005 issued an executive order setting a series of ambitious targets to reduce California's greenhouse gas emissions. Observers suggested that the targets were clear but that the mechanisms were not.[45] Fortunately, the political incentives for developing concrete climate strategies were soon abundantly clear: after a disastrous special election the governor called for in late 2005 and facing a 2006 challenger, Democrat Phil Angelides, who had actually been an early devotee of smart growth—both as a developer and as a state treasurer—Schwarzenegger went on to collaborate with Democratic leaders and environmentalists on a Global Warming Solutions Act, also known as Assembly Bill 32 (or usually, AB 32).[46]

AB 32 was passed in August 2006 and signed at the end of the next month, just a scant few months after the release of *An Inconvenient Truth*, the Al Gore documentary that highlighted both the risks of global warming and the awesome presentation capabilities of PowerPoint. It mandated that California's 2020 emissions be brought down to 1990 levels and established the outlines of a process for getting there, putting much of the authority in the California Air Resources Board. Among the key assignments was to develop a market mechanism to address climate change; while the idea was that many alternatives could be considered, the governor's favorite (and, of course, the eventual winner) was cap-and-trade, a system that sets a target for global reductions but then allows firms to buy or sell credits at auction depending on whether they meet, exceed, or fall below their individual allowance for pollution.

Cap-and-trade eventually set into motion the collection of funds from auction proceeds that were then targeted for various uses. But the key point here is that while AB 32 promoted renewable energy and less-polluting industries, it also put in place the broad conditions for a shift in both planning and the built environment. After all, one main contributor to greenhouse gas emissions (GHGs) was excessive driving, a natural result of placing housing far from employment. In 2008, companion legislation passed that required that metropolitan planning agencies develop Sustainable Communities Strategies to meet specific regional targets for GHG reduction, handing responsibility for coordinating this effort to a new interagency Strategic Growth Council. The council would see its prominence increase when it also gained the responsibility for distributing funds from cap-and-trade to promote the integration of housing and transit.[47]

It is certainly possible to overstate the importance of these shifts in the political economy of the state. It's not like developers completely gave up the lure of building housing in the hinterlands of California's metros—although the appeal of such construction was diminished when the Great Recession hit housing prices far harder in the outlying suburbs than in the urban cores. It's also not the case that corporate leaders in Silicon Valley or elsewhere decided that the market was overrated, that raising the minimum wage was their newest agenda item, or that tackling issues of racism, police brutality, and overincarceration was now priority number one. So one does not want to claim too much movement on the structural side—but we must recognize that it is equally possible to make an analytical mistake in the opposite direction: to not see the ways in which the political economy and built environmental terrains were changing and new possibilities were being created.

Consider, for example, what opened up when business leaders, metropolitan planners, and equity proponents came together in the early 2000s to work together on a Bay Area Smart Growth Strategy Regional Livability Footprint Project: all of a sudden, there was a broad dialogue in which equity was at least given a verbalized place as a co-equal issue with the economy and the environment, and so some movement activists worked to take advantage of the new stage that had been set.[48] Or think about the overall commitment to climate action, something that encouraged business interest in an expanding clean energy economy, provided a counterweight to the political power of older industrial interests, and made clear to the newest and most powerful market players that government action would be needed to achieve profits as well as purpose.[49] Into that opening stepped ambitious political figures, including state senator Kevin de León, who realized the political virtue of tying together the interests of those who wanted a cleaner environment, a growing economy, and more resources for disadvantaged communities—and put it all together in a bill aimed at setting aside cap-and-trade dollars for low-income neighborhoods of color.

Meanwhile, the state was beginning to lean away from the rural and suburban areas that had fueled the rise of the right-wing forces that drove both Proposition 13 and the racialized assaults of the 1990s—and toward its coastal engines of prosperity and soon-to-be thriving city centers. In those dynamic areas lurked business groups more accustomed to diversity, more supportive of urban California, and more willing to promote state intervention to keep the economy ahead of international competition, particularly in green tech. The contemporary national parallel is eerie: the Republican right is often shored up by economically ailing rural towns and racially exclusive suburbs, whereas progressives tend to find their footing in big-city metros in the more thriving and economically sustainable areas of America. Understanding this geography is key to shifting away from the reactionary politics that has gripped the nation—and once had a stranglehold on California.

Untying the Knots

While California's political economy may have been moving in a direction that could better support progressive policy, the state was nonetheless challenged by the governance straitjacket it had placed on itself. The fiscal rules erected by Prop 13, especially the requirement of a two-thirds supermajority to raise taxes, made it difficult to keep up education spending and respond to emerging needs. Worse yet, this restriction on tax hikes was overlaid on another rather odd mandate for a supposedly democratic system: the application of the same two-thirds supermajority threshold to the spending portion of the state budget.

This threshold, adopted in 1930, was a long-standing feature of the state's fiscal system. However, the two-thirds requirement to pass a budget had historically been a rarely tested constraint, partly because a broad bipartisan consensus on investing in California and Californians generally led politicians to find agreement on when to waive the requirement.[50] The right-wing turn heralded by the 1978 passage of Prop 13, however, shepherded in a group of tightfisted Republican legislators who were soon nicknamed "the Cavemen" for their, shall we say, backward-looking attitudes. Since the budget had to be balanced, this gave a small and stubborn minority potential control over the budget process; in both 1992 and 2009—in each case against moderate Republican governors—legislative Republicans used their veto power to delay passage of the budget for so long that the state was forced to issue IOUs to cover its obligations.[51]

Perhaps consensus could have been forged by political leaders with sufficient history, skills, and institutional power to persuade or punish those derailing agreements. However, in 1990, Californians had passed yet another proposition, this one aimed at the ever-popular—or better put, ever-populist—idea of term limits. The ballot measure, Proposition 140, limited those in the state assembly to three two-year terms and those in the state senate to two four-year terms.[52] Resisted for obvious reasons by politicians like assembly speaker Willie Brown—who had been in the assembly for twenty-six years and in the speaker's seat for a decade when the measure passed—the proposition also decreased funding for the legislative staff. The result of the latter feature: the most senior and most expensive staff were cut in the assembly, which "led to an immense loss in policy expertise."[53] Meanwhile, experienced legislators were termed out, opening the path for new committee chairs and legislative leaders who were much less likely to understand all the consequences of the laws they were passing—and also less likely to be informed by experienced staff.

With budget paralysis built into the system and a lack of

legislative knowledge and leverage now added to the mix, one could have at least hoped for an electoral process that was biased toward producing the most levelheaded candidates. But no such luck, partly because the redistricting process—the process by which voters are assigned to areas in which candidates then run—was squarely in the hands of the state legislature. Legislators had incentives to draw districts in their favor—that is, to create boundaries to keep themselves in office. One way to ensure that happened was to let others do the same—that is, to allow both Democratic and Republican officeholders to cluster their party adherents, a process that in 2001 created a situation that virtually eliminated competitive seats.[54] Political stalemate was the inevitable result.

Still basking in his 2003 electoral triumph, Governor Schwarzenegger decided to untangle the mess with a special election in 2005. He placed on that year's November ballot a proposition to make it harder for teachers to get tenure and another to limit the ability of public sector unions to use fees for political campaigns; these conservative favorites were mostly there to limit union power, something that had increased when Prop 13 had the unexpected impact of centralizing spending in Sacramento. Two other proposals sought to shift the fiscal rules: one limiting state spending through a complicated formula and the other putting the redistricting process in the hands of a three-member panel of retired judges. This was a dagger aimed straight at Democratic stalwarts, especially unions and state legislators, who depended on their abilities to draw favorable district boundaries, and they responded with vigor.

Schwarzenegger was confident that, despite the opposition, he could sell the package; a bit like the runner who doesn't realize that he won a race mostly because everyone else was disqualified, he had taken his victory in the 2003 recall clown show as a signal that he really was popular. Maybe he was, but every one of the parts of his reform package went down in defeat. It was a sort of a

dry run for the hubris of the Trump presidency in which the ability to defeat an unpopular Democratic candidate—or better put,
gain a modest electoral college victory while losing by nearly 3 million popular votes—has somehow been reinterpreted as a broad
mandate for change. In such situations, the risks that a leader will
overreach—like "Arnold," like "Donald"—are quite high.

After the 2005 rejection, Schwarzenegger's popularity slipped—
although, as mentioned earlier, he did manage to win reelection
in 2006 when he was challenged by Phil Angelides, a Democratic state treasurer with great ideas but a flat personality and
low name recognition. The pressures for reform, however, did
not disappear—and the inklings of change came in the form of
a 2008 ballot initiative, Proposition 11, that was aimed at setting
up a citizen's redistricting commission for redrawing state legislative boundaries. Soon followed by a 2010 proposition that had
the new citizen's commission take on congressional lines as well,
Prop 11 was supported by good-government types as well as business interests and Republican Party stalwarts who thought that
this would loosen the control of Sacramento Democrats on the
process. Indeed, the state Democratic Party and one of California's two Democratic senators were officially opposed, as were
groups representing major constituencies of color. However, the
proposition eked out a thin victory (51–49) and redistricting took
on a different form.

Among the good-government types pushing Proposition 11
was a newly formed organization called California Forward. The
group was, in part, an outgrowth of the previous consensus-driven
regional collaboratives and drew together many of the same civic
leaders—including former Democratic and Republican legislative
leaders and business executives as well as representatives of labor
and community interests—who had channeled their frustrations
with state government into a penchant for regional governance.
Working with the support of five major foundations—The California Endowment, the Evelyn and Walter Haas, Jr. Fund, the

William and Flora Hewlett Foundation, the James Irvine Foundation, and the David and Lucile Packard Foundation—California
Forward sought to break the governing logjam and so supported
redistricting as well as open primaries, term-limit reforms, and
new budgeting and initiative processes, several of which would
soon come to pass.

Indeed, California Forward was one of the backers of Proposition 14 in 2010, an effort to create a "top two" primary system.[55]
The proposition may have been a good idea, but it actually emerged
from the usual government dysfunction: the budget-held-hostage
negotiation that took place in 2009. With the state issuing IOUs,
Schwarzenegger needed to scrape up just one more Republican
vote to get over the two-thirds budget-passing hurdle. That came
from Abel Maldonado, a rural state senator with ambitions for
statewide office. Convinced that moderates like him would stand
a better chance in an open primary than in the confines of intra-
Republican contests that were increasingly the province of "Cave-
man" politics, he held out for his very own proposition to grease
the electoral skids. Schwarzenegger got his budget and Maldonado got his "top two" ballot measure, which passed in June 2010
with a healthy margin.[56] Maldonado briefly achieved his statewide
ambitions—he was promptly appointed to the lieutenant governor seat by Schwarzenegger when the incumbent vacated—but he
quickly lost the seat when it went to a competitive election, then
ran unsuccessfully for a congressional seat, and finally flamed out
before even really beginning when he tried to run against a wildly
popular Jerry Brown in 2014.

This wasn't the only set of unintended consequences from
structural reform. The adoption of term limits in 1990 reflected a
strong partisan tilt: in a preelection poll, there was a 20-point difference between the support of those identifying as strong Republicans and the support of those identifying as strong Democrats,
a doubling of the margin from a poll just two and a half months

earlier.[57] But as it turns out, forcing out incumbent lawmakers actually set the stage for the arrival of new faces, particularly of left-leaning legislators who were female and/or African American, Latino, or Asian American/Pacific Islander.[58] Perhaps most symbolic of the change was the arrival to the state assembly in 2005 of Karen Bass, an African American progressive who had cut her community-organizing teeth by helping to found Community Coalition, an anchor for Black-Brown organizing in South Los Angeles. Bass quickly jumped up the ranks to be majority whip and then majority floor leader, and between 2008 and 2010, she served as speaker of the assembly—a position that would never have been available to someone so junior in terms of seniority in the past, and one that made her the first Black woman in U.S. history to head a state assembly.

Meanwhile, redistricting reform also worked in ways that were perhaps not intended by the proponents. Republican voters were actually more likely to support the citizen commission than Democrats, and the proposal to take redistricting power away from the legislature had been opposed by the California Democratic Party.[59] But because legislators had been drawing lines to protect incumbents regardless of party—the better to avoid conflicts in Sacramento—the Republican Party, which was steadily losing registration in the state, actually gained from a system its loyal voters derided. Fairer citizen-drawn districts made it possible for more Democrats—who were favored by the majority of the voters—to be elected. When the citizens' redistricting commission finished their work, they were promptly sued by elements of the Republican Party, a suit that was later unanimously rejected by the state supreme court.[60] Frustrated Republicans then placed a referendum on the November 2012 ballot to reject the work of the commission—and that was defeated by a 44-percentage-point margin.[61] Apparently, putting redistricting in the "hands of the people"—as the Los Angeles Chamber of Commerce had pleaded when they supported the redistricting measure—seemed fine until conservative forces realized that voters actually wanted to drag the state left.[62]

And while the top-two primary rule had been pushed by Republican Abel Maldonado to improve his chances as a moderate Republican, the main beneficiaries were the Democratic Party and progressive organizers.[63] Part of the reason was changing party registration in the state: as Figure 4.6 makes clear, after a precipitous fall in GOP strength when the Great Depression and the New Deal rocked American politics, Republican registration held fairly steady in the state until the early 1990s.[64] Interestingly, the lower share of Republican registrants from the 1940s to the 1990s did not seem to work against Republican presidential contenders and Republican gubernatorial candidates, perhaps because of California's long bipartisan tradition. But GOP registration fell more sharply after the 1990s, partly because of the way that decade of racial propositions had left a bad taste with newer registrants of color.

Democrat officeholders were the immediate gainers: not a single Republican has been elected to statewide office since 2006 and not a single statewide office has been held by a Republican since 2010. The party itself has been less of a winner in terms of registrants: Democratic registration also drifted downward until the middle of the 2000s, with the big increase coming in the number of registrants marking themselves as neither Democrat nor Republican, although Democratic registration has staged a small uptick since. Still, the shifting panorama meant that it was far more likely that under a top-two system, the last two standing for the general election would be Democrats—and this, combined with role of independent voters, created an opening to run truly progressive candidates.[65] The tantalizing possibilities helped to draw organizers from straight-out protest toward the mechanics of integrated voter engagement.

Another rule that tilted the playing field away from Republicans

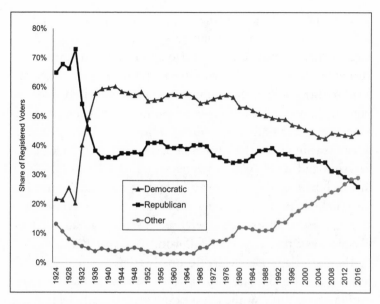

FIGURE 4.6: Party registration in California, 1924–2016.

and toward progressive forces was more intentional: the passage of Proposition 25 in 2010, a measure that reduced the requirement to pass the state budget from a two-thirds vote to a simple majority.[66] This came on the heels of a 2009 debacle in which the state legislature did not pass the budget until one hundred days into the new fiscal year. The legislature had admittedly been facing a tough job: the financial and housing crash of 2008 hit the California economy hard, and even as tax revenue collapsed, the state was on the hook to fill in school funding gaps. Within weeks after the governor signed the 2008–9 state budget, a projected $1.7 billion surplus instead became an $8 billion deficit—and analysts soon suggested that there would be a $27.8 billion deficit by the end of the 2009–10 fiscal year if no immediate action was taken.[67]

Through the latter part of 2008 and early 2009, the governor called special sessions of the legislature to find an agreement. Each successively failed, until February 2009, when the parties agreed to a mix of spending cuts, the largest of which was to occur in K–12 education funding; temporary increases in sales and use taxes, vehicle license fees, and personal income taxes; and some borrowing. The taxes required voter approval in a special election held in May 2009; on the ballot were six budget-related propositions, including the tax hike, but the only one that triumphed was a measure that prohibited pay increases for the state's top officials in any year in which there was a budget deficit.[68] In the end, the governor and state legislators agreed on a package in July 2009 in which half the gap was closed by budget cuts and the rest was filled in by borrowing, a modest $4 billion in new revenues from strategies like selling state property, and a variety of budget tricks, like pushing a payday into the following fiscal year.[69]

The sordid episode seemed to finally trigger some fiscal realism in the state, the first step of which was the passage of Proposition 25 in 2010. While the measure was partially sold on the grounds that it would punish irresponsible legislators—one feature was that legislative pay would be docked for every day a budget was late—the biggest political impact was that it marginalized the "Cavemen" legislative members who held up the budget negotiations during the previous two decades. While the legislature would still need a two-thirds vote to raise taxes, state Democratic leaders would not have to trade off major reforms or district-serving set-asides in order to secure Republican votes to simply pass a budget. The ability to take the state hostage had been limited; in this sense, Prop 25 represents a sort of first crack in the fiscal straitjacket of Prop 13. Progressive forces were soon to challenge the fiscal dysfunction in more direct fashion in the form of Proposition 30, a measure launched in 2012 to persuade voters to raise taxes both on themselves and on those who had profited most from California's widening income divide.

Can't We All Get Along?

California entered the twenty-first century still reeling from both long-term economic changes and the political earthquakes of the 1990s. Economic shifts had created a combination of insecurity, inequality, and working poverty. Racial differences in outcomes were persistent and the state's economic fortunes were increasingly diverging not just by class and race but also by region. Frustration was growing with the policy rules boxing the state in from making good decisions about its future—but this simply fed into a chaotic recall election and the arrival of an action hero to the governor's seat.

Yet all these dynamics were also creating a new context for change. The fact of working poverty created a sympathetic group of "underdogs" for whom policies could make a difference. The changing demography and the persistence of racial disparity meant that the usual "race or class" debates typical of progressives—and so fashionable in today's national debates about the relative importance of "identity politics" and economic policies—were generally moot: both dynamics were key. The shifting economy was also giving rise to a Northern California set of business actors less interested in attacking hapless immigrants in the state's low-wage service industries and more interested in attracting high-tech workers through measures to promote quality of life. A slow revitalization of central cities was getting under way, with the underlying pressures for more compact development helped along when the new movie star governor decided to take action on climate change. This, in turn, facilitated a slow shift of economic activity and political power away from the suburban and rural areas that had been the geographic base for the right-wing populism that had shipwrecked the state—and toward the territory on which progressives could make gains.

Making change was, however, not a straight path. With state

government tied in knots by budget rules and term limits, business and civic leaders launched new public-private efforts around *governance* at a regional level. While the concrete accomplishments of the collaborative groupings that took this on were limited, they did help to popularize the notion that economic prosperity would also require some focus on environmental sustainability and some degree of attention to social equity. Meanwhile, the system of state decision making began to unclog. Term limits had allowed for a new wave of minority lawmakers, and while the creation of a citizen's redistricting commission may have emerged from bipartisan forces, it opened up opportunities for a more popular left. Meanwhile, in the spirit of "two can play at this proposition game," liberal activists in the state launched their own propositions, including one that relaxed the supermajority needed for passing a budget and so facilitated the relative irrelevance of political conservatives.

So the stage was set for change—but actually making change would require vision and movement. After all, the heyday of California, the era in which it bet on itself by investing in both long-time residents and new arrivals, had not resulted from a particular government setup but rather from a broadly agreed-upon social compact that suggested Californians just might all be in this thing together. What had torn that apart and pushed California into the reactionary abyss was a series of well-organized and often grassroots right-wing movements, usually taking advantage of the racialized anxieties of voters frightened of a changing state. A real California turnaround would require a set of social movements that could forthrightly address race even as they clawed their way back from the margins to the near center of political power and reset the terms for a new, more durable, and more inclusive social compact.

5

MAKING CHANGE

In 2012, a California miracle happened: in the state that had ignited a national tax revolt wildfire that burned everything in its path, voters passed a measure designed to close fiscal gaps by (gulp) raising taxes. The measure, Proposition 30, combined higher income levies on the rich with an increased sales tax on the rest, with a sunset clause that had the income tax increase expiring in seven years and the sales tax increase expiring in four. But while some called the measure "Brown-crafted," that was as misleading as the *Newsweek* cover celebrating the singular role of the Democratic septuagenarian governor in the California recovery.[1] In fact, Brown had initially tried to work a tax deal with the state legislature, only to meet the usual Republican policy blockade. He then sought to craft a proposition that he felt was more likely to secure the support—or at least the non-opposition—of the California Chamber of Commerce, primarily by relying on a more regressive approach that promised a more modest and more temporary income tax hike and a more substantial boost in the sales tax.

What finally forced Brown to shift to the winning combination—a more progressive and longer-lasting income tax accompanied by a smaller boost in the sales tax—was an alternative tax measure being promulgated by a group of left-leaning movement organizations. There were not the usual players in the state fiscal drama: the motley collection of activists included the California Federation of Teachers, the much smaller of the two main unions representing teachers in the state; the Courage

Campaign, perhaps best known for its vigorous opposition to Proposition 8, the 2008 measure that sought to strip the marriage rights of same-sex couples; California Calls, a nascent grassroots effort aimed at mobilizing new and occasional voters; and the Alliance of Californians for Community Empowerment, a group that emerged from the ashes of the scandals that took down the national organizing network known as ACORN.

Together, these groups had managed to launch an initiative for a pure "millionaires' tax" to qualify for the 2012 ballot that was polling much better than Brown's plan. There was yet another competing plan, one promoted by multimillionaire Molly Munger and the California State PTA, which would have raised income taxes on most Californians and focused most of the new money on education; this effort was also polling badly, but Munger was convinced enough and rich enough to collect signatures and get it on the ballot, though it eventually went down in ignominious defeat. Recognizing that too many competing tax initiatives could spell doom for them all, Brown found himself forced to the negotiating table, and the seeds of victory were sown: Prop 30 won with an unexpectedly large 11-point margin (55.4 in favor versus to 44.6 opposed), and California's reputation as an anti-tax hotbed was dashed.[2]

After that, the hits kept coming—but now in the sense of celebratory tunes and not the battering-ram measures of the 1990s. Within a few short years, the state had agreed to steer resources from a new cap-and-trade system to environmentally overexposed low-income communities (2012); granted drivers' licenses to undocumented immigrants and passed a bill limiting the cooperation of local law enforcement with immigration authorities (2013); passed an initiative aimed at shrinking the prison population and redirecting cost savings to mental health and drug abuse programs (2014); and adopted a plan to raise the minimum wage to $15 an hour (2016). Behind these policy victories were the same sort of movement actors who had forced Brown's hand on taxes, a sharp turn from the days when advocates for the state's emerging new majority of African Americans, Latinos, and Asian Americans/Pacific Islanders were suffering electoral defeat after defeat. And it is the role of these organizers in making change—in taking advantage of the shifting terrain and crafting forward-looking politics—that frequently goes untold and unrecognized.

This is not to insist that movement organizing was the only element that drove change; it is clear that the economic and structural shifts of the 1990s and 2000s set the broad context for movement work, including the emergence of working poverty, the evolution of business thinking, the rise of urban California, and the slew of reform efforts that helped to break up the governing logjam. But once the path was cleared and the stage was set, some actors needed to step in to make change—and it is the role of grassroots progressive forces that evolved and matured over time that may hold the most important forward lessons for a nation that elected a celebrity president who went on to cause convulsions throughout the social fabric of the nation.

Four themes emerge from this movement part of the story. The first is how organizations decided to both scale up their own work and connect with others through statewide networks; organized labor, environmental justice groups, faith-based networks, and multiracial grassroots advocates proved willing to work effectively with one another and to build an ecosystem for change. The second is the role of a hardheaded analysis of power, a strategy that helped to ease the usual leftist schism between those who emphasize protests and those who stress policy proposals and electoral politics by lifting up the fact that both are important. The third is the key role of geography: progressives recognized that while increasing urbanization might give them an edge, they also needed to stretch into the inland and suburban parts of California—particularly a "fishhook" that ran down the agricultural badlands of Central California and then hooked up through San Diego and Orange Counties.[3] The fourth is the impact of intentionality:

organizers didn't just passively count on demographic shifts but rather developed an "integrated voter engagement" program— one that combined ongoing community organizing with concentrated efforts to get out the vote—to make sure the composition of the electorate would catch up to the changing composition of the population.

A Rose Grows . . .

I have tried to tell the story of California's rise, fall, and rise in close to chronological order, mostly because this is easier for a reader less familiar with the state's trajectory and probably bewildered by the sea of ballot propositions that stand as historical markers. However, such convenience runs the risk of imparting the false sense of a well-behaved continuity to the tale; in fact, there are many breaks in the action and many ways in which civic leaders and community organizers acting in one period were really building on their actions and reactions in the past. Such is the case with understanding the movement momentum in the Golden State in the 2000s and 2010s; a full analysis requires stretching back to a critical turning point: the Los Angeles civil unrest in 1992.

The rebellion in the streets ruptured relations between ethnic groups, paved the way for a law-and-order Republican mayor, and shook the self-confidence of progressives. But it also forced a fundamental reworking of progressive strategies, such that what began as a set of neighborhood organizing groups in the 1990s— usually boasting a few underpaid staff, cramped office space, and an overstressed fax machine—evolved into a statewide infrastructure that could shift policy and deliver votes. It was exactly from the ashes of the unrest that a rose grew in the concrete, that a phoenix of social movement organizing was born in what seemed like the most unlikely and desperate of circumstances.

Of course, this was not written on a tabula rasa: the left had a

long and proud history in the state, having staged a four-day general strike in San Francisco in 1934, fought against Red-baiting
in Hollywood in the 1950s, and launched one of the first successful efforts to organize agricultural employees in the form of the
United Farm Workers in the late 1960s. California, moreover,
was where, in the 1960s, America's universities first erupted with
the Free Speech Movement, Chicanos made their urban presence
known through student walkouts and antiwar organizing, and
the Black Panther Party was born and crystalized into a fierce
symbol of Black pride and community resistance to state aggres-
sion. Particularly in the Bay Area but also in Los Angeles, California was also the home of numerous left-leaning party formations,
frequently quite strict in their discipline and strident in their
beliefs—but often small and limited in their impacts.[4]

Indeed, it was partly that limited reach—and the consequent
inability of the left to scale up and sort of seize the center of the
political debate—that allowed growing frustrations to feed right-
wing populism rather than progressive change. While the Democratic political establishment had sought to include communities
of color as they grew in size and electoral strength—and tried to
absorb some dissident voices into their vote-getting machine—
too many of the efforts seeking to promote social justice and
inclusion for exactly those same communities were more or less
flailing and failing. By the late 1980s and early 1990s, the farmworker movement was stalled, universities were relatively calm,
and anti-incarceration and anti-brutality movements were often overwhelmed by a bipartisan law-and-order ethos. It was an
apt time to resist with a united front, but internecine squabbles
among various radical strains were increasingly about taking the
correct ideological line—even if that resulted in fewer and fewer
members.[5] The battery of racialized propositions that emerged in
the 1990s may have shown the strength of the right, but they also
revealed the weakness of the left: progressives, particularly those
based in communities of color, were on the defense rather than

on the offense. Clearly, an alternative was needed—much as one seems to be needed in the contemporary United States.

Fortunately, there were some emerging exceptions that pointed to a new California. Consider the Justice for Janitors campaign, in which labor sought to reverse a dramatic loss in the rate of unionization in the cleaning industry.[6] Against the backdrop of a changing economy and changing demographics—particularly the decline of African Americans in janitorial work and the rising share of Latino workers, particularly immigrants and women— organizers sought to reenergize the union presence by engaging not just the direct contractors who employed the janitors but also the actual building owners who let those contracts; labor also turned to movement-style tactics, including direct actions like marches and other forms of demonstrations, as a way of build- ing broad public support for economic justice for the janitors. The former strand of work—focused on who owned and not who contracted—reflected and made use of sophisticated corporate analysis; the latter strand—focused on direct action and public appeals—sought to build on the repertoire of organizing activities that many immigrant workers brought from political activities in their former home countries.[7]

The culmination of the early organizing of this sector in Los Angeles came in 1990 when Service Employees International Union (SEIU) Local 399 staged a peaceful march and demon- stration in Century City, a dense commercial and office district on the west side of Los Angeles. When the janitorial workers and their community allies sat down to block traffic—a bit of sacrilege in then car-crazy L.A.—the march was met with physical attacks by police. One bit of bad luck for the recalcitrant building own- ers: James Wood, who was political director for the Central Labor Council of Los Angeles, was marching with the demonstrators and witnessed the full force of the police.[8] Nothing hurts reaction- ary strategy like enraging the second-most powerful labor leader in Los Angeles—who was also the chair of the city's Community

Redevelopment Agency. With pressure building from the calls of irate local officials, including then city of Los Angeles mayor Tom Bradley, and threats of solidarity strikes from another influential SEIU local in New York, the janitors soon secured a multiyear contract.[9]

While the influence of well-connected individuals and sympathetic public officials played a role, the janitors' triumph signaled that there was a new way of making change in California. That new approach—starting from the grass roots, involving poor constituencies, and employing unconventional movement-style techniques—was to soon become standard practice across a range of issues. Its potential strength was demonstrated as the janitors scaled up their own organizing in exactly the ways that progressives in general were soon to follow. After bringing together locals in Oakland and Contra Costa, Santa Clara, and San Mateo Counties, SEIU launched the Cleaning Up Silicon Valley campaign. Its 1991–92 efforts targeted Apple's cleaning contractor, Shine Building Maintenance; using the same sophisticated approach of jumping past the cleaning contractor to the de facto employer, the janitors staged a "fast for justice" at Apple's Cupertino headquarters that ended with Cesar Chavez suggesting a boycott of Apple. The publicity worked, the janitors won, and a victory at Hewlett-Packard quickly followed; "within two years, a majority of Silicon Valley janitors were working under union conditions."[10]

It was against that backdrop of new labor and other organizing that the Golden State's largest city, Los Angeles, exploded in 1992 in reaction to the verdict in the infamous trial of four white police officers accused of viciously beating Black motorist Rodney King. In an eerie forerunner to today, the incident was captured on videotape; in a frightening parallel to today, documenting police brutality against an unarmed Black man was not enough to secure a conviction. The actual days of the unrest are a well-told story: the 1992 uprising topped the 1965 Watts rebellion in terms of its loss of life and property damage, and while the trigger was racist policing, most post-unrest analyses stressed the central role of poverty and desperation in explaining the citywide nature of the looting and arson.[11] But what is of most interest for this narrative is what came after: a sort of reawakening by the local left as progressives realized that their inability to channel the rage that burned down a city into something more politically productive was an indictment of their leadership and not just economic conditions or excessive policing.[12]

The growing awareness that progressives needed a new approach to movement building in the city and the state occurred in the context of a unique opening: this was the beginning of a decade in which the Los Angeles economy was slipping and its business class was fragmenting even as high tech was surging and Bay Area business was on the rise. This structural difference in the political economy of the North and South suggested two different sorts of stages in which to conduct campaigns for social justice. For the policy-oriented left in the Bay Area, part of the challenge was catching up with and altering business and civic proposals for change; the vacuum in Los Angeles meant that organizers could actually be proactive in shaping the course of economic development that was to come.

Into that void stepped a number of innovative efforts. The Los Angeles civil unrest and the racialized politics of the 1990s catalyzed the formation and transformation of community organizing institutions like Community Coalition, Strategic Concepts in Organizing and Policy Education (SCOPE), the Koreatown Immigrant Workers Alliance, Strategic Actions for a Just Economy, the Labor/Community Strategy Center, the Coalition for Humane Immigrant Rights of Los Angeles, Clergy and Laity United for Economic Justice, and the Los Angeles Alliance for a New Economy (LAANE), among others. Anthony Thigpenn, founder of SCOPE and current president of California Calls, reflected, "You think Community Coalition, you think AGENDA/SCOPE, you think LAANE, you think some of the best organizing at organized labor—those are the ones who also came out of that moment where I think many of us, who have been around for a while, realized that we had to do something different, we also had to do something sustained. There were no shortcuts, we had to just dig in and build institutions."[13] By 2000, this cohort of organizations was starting to exercise progressive, people-of-color-centered power at the local level—and they, with allies in the rest of the state, would go on to have policy and political impact across California.[14]

The new connections between many of these efforts were symbolized by emerging labor-community alliances, particularly in the form of a 1996 living wage campaign in Los Angeles led by a broad coalition of union and community groups; one of the main initiators of the campaign, the Tourism Industry Development Council, founded by labor leader Maria Elena Durazo in 1993, was soon reborn as the Los Angeles Alliance for a New Economy (LAANE), a think-and-do tank that would go on to assist efforts to improve labor conditions at the region's airports, ports, and tourist attractions. Meanwhile, in San Jose, the heart of Silicon Valley, 1998 brought its own living wage fight, in this case led by a parallel labor-community think tank founded in 1995 called Working Partnerships USA. Both of these efforts, which soon spawned similar counterparts in San Diego, the East Bay, and elsewhere, were attempts to forge a new sort of labor movement, one that could align with community groups, leverage regional connections and opportunities, and change the public dialogue.[15]

Perhaps the biggest impact of these organizations was to shift the economic debate to how the state and its various metros could actually achieve "growth with equity."[16] Working Partnerships, in particular, played an important role in showing the underbelly of the high-tech economy, pointing early to the growth of temporary employment, foreshadowing many of the issues now raised nationally about the insecurity wrought by the so-called gig economy.[17] Reflective of the divergence in political conditions in the

Bay Area and L.A., Working Partnerships found itself triangulating in the context of business-based groups like Joint Venture, the Silicon Valley Leadership Group, and even the Bay Area Council, often trying to ally with one over the other on issues of common concern. In Los Angeles, LAANE was playing on a less occupied terrain—business was less civically engaged and certainly less forward-looking—and so LAANE could focus on what really had been the secret of California's earlier economic success: leveraging the public sector to improve conditions for those who might otherwise be struggling.

In the 2000s and 2010s, this did not mean a new Master Plan for Higher Education to rescue the lesser skilled or even the build-out of suburbs for a striving industrial working class. Rather, the approach was to start local, to force a widespread recognition of the conditions of the working poor, and to insist that developers and others play a role in fixing the problem. Among the most innovative of the strategies: community benefits agreements (CBAs) that stipulated that the permanent jobs generated from large regional attractions (such as the Staples Center expansion in 2001 in downtown Los Angeles) pay well above the minimum wage. But it didn't stop there, as LAANE then went on to target the ports—key to the logistics strategy for Southern California—through the Coalition for Clean and Safe Ports in the late 2000s, which aimed to improve working conditions for truckers even as both port operations and equipment were upgraded to make for better air quality for nearby impacted neighborhoods.[18]

There was also a sense of their need to scale, hence the concurrent evolution of LAANE and Working Partnerships as well as the East Bay Alliance for a Sustainable Economy (EBASE), an economic and racial justice organization started in 1999 and a local affiliate of the national Partnership for Working Families (as are both LAANE and Working Partnerships). In tight coalition with environmental, community, labor, and faith groups, EBASE helped establish CBAs such as the affordable housing and

local-hire commitments at the Oak to Ninth development project along the waterfront—the largest proposed project in the city
since World War II—in 2006.[19] Replication—learning what was
working in one part of California and applying it to another—was
becoming part of the organizing DNA of progressives.

Back in Los Angeles, labor and its allies realized that any policy
win ultimately depended on the ability to translate community
voice into electoral power. Through the 1990s, Miguel Contreras,
head of the Los Angeles County Federation of Labor, worked to
mobilize rank-and-file members to go to the polls. Labor's enhanced commitment to politics, going well beyond just providing cash to candidates, added a significant punch: in 1997, for
example, the county federation's endorsement of former union
official Gil Cedillo in a special election for a state assembly seat
propelled the candidate from a double-digit trail in the polls to
an eventual electoral margin of more than 20 points.[20] In 2000,
the county federation proved its willingness to challenge politics
as usual, especially the tendency to avoid intraparty challenges of
incumbent officeholders: in a sort of Bernie Sanders–meets–Hillary Clinton moment—albeit with the genders reversed—labor's
preferred candidate, Hilda Solis, took out an incumbent moderate Democrat who had supported Bill Clinton's request to secure
"fast-track" negotiations on NAFTA-style trade agreements.[21]
And in 2002, the county federation's former political director Fa-
bian Núñez was elected to the state assembly and, given the quirk
of short term limits, quickly became speaker of that body, creating
yet another link between the new more militant labor movement
and inside political actors.

Labor also recognized that with much of the organizing and political momentum coming from Latino and immigrant communities, it was important to proactively address the possible tensions
that could emerge between Black and Brown workers. After all,
Latino immigrant janitors were labor's new heroes as the twenty-
first century dawned, but their presence in the industry occurred

in tandem with a diminishing presence of African Americans. For example, in Los Angeles County in 1970, there were more than twice as many African Americans as Latinos who were janitors, but by 2005, there were nearly ten times as many Latinos as Blacks in that occupation, and more than 80 percent of those Latinos were immigrants.[22] In order to ensure that African Americans would not be left behind, to ensure that economic justice squared with racial justice, and to shore up a Black-Latino alliance, the SEIU, the union that had led the janitorial campaign, launched a Five Days for Freedom campaign to sign up thousands of licensed security guards—a sector that was 70 percent African American in the L.A. region. And in November of 2006, more than five thousand guards, many of them residents of South Los Angeles, won the right to unionize.[23]

While labor was a major driver of change, the need for intersectionality—in this case, the weaving together of different identities and different movements—was in the zeitgeist.[24] This was reflected in a sort of doubling back to make sure that Black as well as Latino workers were being organized. But even before that came the realization that immigrant workers, long thought of as unorganizable and hence union competition, were actually mired in the working poor and so eager to protect themselves.[25] SEIU and janitors were clearly in that game, but the Hotel and Restaurant Employees (HERE) Local 11, the United Brotherhood of Carpenters, and the International Association of Machinists and Aerospace Workers also began to invest in immigrant worker organizing as well.[26] The labor movement responded, first in Los Angeles, then in the state, and finally nationally by becoming more supportive of immigration reform.[27] Indeed, in 2000, influenced by the county federation, the national AFL-CIO officially adopted a platform supportive of immigrant rights and comprehensive immigration reform—and its announcement at the Los Angeles Memorial Sports Arena drew an overflow crowd of about twenty thousand supporters.[28] From California to the nation, change was coming—and labor was not the only player.

Deepening the Field

While labor unions and labor-affiliated institutions were clearly playing a central role as the 1990s turned to the 2000s, it wasn't just straightforward economic issues driving an alternative agenda. This was partly because unions themselves had realized the need to broaden their reach—and that meant working against a legacy of distrust in which unions were often perceived as acting in their own narrow interests. Union support for immigration reform had its unionization logic—more secure status would make it easier to organize—but it was also just a way of demonstrating goodwill, solidarity, and, yes, intersectionality.

One effort that helped cement the image of labor as a more reliable partner to California communities was an early flagship campaign of labor-affiliated Working Partnerships USA to provide health care to all children in Santa Clara County, no matter their immigration status or income. Called the Children's Health Initiative, the campaign included Working Partnerships, the county federation of labor, an affiliate of a faith-based statewide organizing network (PICO), and a range of local community groups. The resulting program was launched in 2001 and quickly became a model for community-based health care; by 2005, nine other California counties had similar programs and about twenty were developing them.[29] Most important: it showed community-based organizations that labor could be a strong and important ally even when its own immediate interests—perhaps unionized nurses would benefit, but that was a long causal chain—were not so obvious.

Even as these partnerships were being tested and developed,

California's immigrant rights groups, environmental justice advocates, and others were themselves beginning to work their way through a new sort of politics: a more explicit appeal to the needs of a "new majority" of African Americans, Latinos, and Asian Americans/Pacific Islanders, a majority that was achieved in terms of the state population in 1998.[30] This was a significant departure from the traditional Democratic Party focus, particularly nationally, on the white "swing" voter. As Steve Phillips, author of *Brown Is the New White* and co-founder of PowerPAC+, a group dedicated to mobilizing a multiracial coalition of voters, articulated it, "Our theory of change is premised upon the . . . potential power of the . . . increasing political impact of the various communities of color. And so really seeing that the striving of the particular racial groups for equality and justice and inclusion is a real force for change and really trying to align our efforts and invest in organizations and leaders who come out of those communities and could help both give expression to those sentiments but also channel that energy in ways that can make a tangible organizing difference" is what can lead to impact.[31]

This debate has contemporary resonance, to be sure, particularly as Democratic Party stalwarts wonder whether their 2016 presidential candidate lost to Donald Trump because she failed to capture white working-class voters or whether the failure was due to the undermobilization of voters of color, particularly Black voters in places like Philadelphia, Milwaukee, and Detroit.[32] Regardless of one's position on that question, what is clear is that California organizers decided to take advantage of the state's own demographics and come up with a new and sharper approach to resisting the reactionary politics that had taken center stage in the 1990s. As a result, rather than simply proposing a slightly tamer version of the repressive measures embodied in conservative ballot initiatives, progressives began to push the political envelope and offer hints of a whole new world to come.

The decision to draw more distinct lines was seen in the actions of organizers who marched proudly with the Mexican flag as they challenged Proposition 187 in 1994; traditional Democrats may have worried about alienating an older white electorate, but organizers were seeking to activate voters yet to even naturalize. It was seen in the similar split between movement activists and traditional Democratic interest groups in the fight over Proposition 209, the 1996 measure that sought to eliminate affirmative action in the state's public institutions; mainstream Democrats suggested focusing on how white women would be dinged by the measure, while more progressive advocates tried to emphasize race and use the battle to build ties among communities of color. Lines were drawn again in 2000 when conservatives placed on the ballot a "Defense of Marriage" proposition that sought to confine marriage rights to opposite-sex couples; more mainstream leaders suggested focusing on privacy or divisiveness or anything but marriage, while more progressive forces in the LGBTQ community were willing to risk a loss in order to lift up the fundamental rights of same-sex couples to live in recognized and committed relationships.[33]

Taking a more forthright stand was also seen in the battle against the racism of the criminal justice system. This is a long-standing fight: one strand of Black organizing in the United States has long stressed the way in which the prison system both symbolizes and embodies the persistent confinement of Black lives and abuse of Black bodies in American society.[34] This was certainly the case in California: the "tough on crime" reforms the state had put in place—including mandatory minimum sentences, felony reclassification, and increased parole revocations—expanded the prison population, disproportionately impacting communities of color and especially African Americans.[35] Efforts to curb police abuse of communities evolved into broad efforts to address incarceration; for example, Van Jones and Diana Frappier created Bay Area Police Watch in 1995 to serve victims of police brutality, and that led to the creation of the Ella Baker Center, whose work included efforts to end incarceration, criminalization, and discrimination against Black and Brown communities.[36] The center, along with partner organizations like the ACLU, Critical Resistance Youth Force, and Californians for Justice, led the efforts to push back against punitive laws, like Proposition 21 in 2000, which allowed for juveniles to be tried as adults for certain crimes and otherwise tightened and enhanced sentencing. The proposition won overwhelmingly, but anti-incarceration and pro-justice groups were acquiring the skills to speak to the human and fiscal impacts of such policies, a capacity that would be useful in the 2010s.[37]

As with this particular struggle against juvenile sentencing, progressive forces were losing the fights, but with an eye toward building new skills and a new base to win a longer-term war for human rights and human dignity. Strikingly, the tendency to take a clearer and less ambiguous stance did not lead to what one often associates with progressive opposition: a sort of shrill, leftist shout from the outside. Rather, there was a shift to propositional politics—progressive forces were as likely to craft a community benefits agreement as to protest corporate misbehavior, as ready to naturalize immigrant voters as to defend undocumented migrants, as apt to suggest "restorative justice" as to condemn a system in which justice was noticeably rare. Moreover, many of the activists sought to transform decision making from the inside as well, developing capacities and campaigns to impact politics and policy.

This new proactive positioning can be seen quite clearly in many areas of organizing and policy, but consider two: immigration and environmental justice. The immigration realm is particularly notable, especially since nearly half the noncitizen foreign born in California are undocumented, a factor traditionally associated with low levels of political efficacy.[38] Maybe so, but Prop 187 induced a large number of Latinos who were eligible to naturalize— that is, who had legal status and could become citizens—to file

their paperwork, pay the fees, and engage in the formal political process.[39] Meanwhile, those who could not directly engage
through voting—the undocumented—began to get bolder about
organizing and demanding fairer treatment from local authorities.[40] By March 2006, more than half a million immigrants and
their allies marched in downtown Los Angeles to protest federal
legislation that sought to make it a felony to be in the United
States illegally and criminalized assistance to the undocumented,
signaling a shift in public attitudes.

Pro-immigrant institutions formed or morphed to better capture the emerging dynamism. For example, the Coalition for Humane Immigrant Rights of Los Angeles was founded in 1986 to
provide services to immigrants in the wake of that year's Immigration Reform and Control Act—the Reagan-supported effort
that granted "amnesty" to nearly 3 million undocumented immigrants. But in the context of the mass protests of the mid-2000s,
it transformed into an organizing powerhouse and continues to
play a lead for the state in national politics around immigration
reform.[41] The California Immigrant Policy Center was founded
in 1996 to lean against the hostile winds of Proposition 187 and
a federal welfare reform that limited immigrant access to welfare;
it has steadily expanded both its concerns and the ability to influence decisions in Sacramento.[42] Mobilize the Immigrant Vote
was founded in 2004 to, well, mobilize the immigrant vote, and
thus ensure that political figures would pay a price for not heeding
the legitimate aspirations of communities hoping for a welcoming
hand and not a slap in the face.

The result of these efforts and others has been what political
scientists Karthick Ramakrishnan and Allan Colbern call "de
facto state citizenship."[43] They note that "California today pro-
vides the most integrationist laws in the country when it comes to
unauthorized immigrants living in the state," including in-state
tuition for postsecondary education, drivers' licenses, professional licenses, ever-broadening access to health care, and a piece

of legislation called the Trust Act, signed by the governor in 2013, that limits the ability of local jails to detain immigrants or hand them over to federal authorities except in the case of specific serious crimes. Ramakrishnan and Colbern eloquently argue that "these laws have significantly expanded the access of unauthorized immigrants to what we call 'life chances,' the right of access to an education, health and employment, as well as to what we call 'free presence,' the right to freedom of movement into and within the state through access to identification documents and limited state enforcement of federal immigration law."[44] It is, they argue, a distinctive "California package."

And while lawmakers may claim their share of credit for creating a more welcoming California, Cathy Cha of the Evelyn and Walter Haas, Jr. Fund, a foundation that supported many of the activist groups, notes that "for every single one of these immigration-related policies, political figures have been dragged across the finish line. The story, and the larger narrative in the media, reflects that there was policy or political will to get it done, but the real story is that those victories occurred due to the full-throttle pressure from organizers to sign the bills. . . . All of this was the product of a concerted focus on movement building and establishing a longer-term strategy for change. What was needed—and created—was a durable, sustainable, movement-building infrastructure . . . that could play offense and defense in the long run."[45]

A similar arc of organizers scaling up and garnering influence in the political world can be tracked in another area: environmental justice (EJ). California has been a hotbed of EJ organizing, partly because the racial disparities in terms of exposure to toxics, poor air quality, and other threats are so well documented.[46] For example, in the Central Valley, pesticide exposure of farmworkers and their families has long been a problem.[47] But a 1988 proposal to place a toxic waste incinerator in Kettleman City, a small town of eleven hundred predominantly Latino residents in the

San Joaquin Valley, triggered a revolution in organizing. Kettleman City already hosted one of the nation's largest hazardous waste landfills, a fact that led the landfill owners to believe that they were just more efficiently concentrating risk.[48] Neighbors were not as enthused about the "efficiency," and the resulting battle, assisted by lawyers from the newly founded Center on Race, Poverty and the Environment (CRPE), helped persuade the waste disposal company to eventually withdraw its proposal to build the incinerator.[49]

Meanwhile, in Southern California, a coalition, initially led by Communities for a Better Environment (CBE) and supported by the L.A.-based Liberty Hill Foundation, challenged both corporate actors and the local air quality district about the rules governing an acceptable health risk from new facilities. The regulation, called Rule 1402, had been adopted in the early 1990s, with a threshold cancer risk that was ten times above that recommended by technical staff and even twice as high as business had requested; apparently, in the context of the economic recession of that era, air regulators were worried about anything that might deter investment. But in 2000, after years of struggle, community activists persuaded the air district to reduce the cancer risk standard for new facilities by 75 percent.[50] Their main argument: because low-income communities of color were disproportionately impacted by such permissive pollution regulations, this was a civil rights issue. And their main strategy: mobilizing hundreds of affected residents to attend district meetings held in a far-flung suburb safely distant from the communities under stress from the decision.[51]

The evolution of CBE is as noteworthy as the success, partly because it illustrates a transformation in constituency and purpose that was typical of several other organizations in this period. Originally founded as Citizens for a Better Environment, it replaced "Citizens" with "Communities" to better incorporate immigrants, including those who were undocumented. Originally focused on legal strategies and policy issues, it took up community-based organizing as its main driver for change. Originally based almost entirely in the Bay Area, its locus of operations shifted to Los Angeles as organizing there took off in the wake of the 1992 unrest. Originally doing this work largely on its own, CBE instead embraced the power of alliances and went on to found and anchor two broad regional collaboratives, one in Southern California and one in the Bay Area. And originally stressing the impacts of localized pollution on neighbors, it became actively involved through that coalition on a range of broader issues having to do with climate change.

Along with other EJ groups across the state, including the aforementioned CRPE in the Central Valley, the Asian Pacific Environmental Network (APEN) in the Bay Area, the Environmental Health Coalition in San Diego, PODER in San Francisco, and the Center for Community Action and Environmental Justice in the Inland Empire, CBE became a member of the California Environmental Justice Alliance (CEJA)—an organization that formed in 2001 aiming to link together the many EJ voices to effect state-level policy. And as Roger Kim, a longtime EJ organizer and former head of APEN, notes, "The EJ movement in California became a stronger pole for environmental policy by bringing together an EJ policy vision and political muscle. By paying attention to politics, local organizing, and community-based power building in a way the mainstream environmental movement hadn't, we developed into a progressive force in the state."[52]

One of those moments to demonstrate the emerging political power of the EJ movement came in the 2010 fight over Proposition 23. Prop 23 was an initiative funded primarily by two Texas-based oil companies seeking to derail AB 32, the Schwarzenegger-sponsored effort to address global warming. While the proponents of Prop 23 claimed that this could save jobs, the EJ message was that overturning AB 32 was likely to have its worst impacts on communities of color. Building an independent coalition that worked with mainstream environmentalists but focused on organizing its base in communities of color, the effort seemed to strike a chord: the 57 percent of whites who voted against Prop 23 were eclipsed by the 75 percent of voters of color who rejected the measure.[53]

There were several striking things about the effort. The first was that it signaled where pro-environment votes really were—a fact echoed by a continuing series of polls from the Public Policy Institute of California showing that people of color were far more likely to support policies to address climate change and protect the planet.[54] But the second remarkable thing was the sophistication of the strategy: in fact, many environmental justice proponents were quite skeptical of the cap-and-trade system that was slated as the main vehicle to reduce greenhouse gas emissions. In their view, such a market-based system might actually allow some polluters to maintain if not increase their emissions through the "trade" part of cap-and-trade. But once the state decided on cap-and-trade as the mechanism it would use, a broad swath of EJ organizers remained critical of the market approach but temporarily put that fight to the side to rescue the goals and targets for emissions reduction that were critical to addressing climate change and environmental inequity.[55]

That sort of political flexibility—with an eye toward the pragmatic—has not always been typical of progressives, and it was shown again when some of the groups in CEJA joined with others, such as the Greenlining Institute in the Bay Area, to push new legislation in 2012. That legislation mandated that a quarter of the funds generated from cap-and-trade auctions be devoted to programs that would benefit the most environmentally overexposed and socially vulnerable communities, with a minimum of 10 percent to be spent directly in those communities. By 2015, the state senate and assembly followed up with legislation that directed the state's Air Resources Board to expand by two seats and reserve those new seats for representatives of environmental justice communities and organizations—one of whom was Diane

Takvorian, head of the Environmental Health Coalition, the CEJA partner in San Diego. Advocates had quite literally secured a seat at the table.

The statewide EJ action was matched by some remarkable shifts in local politics. For example, in Richmond, California—a classic older industrial suburb in the Bay Area that by 2010 was more than 80 percent people of color—CBE, APEN, and members of the West County Toxics Coalition organized to stop the expansion of Chevron's Richmond oil refinery. The expansion of the refinery—famous for a 1999 explosion that forced thousands of residents to lock themselves in their houses against potentially toxic fumes—had been approved by the city council in 2008 but eventually got held up in court.[56] While the legal part of the struggle played out successfully, the prior approval by the council convinced local activists that they needed to firm up a tentative grasp on local political power that had been achieved by the election of a mayor from the Green Party, albeit in a three-way race with a perilously small margin of 242 votes.[57] In 2014, the Richmond Progressive Alliance (RPA) campaigned and won three full-term city council seats and one short-term seat, effectively gaining majority control of the city council even as they went against candidates supported to the tune of $3 million from Chevron.[58]

The new shift in progressives' organizing efficacy went well beyond the two areas covered in detail previously. With expanding capacity in the broader field of criminal justice reform, movement organizations began to take the offensive, constructing policy alternatives to what Lenore Anderson, founder and executive director of Californians for Safety and Justice, argued had become an "over-reliance on incarceration, over-reliance on prison."[59] As Anderson notes, "What happened during the 1990s was the selling of a myth . . . that building a bunch of prisons is good for public safety and good for protecting crime victims. And what we needed to do as those who want to advance reforms and reverse the overincarceration era is to have real solutions that are based in what communities actually need to protect public safety, to improve community safety."[60]

That alternative was Proposition 47, a 2014 effort that reclassified low-level offenses and began to chip away at the legacy of California's punitive criminal justice system.[61] As Anderson notes, the measure also "did something unprecedented, which was capturing the money that is saved in prisons in order to directly invest it into community need—and to apply the changes in law retroactively such that anyone in the state of California who has an old criminal record for one of these old felony crimes can get that felony removed."[62] The ability to put new money in community treatment programs as well as ways in which clearing records could facilitate labor market reentry had an economic appeal—as did the idea that overspending on "corrections" was shortchanging investments in education.

With alignment—including within philanthropy—a large network of advocates were able to win Prop 47 in 2014, a remarkable victory in a nonpresidential election year in which voters are usually older, whiter, and more conservative. Part of the reason for success is touched on below—conscious efforts to change the electorate and engage those voters most touched by the disproportionate incarceration of African American and Latinos—but the proponents were also clear about making the sort of bipartisan and multisector appeal that had worked in California's heyday.[63] And just two years later, state voters passed Prop 57—a measure that gave judges discretion about whether to try juveniles as adults and sped up consideration for parole for those who were incarcerated. Strikingly, it won by just about the same overwhelming majority as had Prop 21 in 2000, the measure that helped put more juveniles in prison. The Golden State had not yet come full circle, but it was turning.

All this backing away from the heady stew of "law and order" in a state that once raced ahead of the nation in terms of overincarceration? All this effective environmental justice activism in a

land that had thrived on autos, perfected sprawl, and developed
a record of having one of the nation's highest level of racially dis-
parate exposures to air toxics?[64] All this openness to immigrants,
regardless of status, from a place that had gleefully perfected and
then exported new forms of xenophobia? All this attention to raising wages and improving worker income from an economic system
that had seen its inequality ranking move from the middle of the
states to the fourth worst? And all this impact from movement
groups that had at one time seemed relatively powerless against
the constant bashing from the right-wing forces determined to
shrink the state's fiscal capacity and frustrate the needs and aspirations of new Californians? What had made the difference?

Let's Get Real

Nudging California in a more progressive direction involved
many things, but at its core was a conception of how to understand, build, and wield power. This analysis of power not only
aided understanding of the terrain on which policies would be
won—it reinforced the need to put small differences aside and
gather on the progressive side of the equation new and broader
coalitions.[65] It also implied the need to develop a geographic strategy, one that could build from areas of urban strength but also
influence the great "fishhook" of California—stretching down
from Orange County through San Diego and looping up through
the Inland Empire and the Central Valley—that had been the
residential power base of the right-wing rebellion.[66] And finally, it
made clear that the only way to make change was exactly through
the ballots that had battered vulnerable constituencies through
the 1990s: progressives needed to take the potential of the state's
changing demographics and transform it into the actual strength
of a changing electorate.

Indeed, the losing battles over retrograde propositions in the

1990s convinced many movement activists that they needed to shift from fighting against initiatives to offering proposals that could themselves make their way to the ballot. As Taj James, founder and co-director of the Movement Strategy Center, puts it, "The only time I'd see the progressive coalition assembled was when we were threatened by propositions. That was the only time I'd seen all the capacity assembled at one table and across issues. But that just generated a question: Do we have a proactive vision of what we want? And at that time, there really wasn't a statewide agenda, something that was reflective of the state of the left in both California and the nation. And so the need was there to articulate a proactive vision."[67]

With relatively modest victories for municipal living wages, local environmental justice policies, and other concerns under their belts, a group of social justice organizations from across the state came together in the early 2000s to discuss how to truly transform the state. The effort was led by Anthony Thigpenn, founder of SCOPE, a racial and economic justice organization based in South Los Angeles that had been influential in moving L.A. politics and policy after the 1992 unrest. It was an ambitious undertaking: a multiyear series of convening sought to explore the possibility of joint campaigns and eventually the creation of a statewide alliance. There was no quick agreement on joint campaigns—not surprising given that the groups at the table were coming with different concerns around a variety of environmental, education, and economic issues.[68] But it was from this set of conversations, for example, that the California Environmental Justice Alliance was formed. And perhaps more important was the way in which these conversations created a shared interest in "integrated voter engagement."

Integrated voter engagement (IVE) does involve getting out the vote for elections—but it is targeted at new and occasional voters. It was these voters—who are far more likely to be younger and from communities of color—who were not showing up to defeat the 1990s propositions in California and whose halfhearted (or worse) support for Hillary Clinton were part of the complex set of factors that gave us the Trump presidency. To motivate and mobilize these potential voters, IVE takes an approach quite distinct from the usual political party–based approach to harnessing the electorate—that is, rather than "helicoptering" in outsider specialists to set up field offices, train canvassers, and then shut everything down after the ballots are in, IVE seeks to form a longer-term relationship with voters with lower propensities to participate. It does this by connecting with these voters between elections, partly to ensure their electoral loyalty but also to engage them in political education and other civic actions such as lobbying city councils and legislators for policy change. In this sense, IVE is not just using organizing tools to get out the vote; it is also using an accepted vehicle of democratic participation, voting, to build up a cadre of activists.

One simple way to understand IVE: it is community organizing meets electoral politics, but on equal footing.[69] Partly because of that, it also offers a different sort of engagement around long-term values and not just short-term interests. It's an approach that echoes the arguments progressive organizers had had with more traditional Democratic forces during the battles over undocumented immigrants, particularly around whether to argue that closing education to undocumented children would lead to an uptick in crime—or just that it was wrong. At the same time, the IVE proponents realized that the traditional language—that is, jargon—of the left on these issues was not winning a growing number of converts. So in 2006 the emerging group of social justice organizations going under the name of the California Alliance undertook a significant investment in social-values polling, research, and experimentation to discover which values truly motivated Californians and which values could be tapped to organize a progressive majority.

The effort wound up identifying several new constituencies for outreach. One group was made up of struggling but aspirational people of color whose idea of success was often wrapped up in individual achievement. While members of this group were not "political" in a traditional sense—they had little history of engaging in activism—they did see a role for government in providing a secure platform for seizing opportunity. It was thus a group that could be moved to support progressive reform—but it was not used to thinking in terms of racial identities and political ideologies and so not likely to respond to the sort of large protests, searing slogans, and catchy chants that enthralled dedicated activists in Berkeley or Los Angeles. Another key constituency was what were termed "balanced suburbans"—whites and people of color who had chosen the order and safety of the suburbs but were not enthused by the right-wing politics that had long dominated those locales. Both groups were open to a new narrative that could counter the anti-government sentiment and racial retrenchment narratives that had dominated California's politics—but much like those constituencies being lured into the national resistance against Trump through unorthodox vehicles like the 2017 Women's March or Indivisible, a network seeking to organize localized protest at congressional town halls, the aspiring people of color and balanced suburbans needed a new approach.[70]

Just as the values testing was being completed and summarized in 2008, the state wobbled into fiscal crisis. This was not unique to California—the entire national economy was collapsing—but the Golden State was especially vulnerable because of the prominent role of real estate and construction in the state's economy. Moreover, while the state was rightly proud of its relatively progressive income tax system, this meant that revenue streams were extremely sensitive to the fortunes of high-income earners caught up in the stock market crash. According to Sabrina Smith, deputy director at California Calls, "It was down to the bone; thousands of pink slips being issued to teachers across the state, clinics being closed down, our roads are falling apart so we were reaching this breaking point." With a crisis so large that no one organization or sector could solve it alone—and with battle scars from previous policy and political losses—community-based organizations, service providers, and organized labor saw the need to coalesce.

After all, there were essentially two roads ahead: either service providers and their allies could fight one another over limited resources for vital programs such as education, health care, and social supports—or they could look at the structural problems underlying the state budget crises and dysfunction of Sacramento. As Smith recounts, "In 2010 we began our strategic collaboration with state networks and labor unions. We began a series of sessions to create alignment around the state landscape. We held a session with several policy experts across the state to develop a statewide tax reform agenda that could restore funding for education services for the long haul. In partnership with the California Federation of Teachers and other allies, we conducted research, polling, crafting, and in the fall filed the millionaires' tax."[71]

The "millionaires' tax"—a fiscal fix based entirely on raising income taxes on the rich—was eventually merged with parts of the governor's more regressive approach and reborn as Proposition 30. In the run-up to those negotiations, the California Alliance had been rechristened California Calls, and it became a key component of a broad effort that combined nine social justice networks and unions—Alliance of Californians for Community Empowerment Action Fund, Asian Pacific Environmental Network Action (APEN Action), California Calls Action Fund, California Federation of Teachers (CFT), California Partnership, Courage Campaign, Mobilize the Immigrant Vote Action Fund, PICO California, and Service Employees International Union (SEIU) Local 1021—under the rubric of "Reclaim California's Future." Together with others, those groups helped to collect nearly 1.5 million signatures in less than a month to qualify the new hybrid proposal. On the eve of the election, the proposition was polling under 50 percent—a level that is usually the kiss of death for a proposition, particularly a revenue measure, since late-deciding voters tend to default to "no." But what if those usually deemed "unlikely" to vote in polls actually turned out? The state soon found out, as Proposition 30 passed by a nearly 11-point margin, in no small part due to the four hundred thousand voters mobilized by California Calls.[72]

One part of the secret was getting beyond the usual comfort zone not just in terms of values but also in terms of geography. As Cathy Cha of the Evelyn and Walter Haas, Jr. Fund notes, one of the tipping points for movement building in the state "has been a recognition that the movement can't win in Sacramento with only votes from the Bay Area and LA anymore—it needs the Inland Empire, Central Valley, certainly Orange County, and San Diego."[73] Indeed, California Calls and its allies were explicit about reaching out to the less liberal parts of "fishhook" California and connecting them with assets and capacity from the more developed organizing institutions in L.A. and the Bay Area. By November 2012, when Prop 30 hit the ballot, that infrastructure comprised fourteen anchor organizations and thirty-one individual organizations across ten counties. And this was more than a loose coalition. The more established institutions were engaged in statewide training and capacity building, including equipping each region with the technical capacity to engage voters at scale with phone banks with predictive dialing systems, precinct targeting, and voter lists and precinct maps. In turn, accountability was critical: each region was supposed to hit a certain target number of voters—or find themselves not part of the team.

From a national perspective, one thing that may be especially important about this effort is that it led to building solid organizing infrastructure across the state—just as progressives now need to build such infrastructure in states and suburbs that are sometimes written off as hopelessly red. And it wasn't just about voting for state elections. For example, Communities for a New California, founded by Latino and EJ advocates in 2010, had chapters in the San Joaquin, Imperial, and Coachella Valleys; it was a statewide and regional anchor partner for California Calls even as it achieved its own local credibility by actions like working with others to help force changes in school discipline policy in the Fresno Unified School District.

Likewise, in an area of the Central Coast of California stretching from Ventura to San Luis Obispo—formerly a rural conservative stronghold with an equally right-leaning set of suburbs—Central Coast Alliance United for a Sustainable Economy became a regional anchor for statewide integrated voter engagement, an effort that enhanced its local power to impact living wages, environmental conditions, and immigrant rights. And while the progressive presence in the critical Inland Empire east of Los Angeles County is more nascent, it is not entirely absent—in 2012, for example, voters in western Riverside County elected Mark Takano, an openly gay left-leaning Asian American, to the U.S. Congress, and the area has long been an important hub for environmental justice organizing, particularly by the Center for Community Action and Environmental Justice.

Still, the main point is clear: California progressives had realized that they could not give up on huge swaths of the state and expect to wield power. This was particularly so because until Prop 13 is overturned—a key goal of progressives—any revenue-enhancing strategy needs a two-thirds vote in both the state senate and the state assembly, a goal that requires some support from the suburban and rural locales that had been the base for California's right-wing populism. The growing possibilities of a progressive geographic stretch across the state were illustrated in 2012 when the California Calls affiliates, along with other social justice groups and labor allies, helped to elect a progressive mayor in historically conservative San Diego.[74] Just four years later, both Orange and Fresno Counties, generally considered bastions of GOP conservatism, both went for Hillary Clinton in the 2016 presidential election, with margins of 8.6 percent and 6 percent, respectively.

While geography mattered, so did a commitment to simply getting out the vote. The new confidence in the progressive ability to do voter turnout was tested in 2014 when Proposition 47 was placed on the ballot. Another in a never-ending series of propositions, this one, like Prop 30, actually promised to do some good: as noted earlier, it sought to reclassify some nonviolent felonies as misdemeanors, allowing up to seven thousand inmates to be freed and up to forty thousand records to be altered in ways that would improve employability for ex-prisoners.[75] Slating a "not tough on crime" measure for a nonpresidential election is usually considered risky: off-cycle elections bring out an electorate that is usually older, paler, and less open to claims that high rates of incarceration signal a broken system and not broken individuals. But California progressives were confident that they could actually take advantage of low turnout with the strength of integrated voter engagement—and in a year in which Republicans continued to post gains nationwide, California voters passed the proposition with a nearly 20-percentage-point margin.

So it was perhaps no surprise that the state's progressive activists were bold enough to put a new revenue measure on the ballot in 2016, Proposition 55. The measure, which sought to extend the income tax levies of Prop 30 for another twelve years—that is, to continue the part of the tax package the left had fought for—was supported by many major Democrats but not by the governor. The reason: Brown had campaigned for Prop 30 in 2012 with a promise that the tax measures were temporary, and so he more or less avoided the issue in 2016 (although he was eager to use the fiscal benefits the proposition eventually won to keep the state budget balanced). Opposing the measure was the Howard Jarvis Taxpayers Association, a group named after the famous proponent of Prop 13. It was as though the battle of two Californias—the new and the old—had been joined: a reignited left was pushing to keep high taxes on the rich against the resistance of a Jarvis-inspired right that saw tax cuts as their lodestar. The result: good won over evil with a nearly two-thirds majority.

Winning and Why

One reading of this fiscal and electoral history—one that seems common to observers outside the Golden State—is that this is the legacy of the anti-immigrant rhetoric of the mid-1990s, the subsequent mobilization of the Latino vote, and the way in which demographics shifted politics in a more liberal direction. There are elements of truth to this story. The state's paying more attention to environmental justice issues partly stemmed from a growing Latino Legislative Caucus that included many members whose districts were drenched in pollution. The 2015 decision to pay overtime to home care workers and the 2016 consensus on raising the minimum wage were due, in no small part, to the concentration of Latinos in the working-poor populations. And the governor's willingness in 2013 to sign a law allowing undocumented immigrants to obtain drivers' licenses—a right taken away in late 1993 under Pete Wilson but a measure that Brown himself had resisted early in his term—reflected the fact that the political consequences of doing so had changed.[76]

But the assumption that demographics are destiny is off the mark. After all, Latinos might tend to be more sympathetic to immigrants, but several of the progressive goals and victories described previously—a fairer tax system and a reduction in overincarceration—have less direct emotional connections. Moreover, the growing Latino electorate could have been artfully played against the more stable Black population, particularly by those insisting that the route to Latino political empowerment would be through displacing existing Black leadership; instead, what some thought was just a "presumed alliance" between African Americans and Latinos held more or less steady.[77] Meanwhile, leadership training—including a boards-and-commissions training created by the environmental and social justice organization Urban Habitat in the Bay Area, which has since spread to other places like Los Angeles, where it's being led by the Liberty Hill Foundation—patiently worked people through the system to prepare them for appointed positions and political office. And the broader electoral strategy continues in the form of a Million Voters Project, which seeks to mobilize a million or more new and occasional voters by the 2018 elections, an effort that includes California Calls but also other statewide networks such as Mobilize the Immigrant Vote, ACCE, PICO California, and APEN.

It's also the case that the short history provided here—indeed, any short history—misses some of the key movement struggles that have expanded democracy and equity in California and can leave out many that are ahead. For example, across California, grassroots community organizing groups—many of which are rooted in tenants' rights organizing from the 1970s—have been working to promote affordable housing. For example, in 2001, housing advocates in Los Angeles successfully pushed the city to create a housing trust fund to finance the construction of affordable housing and, in 2009, nearly secured a mechanism to finance the trust fund—an inclusionary zoning ordinance that would have collected fees from market-rate housing developers. That effort was derailed when one such market-rate developer—Geoff Palmer, who would go on to be the ninth-largest individual donor supporting Donald Trump's presidential campaign—successfully sued the city over a similar but smaller-scale ordinance.[78] Advocates in the Bay Area have had slightly more success in passing local inclusionary zoning ordinances over the years, and also strengthened the rights of tenants as cities became less affordable for the low-income families who had lived there for decades.

There was also the critical role of the LGBTQ movement in

California. June 1978 saw the passage of the fiscally disastrous Proposition 13, but later that year, in November, came an initiative to force openly gay and lesbian teachers, aides, and administrators out of public education. The successful fight to defeat this homophobic initiative pulled together a wide range of gay and straight allies and helped to propel the organizing and political career of Harvey Milk, a San Francisco supervisor who debated the author of the initiative in a series of events through the campaign season.[79] But LGBTQ organizing soon became understandably consumed with combating the AIDS crisis, a task that involved working to set up clinics, securing medical services, and garnering the needed federal, state, and local attention to funding and research. As the crisis became less acute, many turned to fight for gay rights in general and domestic partner rights in particular. But the community was rocked on its heels in 2008 when California voters managed to simultaneously contribute their electoral votes to the ascendance of the first Black president *and* pass Proposition 8, a measure designed to roll back the rights of same-sex couples to wed.

Some LGBTQ advocates were struck by initial exit polling that suggested that African Americans (and Latinos to a lesser degree) were much more likely than whites to vote against marriage equality—perhaps a new majority of progressives was not in the offing.[80] But many in the movement also began to understand that while some voters of color may have supported Prop 8 out of religiosity, the LGBTQ movement was also seen as overwhelmingly white and not concerned with challenges facing many who were less economically advantaged or who were facing issues of overincarceration, uncertain immigration status, and a host of other racialized disadvantages—a perception shared by many lesbians, gays, and transgender people of color. For those key leaders in the LGBTQ movement who had been deeply influenced by both the alliance building of the 2008 Obama campaign as well as the intersectional work pioneered by Milk—who was an advocate for

labor unions and minority groups as well as gays and lesbians—
the critiques resonated and so it was a time to reflect and regroup.

From that came a realization—that you can expect support for
your struggle only if you show up for the struggles of others. That,
in turn, led to Camp Courage, an attempt to take the training
techniques used for Obama volunteers and create the basis for a
new movement not just for marriage equality but for total equality as well. As one of the leaders, Torie Osborn, put it in a closing
speech in one of the ten camps conducted over 2009:

> You probably think this weekend is about marriage equal-
> ity. That's why you signed up. . . . Sorry. You've spent the last 36
> hours at Camp Courage under false pretexts. This is not about gay
> marriage. . . . What is being launched at Camp Courage is about
> something bigger. . . . The people who brought us Prop 8 are the
> same people who cut taxes on the wealthy to decimate the safety
> net. They are the people who took California schools from first to
> worst, who filled our prisons beyond capacity with people whose
> only crimes are poverty and addiction, who sent to war working
> class sons and daughters who have no other path to citizenship,
> college or an economic future. . . . The American Dream is on
> life support. Although we haven't stopped to realize it, our anger
> at being denied our equality is shared by millions whose dreams
> have also been stolen.[81]

It was a profound example of exactly what was needed to build
bridges—a willingness to stand in solidarity, to speak to common
fate, and to be explicit about a social compact. So it was perhaps
no surprise when the Courage Campaign, which had been crucial
in the fight against Prop 8—which was eventually declared unconstitutional by a federal judge in 2010 but remained in place until a decision on somewhat different grounds by the U.S. Supreme
Court in 2013 allowed same-sex marriages to resume—joined
with many others in the 2012 campaign to support the fiscal relief

in Proposition 30, a measure that seemed, at best, marginally related to gay rights per se.

Intersectionality went both ways. Many in the immigrant
rights movement had stayed away from LGBTQ rights, partly
because of the conservatism of their own constituencies as well as
the support of immigrant-friendly but gay-wary Catholic organizations and charities.[82] However, seasoned leaders came to better
appreciate the power of alliances and youth-led LGBTQ forces
within the immigrant rights movement, particularly the so-called
DREAMers who quite literally borrowed the trope of "coming
out" and forced the movement to confront its engagement with
the LGBTQ movement.[83] This new sort of intersectionality—in
this case really led by youths—built on previous efforts, such as the
way the labor-Latino alliance had helped create a more welcoming
labor movement *and* allowed immigrant activists to see their work
in the context of a broader arc of social and economic justice.[84]

Another key force in the state helping change happen: philanthropy. Historically, California funders had followed the national
norm and so stayed away from direct politics and policy. But key
to the Los Angeles awakening I detailed previously was the L.A.-
based Liberty Hill Foundation, a smaller fund that bet long-term
on emerging regional efforts to pass a living wage, secure environmental justice, reform the transit system, and secure LGBTQ
rights.[85] And it wasn't just small explicitly left-wing funders and
certainly not just Los Angeles: up north, the San Francisco Foundation financed and helped convene a Bay Area Environmental
Health Collaborative that pressed for major improvements in
disadvantaged communities. Numerous other funders helped to
support training community activists to serve on boards and com-
missions, and some, like the Evelyn and Walter Haas, Jr. Fund,
were instrumental in supporting the immigrant rights infrastructure that helped to change hearts, minds, and policies in the
Golden State.

One of the biggest shifts in the philanthropic landscape came when the state's largest health care funder, The California Endowment (TCE), launched a ten-year initiative in 2010 to promote health in fourteen low-income neighborhoods in the state. Like many funders, TCE arrived laden with theories of change, defined goals, and complicated matrices to evaluate outcomes—but it quickly realized that listening to community actors might be the best way to empower change. From that came campaigns to change school discipline policies that disproportionately penalized Black and Latino youths as well as efforts to reform city planning in Fresno and extend state-funded health care to undocumented immigrants. All moved forward, but the latter was especially surprising given the national turn against immigrants: in 2015, the governor agreed to expand Medi-Cal, the state version of Medicaid, to cover undocumented youths. By early 2017, TCE had become the largest funder of "systems change" efforts—primarily grassroots organizing, policy advocacy, and coalition building—in the state, and indeed the largest non-national foundation in the country in terms of its spending to support social justice.[86]

And it hasn't been just one flagship foundation. Coming out of a successful collaboration aimed at increasing California's participation in the 2010 census, a group of like-minded funders launched an ongoing initiative, the California Civic Participation Funders. Now comprised of ten foundations—TCE, the California Wellness Foundation, Evelyn and Walter Haas, Jr. Fund, James Irvine Foundation, McKay Foundation, PowerPAC Foundation, Progressive Era Project, Rosenberg Foundation, Tides, and Women's Foundation of California—the California Civic Participation Funders are putting their own specific concerns around criminal justice, immigration, and gender justice to one side to focus on bolstering the capacity of nonprofits to engage underrepresented populations in elections—and, perhaps more important, between elections—in four counties: San Diego, Orange, Riverside, and San Bernardino.

In San Diego, leaders from the ACLU, several community organizing groups, the region's own labor-affiliated think-and-do tank, the Center on Policy Initiatives, as well as the Environmental Health Coalition and San Diego LGBTQ Community Center, came together to form Engage San Diego to coordinate their civic engagement efforts and strategies.[87] In Orange County, the initiative helped to spark a Latino-Asian-labor alliance that coordinated a public education campaign to push for district-based city council elections in Anaheim.[88] As for the sprawling Inland Empire, a place in which the organizing infrastructure has historically suffered from underinvestment, and where the physical and political distance between groups has been significant, funders supported a facilitator that led a long-term process to build relationships and trust.[89]

What the funders learned was an old axiom attributed to famed California organizer Fred Ross: "Short-cuts usually end in detours, which lead to dead-ends."[90] The story of California's movement building—one key element to the way the state has been transformed—is not about a single instance or a magic moment but rather about a long-term commitment to authentic base building, leadership development, civic engagement, effective policies, intersectional networks, and unexpected allies. It's also an illustration of how a hardheaded analysis of power and a disciplined approach to changing the electorate can translate anger into action, resentment into resistance, chagrin into change. It's a lesson needed for a national political scene in which short-term strategies often dominate; we will not be saved or doomed by a well-written tweet, an Instagram share, and a perfectly reported scandal but rather by a patient commitment to building governing power in cities, metros, and states across the nation.

Movements to Match My Mountains

In his celebrated history of the American West, *Men to Match My Mountains*, Irving Stone discusses the role of key individuals, like John Sutter, James Marshall, and Brigham Young, in opening up a new part of America.[91] A bit lost on Stone was the irony of their triumph: the West was won, after all, by taking land belonging to someone else (i.e., Mexicans), who had themselves taken it from others (i.e., indigenous people). But it was exactly that sort of hubris—in this case, trying to take back the political terrain that had been seized by the populist right—that progressive forces demonstrated as they picked themselves up from the dark decades of the 1980s and 1990s and worked to build an effective strike force for justice in California.

The story of this transformation took place on a terrain that had been altered by economic and social forces. The evolving demographics of the state, the drift of business dynamism to the North, the emergence of more sympathy for the working poor, the recognition that class and race were not separate dynamics, the slow transition toward stronger cities and more compact development, the emergence of regional collaboratives highlighting not just the economy but equity and the environment as well, and the reworking of a set of government rules that had long encouraged paralysis and not decision making—all these played a role. So, too, did particular individuals; while I have stressed that Governor Brown was not the singular reason for California turning around, it did help to have a stubborn governor who finally got sick of having the government held hostage by Republicans and so turned to more liberal forces to repair the state's finances. Finally, there was simply something about the times: the desire to address climate change, which animated Schwarzenegger as well as Brown, created a new possibility of common ground between environmental, social justice, labor, and business groupings and facilitated an opportunity to develop and maintain unique cross-sector political relationships.

But none of this was automatic, and progressive organizing played a key role in California's turn. Staggered by the 1992 civil unrest and reeling from the steady drumbeat of racial propositions of the 1990s, a battered left hunkered down. Work became more intersectional, linking immigrants and labor, environmentalists and social justice proponents, and community actors and policy makers. Opposition evolved to proposition: rather than merely arguing against the newest inane right-wing idea, groups were rolling out concepts like living wages, community benefits agreements, immigrant-friendly policing, and environmental equity. And rather than playing defense by appealing to groups of voters that had abandoned the old social compact when new residents arrived, progressives began to frame issues to mobilize those Californians who were often hurt by politics but did not always participate.

This turn to serious electioneering led to the adoption of integrated voter engagement, a strategy aimed as much at organizing as at voting. A first step in the process was developing a shared analysis of power; a second was understanding that victory could come only if progressives had geographic reach, including and perhaps especially to those areas that had been right-wing strongholds; a third was realizing that everyone had to go beyond the usual suspects, something that required outreach based on values and not slogans; and a fourth was recognizing that it was critical to mobilize those already close to being on your side—in California, that meant low-income communities of color—rather than spending all your efforts reaching for an imaginary middle or "swing" voter. It took time—leadership development and civic engagement do—and it ripened in the context of a crisis that made multiple actors see more clearly their own shared interests in coming together rather than peeling apart.

And isn't that a recipe for America today—and doesn't it call for making sure that we get the story right? For if the takeaway from California's descent and revival is that voters were brought to their senses by an old and experienced governor, the strategy for a nation convulsed by reaction is to search for exactly the right sort of leader. If, in fact, the governor was brought to his political senses by a nascent progressive movement, then there is reason for progressives nationwide to double down on understanding power, taking geography seriously, developing long-lasting alliances, constructing an alternative values-based vision, and working to get the people out when the vote really counts. It is arguable that if the national left had done just a bit more of all that, the Obama presidency could have been bolder, the Tea Party could have been countered, and the Trump phenomenon would have been less able to fill the gap. What happened in the Golden State need not stay in the Golden State—but it is important to grasp the lessons and equally important to apply them in ways tailored to other settings.

6

WHAT HAPPENS IN CALIFORNIA . . .

The election nights of 2008 and 2016 could not have been more different. On the former, Barack Obama delivered a victory speech in Grant Park to a crowd flush with a sense of pride and possibility, hopeful that we might just be getting ready to get past our political polarization, reaffirm our basic social compact, and work together as one to address our national challenges. On the latter, even a victorious Donald Trump looked stunned as he stumbled onto a New York hotel stage to claim the win. And while pundits began a frantic effort to understand the importance of interventions by the FBI director or even Russian hackers, the underlying drivers of the election results were simple: fear of demographic change, anxieties over a malfunctioning economy, and a level of social disconnection reified by vastly different perceptions of facts and, indeed, reality.

California immediately declared resistance and the reasons were clear: aside from what was at stake in terms of hard-fought policies on climate, immigrant integration, and even economic justice, civic leaders realized that the Golden State had been here before. Indeed, if you'd blinked and been transported back in time, you might have thought you were in 1990s California, reeling from an economy that was underperforming, wracked by a class divide that was widening, stressed by views that newcomers were alien invaders, and vulnerable to opportunistic political figures proffering a populist agenda that would turn out to be a cover for enhancing corporate gains.

But if California was America fast-forward in terms of demographic shifts, economic transformations, and political disruptions, the view from what was supposed to have been the rubble of a right-wing assault does not look all that dystopian. The sense of coming apart has been replaced in the Golden State by the outlines of a sort of "new deal" for the twenty-first century, one that promises renewed and more inclusive investments in physical and social infrastructure. The racial and intergroup tensions of yesteryear are not completely dissipated, as can be seen in continued struggles over policing and education reform, but California is less susceptible to the racialized anxiety that once drove its politics. And tackling climate change—which should be everyone's concern—has become a central commitment for the state, along with a recognition that the most effective path to addressing environmental conditions is through a focus on problems afflicting the state's most disadvantaged populations.

While it all sounds good now, the process of getting there was nasty, brutish, and anything but short. A shifting economy changed the nature of poverty and the composition of business, even as frustrations with the structure of governance helped to set in place new rules. Onto that reworked stage stepped a series of innovative social movements that were able to get past their own divisions, develop a geographic strategy for change, and take power and elections seriously. Change was not automatic: it required new strategies and new alliances—and a whole lot of painful learning. And since there is no good reason why the national body politic should be raked over the same hot coals that nearly torched the Golden State, some lessons should be drawn from that rocky ride.

How We Got Here

The history in this book is nuanced but the basic story is not complex: California worked when it had a social compact that welcomed and integrated newcomers, a broad set of infrastructure investments that facilitated that process, and an economy that functioned to create platforms of opportunity. That commitment assumed a particular economic, social, and racialized form—including a booming industrial economy overly reliant on military spending, suburban housing built for a mostly white middle class, and highways that wrecked the environment even as they facilitated escape from city environs. It was an economic and social landscape with economic risk, social exclusion, and environmental stress built right in—contradictions that would cause an undoing further down the historical road. But it reflected a sense that at least some of us were in it together, along with a broad recognition that government should play a role *and* that investments in human capital—particularly through high levels of K–12 spending and improved access to higher education—were key. There were always right-wing forces tearing at that broad common understanding, lurking in the shadows of reason, and cooking up conspiracy theories about communists, collaborators, and so much more—but they were constrained by the state's political traditions that tended to reward moderation and bipartisanship.

California began to fall apart when its sense of commonality began to slip. Some of that drift was the result of demographic change; increasingly, the new Californians were ethnically different from the old Californians. Discomfort with the shifting hue of the California populace was exacerbated by worries about a society under challenge: civil rights militancy, Vietnam War protests, and urban riots fed into concerns about "law and order." The economy began to seriously underperform as early as the 1970s, with unemployment rising even as inflation drove housing values and property taxes. An attempt to equalize spending across school districts added fuel to the fires of resentment as it gave the appearance that any revenue increases wrought by housing inflation were heading out of middle-class neighborhoods and to those militant minorities seeking to barge their way into the California Dream.

It was a recipe for a tax revolt—and so one occurred in 1978. Building from previous attacks on housing desegregation and school busing, right-wing populists stoked anger with tales of an overreaching government serving the new demography. Prop 13 passed, ripping an immediate hole in state and local budgets and making it more difficult to enhance state resources in the future. Frightened of the forces that had just been unleashed, state leaders decided to cushion the blow by backfilling lost revenues—and Californians began to think taxes could be cut painlessly, a delusion that soon infected national politics. But this could not last long and the state's fiscal and other vulnerabilities were revealed when deindustrialization, once masked by the defense spending that continued to drive the California economy forward through the 1980s, began to ripple its way through the state's economic structure.

By the early 1990s, it was clear that something needed to be done. California could have tried to mend the social fabric, restore the commitment to infrastructure, and head into the millennium with a stronger, more-skilled, and better-prepared workforce. Instead, voters ponied up for a series of ballot propositions that threatened immigrants, killed affirmative action, derailed bilingual education, and criminalized youths. But in what seemed like the darkest of times, a remarkable thing happened: a new sort of progressive politics was born.

Facing the onslaught of "racial propositions," organizers fought back, rejecting a moderate politics of assuaging the median voter with something just a bit less draconian and instead trying to offer a new set of alternatives focused on living wages, immigrant integration, and de-incarceration. Getting there required a new sort of intersectional politics—alliances between labor and immigrants, between communities of color and environmentalists, between inside policy makers and outside agitators. It also required a growing recognition that demography would *not* become destiny without a clear strategy—that translating the growing Latino and

Asian American/Pacific Islander presence into being part of an effective and progressive voice required integrated voter engagement. That meant moving from opposition to proposition, from Pyrrhic stands to pragmatic policies, from accepting a role at the margins to moving boldly to take the main stage as with the 2012 showdown over the millionaires' tax.

Movements were key but they were not the whole story. The state's business class changed, particularly as the economic dynamism shifted north and facilitated the ascendancy of a more liberal (at least on social issues) civic leadership in the Bay Area—one rooted in high tech, open to immigration, entranced by the green economy, and largely nonplussed by attempts to raise the wages of service workers. For a left correctly angered about the poles of wealth generated by the high-tech sector and worried about the unfettered power of large firms, this was a wary phenomenon. But consider that some of the recent national "victories" that are partly attributable to movement organizing—like slowing the brakes on draconian immigration policy in Arizona, forcing out an anti-gay governor in North Carolina, or resisting the initial version of the Trump travel ban against immigrants from seven Muslim-majority countries—also have their roots in a set of businesses that reacted negatively to right-wing policies.

Another key part of the California story has to do with its geographic reconfiguration. Partly because of the need to address climate change, California's longtime love affair with sprawl is on the wane. The new built environment—more city, less suburb, more transit, less auto—has shifted power and dynamism from the right-wing base in the suburbs and far-flung rural areas of the state. Nationwide, a similar geographic sorting is under way but it is more nascent, and so the old empire—meaning the South, rural America, and the battered industrial Midwest—has struck back. In the last election, the counties that voted for Hillary Clinton tended to be in larger metro areas that produced nearly two-thirds of the nation's GDP in 2015; Trump country represented an anemic 36 percent of the nation's productivity, and the Trump economic coalition was also built on older, threatened industries such as mining and fossil fuels.[1] It is clear where the national future is, but getting there will require a careful attention to fortifying the current geographic base even as progressives reach out to the less dynamic areas that are under stress.

As for California, achieving a just, sustainable, and economically vibrant future will require much more work: poverty remains an issue, the historic legacies of overincarceration limit community potential, and the new focus on compact development will collapse into gentrification unless there is a twenty-first-century commitment to housing as robust as that which gave the state its suburbs. But while work remains, it would be missing the forest for the trees if one did not conclude that it has been a remarkable shift. Fiscal balance has been more or less struck, immigrant rights are being extended, not eroded, and the state is engaged in an ambitious albeit imperfect program to tackle both climate change and climate equity. Education spending is headed to the least-advantaged communities, the prison population is shrinking, and while traditional business advocates offer the usual resistance to labor-friendly policies—it's still capitalism, after all—the passage of a statewide minimum wage was remarkably conflict-free and some Silicon Valley entrepreneurs are interested in whether a universal basic income might address a world in which work really will disappear.

In the era of Trump, this has positioned the state as a key point of resistance: bold enough to believe that the future is once again being forged on the left coast and rich enough to stand up against a federal government focused on dragging America back to an era in which greatness was measured by who was excluded from opportunity. Texas was once determined to sue the previous president, Barack Obama, on nearly every policy and continues to boast that it is the true national alternative going forward. But its model—based on cheap energy, urban sprawl, and political disenfranchisement—does not seem like a recipe for the national long haul.[2] What California is stumbling toward—still evolving, still incomplete, still vulnerable to its own reactionary voters—is a path to a new American future, one in which the nation becomes more prosperous *and* more sustainable, more diverse *and* more cohesive, more engaged *and* more agreeable. It matters that the state gets there and it matters that the country learns from its path.

What's Next

Fulfilling its national role will require that California both defend what it has achieved *and* develop new policies that point the way to the future. On the defense side, one key element will be protecting the roughly 2.8 million undocumented Californians who are deeply embedded in the state; various efforts are under way to have state and local governments provide legal assistance to immigrants facing deportation.[3] Another crucial battle: California has already strengthened its targets for greenhouse gas reductions and, in the wake of President Trump's rejection of the Paris climate agreement, Democratic governor Brown—whom the *New York Times* described as "America's de facto leader on climate change"—has offered to host a global climate summit in California.[4] Yet another key struggle: the Trump administration's talk of tax reform has included discussion of the elimination of the deductibility of state income taxes, meaning that the state's bite on the rich—which is now partly offset by the fact that higher taxes in California get written off on federal taxes—would bite all that much harder and make California's efforts to retain business a bit harder.

However, defense is not enough: California needs to ensure that progressive policies actually bring improvements in people's daily lives. For example, the new infill development coming in California's urban centers has its benefits, but it has also displaced many lower-income renters from their homes—sometimes straight into homelessness.[5] In San Francisco, the average cost of a two-bedroom apartment rose by more than 70 percent between January 2011 and December 2016.[6] Partly as a result, families have fled the city: children now represent only 13 percent of the city's residents, slightly above half the national average; one startling statistic is that San Francisco now has about as many dogs as kids.[7] Los Angeles has faced similar pressures as the downtown has recovered and adjoining neighborhoods have zoomed in value—and hipster appeal. The shift has been pushed along by the rollout of rail-based mass transit financed largely out of local sales taxes.

Even far from the burgeoning centers, the share of income eaten up by housing costs has been on the rise.[8] A state that once committed itself to producing a housing stock that, despite the attendant problems of its sprawling nature, was at least generally sufficient to meet rising demand has largely retrenched. The state Department of Housing and Community Development reports that housing production between 2006 and 2015 was adding only about eighty thousand homes annually, a far cry from the average two hundred thousand units being generated each year between 1955 and 1990.[9] Between 2008–9 and 2014–15, California's annual state and federal funding for affordable housing production and preservation fell by more than $1.7 billion—a 66 percent reduction.[10] Cap-and-trade dollars have filled in a bit with funds going to an Affordable Housing and Sustainable Communities Program intended to support housing near transit, but this is limited and insufficient to address the state's housing crisis.

While September 2017 saw the passage of new legislation that may begin to turn the tide—by seeking to increase housing stock in all California cities, particularly for lower-income families, and to provide new bond money for affordable housing—the housing dilemma is a perfect illustration of what is fundamentally at stake: California has abandoned an old model of suburban sprawl that was environmentally unsustainable, but it has not yet developed a new model that is economically sustainable.[11] A similar dynamic of the old and the new is at play in the economy. A state that once advanced by shoring up the middle of the economy has instead been distracted by the glitter of high tech, entertainment, and finance. Steady work is increasingly being replaced by the gig economy, in which what is really being "shared" is stress and insecurity. Uber is a perfect symbol of the rapid shifts in this new economy: it has helped to disrupt and to some extent destroy the old taxicab monopoly, but the workers who are helping them do that are themselves slated to be replaced by driverless cars.

While California can be proud of raising its minimum wage, that is not really an economic strategy to propel people into the middle class. There is increasing conversation among some elite business leaders as well as progressive thinkers of a universal basic income (UBI)—basically, a strategy to guarantee a certain standard of living regardless of whether one has steady employment.[12] Some offer quite reasonable critiques of UBI, for example, that it could become a recipe to weaken key social programs and that the concept ignores the fact that work generates meaning and identity as well as income.[13] But whatever the merits of universal basic income as a policy, it is at least an attempt to come to terms with the real "new" economy.

A similar dose of realism is needed with regard to job creation: much like defense spending spilled over to spur aerospace and manufacturing, state policy intended to propel the green economy can give California entrepreneurs an international jump start and California workers steady employment in that sector.[14] And, of course, no one will be able to secure the jobs in the green or any other sector of the economy without a new master plan for public education, one that understands that given the persistent racial and income disparities in California, moving forward requires a focus on those who have been left furthest behind.[15]

The good news is that recognizing these dynamics, the California legislature passed a shift in school spending in 2013 that, for a change, made sense: spend more on those who need it. Originally proposed by Governor Brown—but building on years of preparing the political ground through community-based organizing for more equity in educational resources spending—the so-called Local Control Funding Formula (LCFF) steers more dollars to school districts with higher concentrations of low-income children, English learners, and foster youths.[16] Implementation has not always been easy—community groups have had to fight to ensure that district-level enhancements in funds actually get directed to the neediest schools and students within a district—but there is a different tone being set about how to best leverage resources for maximum social benefit.[17]

Of course, the eventual challenge will be about not just shuffling what is available for education spending but actually increasing what the state spends. In the 1950s and 1960s, California was regularly among the top-funded states in terms of basic education; it is now generally ranked in the bottom ten in terms of inflation-adjusted spending per pupil in kindergarten through high school.[18] While funding was strengthened by the extension of taxes on higher-income Californians in the 2016 elections, a firmer base of revenues is needed. And the fat, juicy target—one that would also symbolize finally putting to rest the right-wing, anti-government tax revolt that shredded California's finances and future—is the overturning of Proposition 13.

Prop 13 has worsened the state's problems in many ways. The ability to continue to pay low taxes even as your house zooms in value has benefited those who are better off and own more expensive homes, a fact made clear in a 2016 study by California's Legislative Analyst's Office, which found that nearly half of Prop 13's benefits to homeowners went to households making more than $120,000 a year.[19] It's also given an unfair advantage to business, partly because a reassessment occurs only when a property changes hands. As a result, Chevron and Intel are paying taxes essentially based on the 1975 value of some properties they hold (with annual increases in assessments and taxes held to no more than 2 percent). And businesses can take advantage of a quirk in the law: if you buy the business entity that owns the property and no new owner takes a majority position, no reassessment is triggered. This loophole was best publicized when Michael Dell—yes, of Dell Technologies—purchased a seaside hotel in Santa Monica, then ripped up the deal and restructured it to bring in his wife and two investment advisers so no one would take a majority position, thereby shaving $1 million a year from his property tax bill.[20]

The estimated increase in revenues from a so-called split roll—that is, preserving the protections for homeowners as well as agriculture and apartment owners but allowing market-based assessments on commercial and industrial property—is a relatively modest $9 billion annually.[21] But the meaning of this move would reverberate beyond the dollars collected. Directly tackling Proposition 13 would signal a new political economy in the state. It would suggest that conservative populism can no longer be used to mask schemes to enhance corporate interests or enrich the wealthy. It would signal that the state recognizes the need for a more stable source of funds for investment in the future. And it could start a conversation about the underlying and rather dangerous premise of Proposition 13: a generational divide frozen in place by a haywire tax system protecting older Californians as a poorly functioning housing market penalizes the young.

There are myriad other policies that should be part of California's next agenda. The state has committed to reducing its prison population; it now needs to offer more resources and strategies to ensure reintegration of the formerly incarcerated into the economy and local communities. The state has acted boldly on climate change but it also needs to address community-based critiques about cap-and-trade worsening local pollution and worries about how the logistics industry in Southern California is endangering the lives of nearby residents.[22] The state has improved the situation of undocumented Californians, including through the October 2017 signing of so-called "sanctuary state" legislation further limiting local police and sheriff cooperation with Immigration and Customs Enforcement (ICE), and it has begun to make an overall commitment to immigrant integration; next steps could be increased investments in adult education, particularly English classes, enhanced job-training systems to better support the working poor, and even new avenues for formal voting in local elections.[23]

The state has adopted a more equitable approach to spending on K–12 education; a key next step will be expanding the community college system and making it free, something that would benefit lower-income students of color and can further economic development and growth. The state has boosted the minimum wage, but it should now extend other critical worker protections, including portable benefits, affordable childcare, and vigorous enforcement against wage theft.[24] The state has embraced a new and more compact form of development, but reducing the displacement caused by gentrification will require an expansion of land trusts, rules against eviction, requirements that developers build or contribute to affordable housing, and a vibrant housing movement to make all this happen. Moreover, the state will also need to ensure that a new urban emphasis does not leave inland California behind, worsening some of the geographic disparities highlighted in earlier chapters.

It's a long list of particular policies, but it is motivated by a simple recognition: the California Dream emerged from an earlier commitment to create platforms of opportunity for both those who were already living in the Golden State *and* those who were still to come. That led to a commitment to create sufficient housing to accommodate growth, to work toward an economy that could deliver jobs and income for those in the middle, and to support a first-class education system that trained workers and leaders for the future. Creating the California Dream, version 2.0, will require recognizing the Achilles' heel that has plagued both California and the nation: the state's fortunes slipped when the racism of its own residents got the better of them. California can do better, but only if Californians realize that what is at stake today is not just the size of the deficit or a specific set of policies but the outlines of a new social compact that includes everyone.[25]

And if you think about it, that's exactly the challenge facing America. With an economy still stumbling its way out of the Great Recession, with uncertainty about job prospects affecting older and younger workers alike, with both red states like Florida and blue states like New York threatened by the rising seas from climate change, 2016 seemed like an appropriate time to come together. Instead, like California in the 1990s, voters chose to tear themselves apart in a sort of last gasp of a collapsing racial order. And as in California, racist and anti-immigrant pandering will cost us in terms of our moral values and social cohesion *and* also in the dollars and cents of productivity and income lost to discrimination, incarceration, and unequal education.

The way out does hinge on rejecting bad leaders, but this is not enough. Too many progressives hoped that electing Barack Obama would turn the American corner, offering a way past the legacy of racism and social disconnection and toward a sense of common destiny. Instead, we got political paralysis—and as in the Golden State in the 1980s and 1990s, a revitalized right-wing determined to hold progress at bay. Jazz poet Gil Scott-Heron once sang that the only way to "take this world and make it what it need to be, want to be, will be, someday you'll see" was through realizing "that there ain't no such thing as a superman." The real need is not for a great leader but for many leaders, not for winning at the top of the ticket but for winning across the board, not for pinning our hopes on one speech, one candidate, or even one big march but rather counting on the grassroots organizing that brings people together face-to-face, race to race, and place to place to see their common future.

Learning from California

In the chaos that was triggered by the election and then ascendance to the presidency of Donald Trump, it was easy to lurch from tweet to tweet, crisis to crisis, with attention focused mostly on whatever odd utterance and misguided public policy had become the subject of the day. But in the midst of the panic, I found myself reminded of Los Angeles in the days after the 1992 civil unrest. Against the backdrop of a city ripped asunder, leaders and activists flitted from meeting to meeting, thinking that perhaps just one more meeting would actually provide a path forward. In the midst of yet another urgent gathering, one activist leaned back and uttered words that aptly described the situation then and now: "There's an immediate need to think long-term."

What followed were campaigns to secure a living wage; efforts to build bridges between immigrants, community organizations, and labor; and the patient creation of an electoral strategy to shift the state. Even as protest marches, social media shaming, and active pressure on political figures become main tasks of today's national resistance, it is key to keep our eyes on the long-term prize: a social compact that will secure our intergenerational future. To do this, we will need to understand that systemic racism has created a sinkhole that prevents us from addressing our big economic and generational challenges. We will need to accept that making America great requires a consensus about our mutual responsibilities to one another and a new commitment to public investments aimed at promoting success. And we will need to realize that while economic structures and political rules will set the terrain, what really drove change in California—and can for the nation— are social movements and community organizing.

Can the rest of the United States learn from the California story? The Golden State has its own peculiar history and there is no one size fits all: for every "California package" on immigration, there is a Utah Compact—a 2010 agreement among religious, business, law enforcement, and community leaders designed to cool the heat in the immigration debate—that fits like a glove for that much redder state.[26] Partly because of this, it can be hard to accept the advice of others, particularly those who seem to have the advantages of a high-tech economy, beautiful weather, and a politics now less tainted by racial anxiety. Hearing that California is America fast-forward can just seem like an arrogant and uncaring boast, a sort of taunt across the other side of history.

But no matter how the message may be received, Californians have a special responsibility to communicate what they have learned. After all, like it or not, California already has a long history of exporting. Not all of it has been bad: under the Clean Air Act, California was allowed to set stricter emissions standards for vehicles, which drove manufacturers to craft cleaner vehicles nationwide. Still, as noted in Chapter 3, plenty of bad was shared: the state's tax revolt spilled beyond its borders, as did its three-strikes laws, attacks on affirmative action, and anti-immigrant hysteria. And having been through its own misguided attempt to restore greatness through generational protection and racial exclusion, California can offer a dozen takeaways to help our nation toward justice instead of reaction.

The first is to *anticipate and counter the dynamics of the generation gap*. The fight to starve California of resources, embodied in the form of Prop 13, began just as the racial generation gap—the difference in the ethnicity of elders and youths—was beginning to widen in the state. The initial shot was not directly racist but it was close: on the heels of voting to reinstate housing and school segregation came an effort to explicitly protect older (read whiter) homeowners, which eventually forced a retreat from the sort of state spending on education that was critical to an earlier generation's success. What followed got more directly racial—round up the undocumented, ban affirmative action, end bilingual education, lock up criminals for life—but it was all stirred into existence as the gap was widening and dis-ease was growing.

Why is this relevant to the nation? Consider Figure 6.1, in which I chart the gap—the difference between the percentage of seniors who are white and the percentage of youths who are white—for California from 1970 to 2015, side by side with the corresponding percentages in the United States from 1990 to 2035.[27] Look closely at the California peak in the mid-1990s and the U.S. peak in 2016: it is not an exaggeration but rather a bit of an empirical reality to say that America just went through its "Prop 187" moment. We need to recognize how the tensions that occur when the gap is growing can lead to attempts to limit new voters' power through overincarceration, suppression of voting rights, and other means. To counter this, we need to restore the hopes for generational connections that were lifted up in the Obama campaign and are the everyday work of faith-based and other values-driven community organizing.

The second big lesson from the California experience: *understand the key role of social movements.* The combination of economic distress and demographic change is part of the explanation for Proposition 13 and Proposition 187—and for the triumph of Donald Trump in the 2016 presidential elections. Still, none of those toxic efforts would have succeeded without a vibrant right-wing social movement that was ready to exploit the moment. Similarly, one could explain California's swing back to fiscal and political sanity by a series of structural forces: a business class that began to see less profit in dividing the state by race and sector, a shift in the political rules of the game that reduced the "veto power" held by the Republican right, and an impending climate crisis that created opportunities for new coalitions and new leadership. Those factors were critical—and the left ignores them to its peril. But that sort of analysis of the terrain rather than the actors would also gloss over the careful movement-building enterprise

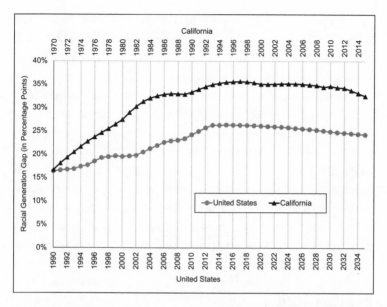

FIGURE 6.1: Racial generation gap in California and the United States.

that changed the political calculus and made it possible to secure drivers' licenses for immigrants or beat back an oil-company-sponsored attack on the state's climate laws.

What does this imply for America going forward? When Obama won in 2008, policy advocates rushed to D.C. to push for their favorite programs; meanwhile, the right wing launched a grassroots insurgency—namely, the Tea Party (albeit with funds from the Koch brothers and others who stood to gain, opportunism that was simply par for the course). The result was a liberal president who found himself not just sharply constrained but forced to hand over the seat to his polar (and polarizing) opposite. If resistance in the current era is conducted largely by the advocacy of interest groups or the machinations of political figures, this will not be enough. Judging from the millions who showed up for women's marches around the country on January 21, 2017, the country is ready to be organized—but turning that moment into a movement will require grassroots organizing, base-level leadership, and new avenues for civic engagement. All of this will require funds—and, as in California, the role of the philanthropic sector and individual donors could be crucial.

The third big lesson: *change takes time.* California may have been slapped to its senses by a roller-coaster ride through anti-immigrant hysteria, economic distress, and government dysfunction. But it took a while: for example, the arc from Proposition 187 to the 2013 Trust Act limiting the cooperation of local jails with federal immigration authorities took just under twenty years. Americans tend to want quick fixes—but we did not get into the national mess easily, nor will we depart simply by impeaching a particular president (as tempting as that may be). After all, the national conservative movement has deep roots: one early salvo was the famous 1971 memo from future Supreme Court justice Lewis Powell arguing that American business was under attack and laying a multistrategy long-term agenda to restrain government and shift education, politics, and the courts in a direction more favorable to capital.[28]

Conservatives proved to be patient warriors, taking a multifaceted approach that involved on-the-ground troops, a strong base in churches and communities, a link to electoral organizing, and a funded network to spread its ideas that included, for example, the American Legislative Exchange Council (ALEC) and the Koch-funded Americans for Prosperity. California's progressive approach was less well financed—right-wing movement builders gain from shilling for well-financed corporations—but it took an equally patient march through institutions so that, for example, an immigrant rights organizer who cut his teeth on resisting Proposition 187, Kevin de León, could end up as president pro tem of the state senate, a labor organizer like Antonio Villaraigosa could end up as mayor of Los Angeles, and a grassroots activist on community health like Karen Bass could end up as speaker of the assembly and then a representative to Congress. The Trump presidency—and the apparent desire to wreak havoc on nearly every social gain—creates a sense of urgency that demands a defensive posture. But while a crisis can be a turning point, panic is not a strategy. So any sort of immediate defense must be tempered with the development of an infrastructure of leaders, organizations, and institutions that can win over time.

The fourth lesson: *build intersectional movements that are less susceptible to infighting.* As I have noted, 2008 was a key year for movement builders in California. Obama won handily—yea!—but Proposition 8, a measure to eliminate "gay marriage" in the state, triumphed as well. With polling data indicating that African Americans were far more likely and Latinos slightly more likely than whites to support the marriage ban, one could have imagined a retrenchment by LGBTQ civic leaders away from issues that concerned communities of color. But rather than reaching toward recrimination—and with the proper amount of pushing from LGBTQ folks of color—many organizers focused on marriage equality began a process of both fortifying their own grassroots organizing and reaching out to others. Meanwhile, immigrant rights organizers chagrined that immigrant voters had favored homophobic policies took on the challenge of self-education and bridge building.

As is especially apparent with the election of Trump, there is nothing like facing a common threat to bring people together. But unity can be short-lived without an intentional focus on threading together different concerns and issues. Deportation and overincarceration are points on the same racialized continuum, union bashing and voter suppression are both aimed at disenfranchising community voice; and forcing fossil fuels on the planet and denying women control over their own bodies both reflect a bully's approach to nature and people. But actually seeing how all that comes together as a whole involves intentional and intersectoral leadership development, an avenue that opens a role for both organizers and philanthropy. And while a focus on such intersectionality does seem to come more naturally to millennials, those of us who are, shall we say, more seasoned and perhaps more accustomed to the siloed separate movements of the past might find inspiration in the lyrics one of our generation's poets, Bob Dylan: "Ah, but I was so much older then. I'm younger than that now."[29]

A fifth lesson: *untangle the rules that bind.* In California, conservative forces locked in their anti-government agenda with mandates that required supermajority votes on raising taxes or even passing a statewide budget. Some of these rules had existed on paper but had not always been followed in an earlier era of bipartisan moderation; Democrats and Republicans usually found an approach to a compromise, particularly at the local level. But as the generation gap widened, economic growth slipped, and political polarization sharpened, these illogical constraints forced a series of fiscal crises. Finding a correction involved lifting restrictions on budget decision making; helping to push along change were term limits, which brought into Sacramento a new crop of legislators of color, and a citizen-driven redistricting process that allowed a "new majority" to better realize its voice at the ballot box.

Nationally, the rules restraining progress are evident. Part of it is the gerrymandering that has locked in a Republican advantage: for example, in 2016, the GOP secured just over 49 percent of the votes cast in House races but wound up with more than 55 percent of the seats.[30] Part of it is the active efforts at voter suppression, with ID requirements and other restrictive laws holding back the will of the public in at least twenty states during the 2016 election.[31] And part of it is the role of money in politics, particularly the infamous Citizens United ruling that, in fact, was designed to diminish the power of citizens who might be united against determined corporations. All of these must be vigorously challenged for a more forward-looking agenda to be realized.

And this leads to a key sixth lesson from the California experience: *pay attention to geography.* Part of this is scaling:

organizations like LAANE, Working Partnerships, and the Social Equity Caucus tried out new ideas like living wage laws and
community benefits agreements at the metro level, then sought to
link together and extend their influence and ideas across to the
state. This was sometimes facilitated by a shifting metro environment as business actors hoping to restore regional competitiveness
sought collaborative deals with labor, community, and local officials. But the big geographic realization for progressives in the
Golden State—one that impacted the whole framework for integrated voter engagement—was that bottling up organizing on
the coasts and in the cities was leaving a large swath of rural and
suburban California vulnerable to right-wing politics.

That geography is also a strategic concern at the national level
should be apparent to all observers: the 2016 elections saw one
candidate gain an electoral margin of more than 2 percentage
points and still be defeated because those overwhelming margins
did not accrue in the "right" states. But the local imperative was
evident to conservatives well before 2016 as they fought during
the Obama years to win seats in state legislatures, racking up a
net gain of more than nine hundred such seats for Republicans
between 2008 and 2016.[32] To regain national footing for progressives requires the resurrection of a fifty-state strategy—and
in some states, like Texas, that will require metro-level efforts to
build from an urban base, gain footholds in the suburbs, and use
that to leverage power in the capital.[33]

A seventh lesson: *work to pull in some part of the business class*,
as challenging as that might be. In California, many corporations
have benefited from Proposition 13 and business leaders seem
to view it as a symbolic bulwark against taxes and overspending.
New and growing sectors of the economy, especially in high tech,
are riddled with libertarians who are instinctively against government, unions, and other institutions associated with what they see
as the "old economy." Yet, the business dialogues that were part of
the regional collaborative efforts in California did give rise to at

least a verbal acknowledgment of the importance of equity. Part of that was pure politics: making progress in progressive California meant demonstrating how the less advantaged could gain (or at least, not lose) from any public policy. But there are also business leaders at the local, metro, and even state level who are legitimately worried about the way in which inequality is choking off a middle class that is crucial to long-term prosperity.[34]

Getting business leaders to understand how inequality is an economic drag and why they should come on board to address issues of equity and inclusion is key to moving national politics as well. When a Republican elected as governor of North Carolina in 2012 promptly overreached on immigration, voting rights, and a woman's right to choose, a protest effort called Moral Mondays was launched to great fanfare, lifting up public consciousness but not always able to force the governor and legislature to change their ways. When the same governor overruled the efforts of the city of Charlotte to protect its LGBTQ city residents, PayPal, Deutsche Bank, and the National Basketball Association pulled business out of the state and the governor went down in narrow defeat. Similarly, when newly inaugurated president Donald Trump sought to restrict the arrivals of refugees and others in early 2017, airport protests were important, but equally key was the opposition of high-tech companies such as Google, Facebook, and Microsoft.[35] The task ahead is to translate the obvious corporate commitment to diversity and difference—because it leads to innovation—into more solid support of inclusion.

This entreaty to business is precisely what makes an eighth lesson so crucial: *offer up a compelling, practical, and progressive economic vision.* California has certainly not gotten this right; too much of the economic structure of the state remains dependent on a combination of high-tech wealth and low-wage services. In that context, raising the minimum wage can lift the floor, but it will not necessarily grow the middle. Supporting regional clusters, expanding the community college system, and leveraging public

spending on transit all offer hope going forward. So, too, does the
so-called green economy, in which an advanced and advancing
part of the economy has the possibility of developing new global
and national markets by blending together sophisticated engineers with those who work to retrofit buildings, rejigger the electric grid, and install solar panels.[36]

What a more inclusive economy could look like is still very
much up for discussion—but what is crystal-clear is that the failure to articulate a coherent economic vision creates two risks. The
first is that it leaves an opening for xenophobic economic national-
ism; if there is no reasonable alternative, banning immigrants and
shutting down trade may sound better than doing nothing at all.
A second risk is that without a clear program, the sort of collaboration with business envisioned earlier in this chapter is bound to
be problematic; when one part of a coalition has an agenda and
the other has grievances, the agenda usually wins. Fortunately, the
Roosevelt Institute, the Economic Policy Institute, the Center for
Community Change, and other left-leaning institutions have offered progressive economic programs that make sense (and have
common elements); moving these into the middle of the debate
will be crucial. Bottom line: progressives have to be clear what
they are for and not just what they are against.

Which gets us to a ninth lesson: *do not move to the middle,
move the middle.* During the period in which racial propositions
hit their peak in the 1990s, the strategy of moderate Democrats
was to poll and focus group their way to a message that still de-
monized immigrants and people of color but just a little bit less
than the other guy. But trying to sway voters to keep undocumented children in school because they would otherwise be
swarming through your neighborhoods basically just queues up
an argument to try juveniles as adults. What was needed in California was a real alternative that could offer a positive vision for
a new economy, celebrate the contribution of immigrant Californians, explain why overincarceration was a threat to public safety,

and indicate how addressing environmental injustice was critical to addressing climate change.

Moving the middle in an authentic way will be a difficult balancing act at the national level. The argument that the only way to create a bigger tent is through the lowest common denominator still holds sway in some circles; consider the argument that what doomed the Democrats in 2016 was "identity politics."[37] Yet the challenging issues of race must be tackled with honesty and integrity—rather than avoided—lest politics be left open to the corrosive effects of division. At the same time, moving the middle will require an inclusive attitude toward those whose principles are not (yet!) fully formed. In discussing her own ambivalence about the January 21, 2017, Women's March on Washington, Alicia Garza, a California-born (naturally!) co-founder of Black Lives Matter, notes, "That a group of white women had drawn clear inspiration from the 1963 March on Washington for Jobs and Freedom, yet failed to acknowledge the historical precedent, rubbed me the wrong way." But she goes on: "I decided to challenge myself to be a part of something that isn't perfect, that doesn't articulate my values the way that I do and still show up, clear in my commitment, open and vulnerable to people who are new in their activism. . . . [For if] our movement is not serious about building power, then we are just engaged in a futile exercise of who can be the most radical."[38]

And this leads directly to a tenth lesson: *be clear about analyzing and building power*. The right-wing movements that derailed California were nothing if not strategic. The left that eventually responded had to learn to stop complaining about communities being left out of the decision making and instead conspire to build the strength to ensure the inclusion of those same communities. That meant utilizing a keen understanding of power to become more strategic about which targets to choose, when to choose them, and which alliances to form and why. It also meant becoming relatively unromantic about the shifting loyalties of elected "friends": politicians respond to incentives and their good intentions need to be reinforced with the organized power of social movements, a lesson surely learned from the disappointments of the Obama years.

To be sure, progressive think tanks, elected officials, and philanthropic allies all have a role to play. But to be effective, they will need to grasp that what fundamentally drives policy decisions is not the eloquence of the argument or even the accuracy of the data—something being driven home in the political cacophony and alternative facts of the Trump presidency—but the underlying distribution of power across a wide range of arenas, including the legislative, judicial, and administrative areas of contested decision making.[39] Movements matter and engaging in serious power analysis was a useful tool for California's grassroots organizers. If today's resistance is serious about changing America—and not just disrupting Trump—it will need to adapt similar strategies to local conditions, couple them with programs for leadership development, and dig in to win the local and state offices that can turn a nation.

And this is why the eleventh admonition is so important: *change the electorate.* Key to steering California away from the lure of right-wing temptation was the mobilization of a new set of voters. Some of this was helped along by demographic change, especially as young U.S.-born Latinos and Asian Americans/Pacific Islanders kept turning eighteen. But it wasn't just the inevitable grind of the aging process: efforts were made to step up naturalization, encourage registration, and attract the interests of new voters. For while demography was important, it was also not destiny. Organizers also helped put in front of the emerging electorate issues that motivated them, such as increasing taxes on the wealthy to protect education (Prop 30) or fighting oil companies to protect climate legislation (Prop 23). Integrated voter engagement,

which kept up contacts between votes rather than simply helicoptering in precinct walkers at ballot time, was another part of the
transformative recipe.

The national implications are straightforward: as Taj James,
founder and co-director of the Oakland-based Movement Strategy Center notes, "The California story is a way to understand
the national moment. For many, the issue is how to engage the
white working class—how to feel their pain and bring them back
into the fold. But we didn't get where we are now by responding
to the Prop 187 voters. Instead, we participated in engaging the
new majority who were not the folks participating actively in the
political process. . . . We moved forward by becoming more democratic and majoritarian."[40] This means tapping into the nearly
9 million lawful permanent residents who are eligible but have not
yet naturalized; combating voter restrictions every time and ev-
erywhere they crop up; and running issue-based campaigns that
can improve turnout, particularly among the young. We also cannot assume that America's politics will change in step with its hue,
particularly in light of the right's campaign to restrict new voices
through deportation, incarceration, and voting restrictions. Skin
color and ethnic background are not full stand-ins for political
preferences—ideology is forged by hard work, not implanted by
DNA. But the constituencies are there to be developed and mobilized to put victory within grasp: as much as was made about
Donald Trump's ability to tap into white non-college-educated
voters, it is also the case that a better ground game to move Black
voters in Milwaukee and Detroit and non-Cuban Latinos in Florida would have yielded a very different outcome.

The twelfth and final lesson from the California experience:
keep your eyes on the social compact. From the 1970s to the 1990s,
what unraveled in the Golden State was not just a set of investments and public policies but the very notion that society was
more than the sum of its self-interested parts. Protecting one's
tax assessment became more important than educating the next

generation; pandering to anti-immigrant sentiment to continue your reign as governor was more compelling than keeping families together; escaping to racially homogenous suburban housing sounded better than confronting racial injustice and the damage to the urban fabric that was driving crime and despair.

Stoked by fears and organized by the right, voters refuted the California ethos that had fueled the state's remarkable postwar rise. A dizzying descent ensued, with observers and residents suffering from a plunge into social conflict and political chaos. Making California great again, unlike the divisive national project of a similar name, has required restitching the state. Movement organizing, conducted on a landscape impacted by economic shifts and demographic change, has been a key element in restoring a sense of the commons. Political reforms have slowly helped to make governance more democratic and more effective. Despite imperfections and constant challenges, a bit of the luster once attached to the Golden State is gleaming again: a California that once led the way in fiscal and racial backlash is now poised to function as a state of resistance.

State of Resistance

So why do I care so much about the state, its future, and its potential impact on America? I'd love to cast it in broader and seemingly neutral academic terms, riffing on how I and others have seen the risks of racism to social cohesion, bemoaned the impacts that has on economic well-being, and realized the importance of movement building to the national future. That's all correct, but there is a simpler truth at work as well: my own story is embedded in California's broad historic arc.

I was born in New York, the son of an undocumented immigrant father from Cuba and a Tampa-born mother who grew up in Spanish Harlem. When I was six months old, my family moved west, eventually landing our own little piece of the California Dream: a modest tract home in a sprawling working-class suburb just east of East L.A., a place where the smog was abundant but the opportunities were sometimes scarce. I took to school, but college counselors—not seeing the potential in the son of a Latino janitor—skipped over me when it came time for college-going advice. Still, I got lucky: California's Master Plan for Higher Education meant that the public universities were expanding and affirmative action was there to force the system to take a chance on a kid who did not fit the typical profile. I eagerly enrolled in the university, and like many other college students, I got swept up in social justice concerns, organizing with and for the United Farm Workers. And in 1978, just after Proposition 13 had swept its way to victory, I was asked by fellow classmates to give the student address at our college graduation.

I spent my scant few minutes not honoring my parents—although in retrospect, I should have (sorry, Mom and Dad, and that's one of the reasons this book is dedicated to you). Instead, I pined at length about how I thought Prop 13 was likely to shipwreck the state. Because I realized then—as I do even more viscerally now—that what made the California Dream possible was not just the energy of those who had arrived but the infrastructure Californians had inherited. The state had taken on the big challenges of energy, water, and housing; it had focused on generating an economy that could produce both enormous wealth and a large middle class; and it had expanded education in a way that made it possible for people like me to succeed. Many of us had to fight our way in—battles around university admission, public school spending, and access to jobs and housing were part and parcel of a struggle against the racial restrictions that limited the reach of opportunity. But the state's philosophic footing—what moored the state itself—was the idea that a social compact could and should connect generations and geographies, ethnicities and economic classes, in a common destiny.

What America needs now is more of that California Dream and the compact that drove it. It embodied and supported a willingness to invest in those who were here and to welcome those who were soon to arrive—exactly the logic behind a comprehensive immigration reform aimed at legalizing the undocumented and setting up new migration flows for the future. It was reflected in a commitment to housing, education, and job growth—clearly the prerequisites for working with communities, business, and the public sector to develop an economy that can work for all. It offered a chance for people to come, remake themselves, and rebuild their lives—certainly part of what is needed to shrink our prison population and create paths to successful reentry. It embraced the beauty of the Pacific Coast and the Sierra Nevada and eventually fueled some of the strictest environmental laws in the nation—surely a centerpiece for honestly addressing the climate crisis.

To perfect this dream—and to defend its future—California has declared itself a state of resistance. Lawsuits will be filed against an overreaching and reactionary Washington, political figures will speak out for the state's progressive achievements, and movement organizers will try to hold the state's policy makers honest to their supposed social justice ambitions. The state is big and powerful: with the world's sixth-largest economy, it will have the resources and, quite frankly, the will to respond to threats and to further its own agenda. For example, in 2017, Governor Brown responded to the Trump administration's rejection of the Paris climate accords by traveling to China to meet directly with that country's president on climate policy, hardly the reaction of a timid or underpowered executive.[41]

But resistance cannot come from just one state—and it cannot be targeted at just one politician. After all, Donald Trump may represent a sort of apogee of right-wing and personal opportunism, but he is reflective of an era in which division, difference, and deception have become the calling cards of modern political discourse. That he secured the support of many—indeed, of any—is a testimony to the cleavages in the country and the craven willingness of a political party to support anyone who could win. The fight ahead is not about eliminating the influence of one leader but about ridding the nation of the toxic anxiety that once gave us Proposition 187 and has now bestowed on us a destructive presidency.

So how do we avoid a repetition of California's once fall from grace? How do we learn to turn to one another rather than away, to engage civically rather than withdraw in cynicism, to embrace what's new rather than cling to what's old? This is the challenge facing Americans—and the real measure of the state of resistance will be how we address it as a nation. Ultimately, the country's political health will not be improved by cable news spats but rather by organizing communities, lobbying policy makers, and persuading new leaders to run for public office. Achieving change will require purpose and passion but also patience. So dig in for what one hopes will be a resurgence from America's own dizzying descent—and let us work together to resist, recover, and rebuild a more prosperous, inclusive, and sustainable America.

ACKNOWLEDGMENTS

More than any book that I have written, this one is deeply personal in two ways.

The first is my own history. I was born in New York but my family moved to Southern California when I was six months old—I am a nearly native Californian. I grew up when times were good but came of age as the state decided to shortchange its future, symbolized most dramatically by Proposition 13's impact on our fiscal strength. I witnessed the state's self-defeating attacks on its own people, evidenced by propositions that threatened immigrants, stripped affirmative action, banned bilingual education, and criminalized youths. I have worked with the social movements that challenged that era of reaction, helped to usher in a new and more hopeful approach, and are now fighting back to protect what's been won; the state's arc from descent to resurgence to resistance has defined my adult life.

And that gets to the second reason that this book is personal: my kids. Both millennials and both progressive, they are angry—like so many their age—that America has bequeathed them not only an ailing economy but a failing political system as well. The Trump victory was a sort of ultimate insult to their sensibilities and their futures, and they and so many others are ready to resist but not always quite sure how. In the days after the election—after first crawling into a ball of pain—I quickly realized that California offered a playbook for change. So as important as it was to hit the streets, it made sense to hit the keyboard as well, all in the hopes of shortening the strange national trip ahead.

For educating me about California and its possibilities, I have gratitude for more thinkers and doers than I can possibly list. Among the most important have been a mix of folks from the academy, journalism, philanthropy, and community and labor organizing, including Carl Anthony, Angela Glover Blackwell, Ron Brownstein, Cathy Cha, Donald Cohen, Clare Crawford, Amy Dean, Bill Deverell, Amy Dominguez, Peter Dreier, Maria Elena Durazo, Juliet Ellis, Bill Gallegos, Marqueece Harris-Dawson, Antonia Hernandez, Madeline Janis, John Kim, Stewart Kwoh, Steve Levy, Martha Matsuoka, Joseph Tomás McKellar, Harold Meyerson, Dowell Myers, Penny Newman, Torie Osborn, john powell, Michele Prichard, Laura Pulido, Karthick Ramakrishnan, Connie Rice, Bob Ross, Angelica Salas, George Sanchez, Peter Schrag, Kevin Starr, Diane Takvorian, Anthony Thigpenn, and Kent Wong.

For their specific comments on the content of this volume—as well as for informing my ideas over the years—special thanks go to Chris Benner, Richard Healey, Mari Ryono, and Dorian Warren. And for her expert guidance on moving this from idea to proposal to pages, including a persistent focus on putting the story and not the details at the center, a very special shout-out to zakia henderson-brown of The New Press.

While the research process was steady, the book itself was written in bursts, during focused stays at Mesa Refuge in Point Reyes Station, the Center for Advanced Study in the Behavioral Sciences at Stanford, and Casa Morello (okay, it's really just the seaside home of my colleague Rachel Morello-Frosch) in Santa Cruz. At Mesa Refuge, I was able to write along with two new friends also enjoying the writers' retreat, Cameron Russell and Andrew Boyd; thanks for your support and encouragement, and hope to do a joint authors' event in the near future.

There is one name on the jacket, but there were many hands in the mix, particularly from the USC Program for Environmental and Regional Equity (PERE). Rhonda Ortiz is our managing director and she, well, managed and directed, assigning staff as needed to make this book happen. Research director Jennifer Ito boasts a history of having worked for community organizations on the front lines of California's resistance; she contributed significantly to the analysis of the 1990s and the movement building that followed. Vanessa Carter was my writing buddy, supplying raw material, snappy phrases, and a smiling insistence that we actually stick to the project timeline. Lauren Portillo employed tenacity and grace to steer away "urgent" meeting requests and protect my time to research, think, and write; she also arranged travel and reimbursements, critical for the, shall we say, barely organized professor. Senior communications specialist Gladys Malibiran worked to ensure that the language I used in the text would be accessible and consistent with getting this book and its message out of the academic ivory tower and into a world still craving hope and change.

Also from PERE, senior data analyst Madeline Wander stepped in to help meet key deadlines when Vanessa Carter had to step out for a few months. Pamela Stephens, data analyst extraordinaire, provided precision and creativity with large data sets; she was also remarkably patient as I popped my head into her office to suggest yet another interesting data point. Víctor Sánchez, who graduated from USC Price School of Public Policy in the course of writing this book, brought a passion and practicality to researching the especially bad days of California policy. Many other graduate students, including Natalie Hernandez and May Lin of USC, Melody Ng of UC Berkeley, and Carolyn Vera of UCLA, provided fastidious background research, fact-checking, and editorial assistance. And thank you to the rest of the staff and students who have contributed to the thinking and doing of this book in less direct but equally important ways.

Much as philanthropy played a role in the transformation of California, the foundation world was key to providing the resources to do this book. Special thanks to the Ford Foundation, the James Irvine Foundation, the California Wellness

Foundation, the Roy & Patricia Disney Family Foundation, and The California Endowment for supporting this research. Thanks to them also for facilitating the constellation of work in which I and USC PERE have been engaged: an effort to understand California's history, demography, and economy and to use that to support the social movements that can change the world.

Finally, the biggest thanks go to my family. To my wife, who released me for weeks at a time to do one of my favorite things: hole up and write for days on end. To my children, whose creativity inspires my own and for whom I hope to leave California better than I found it. And to my late parents, who took a risk on coming to this state in the first place.

Manuel Pastor
Los Angeles, California
October 2017

NOTES

1. America Fast-Forward

1. Tara Golshan, "Hillary Clinton's Concession Speech Full Transcript: 2016 Presidential Election," *Vox*, November 9, 2016.

2. Kevin de León and Anthony Rendon, "Joint Statement from California Legislative Leaders on Result of Presidential Election," California State Senate Majority Caucus, November 9, 2016, sd24.senate.ca.gov/news/2016-11-09-joint-statement-california-legislative-leaders-result-presidential-election.

3. Paige St. John, "Prop. 47 Puts State at Center of a National Push for Sentencing Reform," *Los Angeles Times*, November 1, 2014, sec. Local/California Politics.

4. Radley Balko, "Raid of the Day: The 39th & Dalton Edition," *Huffington Post*, February 5, 2013, sec. Politics; John L. Mitchell, "The Raid That Still Haunts L.A.," *Los Angeles Times*, March 14, 2001.

5. Ruth Wilson Gilmore, *Golden Gulag: Prisons, Surplus, Crisis, and Opposition in Globalizing California* (Berkeley: University of California Press, 2007).

6. The measure used for this ranking is the Gini coefficient, a standard indicator of income inequality.

7. Data is for 1990 to 1992 from the U.S. Bureau of Labor Statistics, Total Nonfarm Employment, 1939 to 2016, www.bls.gov/sae.

8. Data is for annual average employment in durable manufacturing, taken from the Bureau of Labor Statistics at www.bls.gov/data.

9. Daniel Martinez HoSang, *Racial Propositions: Ballot Initiatives and the Making of Postwar California* (Berkeley: University of California Press, 2010).

10. Peter Schrag, *Paradise Lost: California's Experience, America's Future* (New York: The New Press, 1998).

11. Joe Mathews and Mark Paul, *California Crackup: How Reform Broke the Golden State and How We Can Fix It* (Berkeley: University of California Press, 2010).

12. Historical data on demography are taken from the U.S. Census; for the data on the United States beyond 2010, I use the 2014 census projections available at www.census.gov/population/projections.

13. Assistant Secretary for Public Affairs, "About the Epidemic: The U.S. Opioid Epidemic," U.S. Department of Health and Human Services, December 22, 2016, www.hhs.gov/opioids/about-the-epidemic.

14. Michael Hiltzik, "If California's a 'Bad State for Business,' Why Is It Leading the Nation in Job and GDP Growth?" *Los Angeles Times*, July 22, 2016.

15. Joel Kotkin, *The New Class Conflict* (Candor, NY: Telos Press Publishing, 2014).

16. Ari Bloomekatz, "Census Analysis: Number of Nonwhite Children in L.A. Area Declines, Bucking Nationwide Trend," *Los Angeles Times*, April 7, 2011.

17. Data for the figure come from the California Department of Finance for 1970–2009; the relevant files are available at www.dof.ca.gov/Forecasting/Demographics/Estimates/Race-Ethnic/1970-89; www.dof.ca.gov/Forecasting/Demographics/Estimates/Race-Ethnic/2000-2010; and www.dof.ca.gov/Forecasting/Demographics/Estimates/Race-Ethnic/1990-99/documents/california.xls. The data from 2010 and after come from annual versions of the Public Use Microdata Sample of the American Community Survey, downloaded from Integrated Public Use Microdata Series (IPUMS). Steven J. Ruggles, Katie Genadek, Ronald Goeken, Josiah Grover, and Matthew Sobek, *Integrated Public Use Microdata Series: Version 6.0 [Machine-Readable Database]* (Minneapolis: University of Minnesota, 2015).

18. Manuel Pastor and Deborah Reed, "Understanding Equitable Infrastructure Investment for California" (Public Policy Institute of California, San Francisco, June 2005), www.ppic.org/main/publication.asp?i=613; Manuel Pastor, Justin Scoggins, and Sarah Treuhaft, "Bridging the Racial Generation Gap Is Key to America's Economic Future " (PolicyLink, Oakland, CA, 2017), nationalequityatlas.org/sites/default/files/RacialGenGap_%20final.pdf.

19. Dowell Myers, *Immigrants and Boomers: Forging a New Social Contract for the Future of America* (New York: Russell Sage Foundation, 2008).

20. Roger Kim, interview with Jennifer Ito, research director at USC PERE, April 20, 2016.

21. Chris Benner and Manuel Pastor, *Equity, Growth and Community: What the Nation Can Learn from America's Metro Areas* (Oakland: University of California Press, 2015).

22. Alex Johnson, "'California Will Launch Its Own Damn Satellites,' Governor Tells Trump," NBC News, December 16, 2016, sec. U.S. News.

23. Selena Larson, "Tech Workers Pledge to Never Help Trump Build Muslim Registry," CNNTech, December 13, 2016.

2. From Dream to Drag

1. David E. Hayes-Bautista and Gregory Rodriguez, "A Tale of Two Migrations, One White, One Brown," *Los Angeles Times*, March 17, 1996.

2. Kevin Starr, *California: A History* (New York: Random House, 2005), 237.

3. Isaac William Martin, *The Permanent Tax Revolt: How the Property Tax Transformed American Politics* (Stanford, CA: Stanford University Press, 2008).

4. Starr, *California*, 169.

5. Marc Reisner, *Cadillac Desert: The American West and Its Disappearing Water*, rev. and updated ed. (New York: Penguin Books, 1993).

6. See Starr, *California*, 182. The preference for cars led to the demise of the Los Angeles area's Red and Yellow Car rail system. Ironically, in recent years, some of the right-of-way for that earlier system has been used to build out this era's "new" transit system. See Scott Harrison, "Tracking the Slow Decline of the Pacific Electric Railway Red Cars," *Los Angeles Times*, January 2, 2016, sec. Local.

7. Francisco E. Balderrama and Raymond Rodriguez, *Decade of Betrayal: Mexican Repatriation in the 1930s* (Albuquerque: University of New Mexico Press, 2006).

8. Kathryn S. Olmsted, *Right Out of California: The 1930s and the Big Business Roots of Modern Conservatism* (New York: The New Press, 2015), 16.

9. Ibid., 17.

10. Ibid.

11. Gabriel Thompson, *America's Social Arsonist: Fred Ross and Grassroots Organizing in the Twentieth Century* (Oakland: University of California Press, 2016), 32.

12. Ruth Milkman, *L.A. Story: Immigrant Workers and the Future of the U.S. Labor Movement* (New York: Russell Sage Foundation, 2006).

13. Kevin Starr, *Embattled Dreams: California in War and Peace, 1940–1950: Americans and the California Dream* (New York: Oxford University Press, 2009).

14. Matthew H. Hersch, "Equitable Growth and Southern California's Aerospace Industry" (Washington Center for Equitable Growth, Washington,

D.C., November 2015), equitablegrowth.org/report/equitable-growth-and-south ern-californias-aerospace-industry.

15. Deborah Cohen, *Braceros: Migrant Citizens and Transnational Subjects in the Postwar United States and Mexico* (Chapel Hill: University of North Caro-lina Press, 2011).

16. Calculations are by the author utilizing data from the Bureau of Labor Statistics, www.bls.gov/data.

17. This was on top of a perhaps surprising increase during the 1930s, a period in which the Depression seemed to hit even harder elsewhere: reflecting the new Dust Bowl refugees and others, the total decadal population increase in California was larger than in any other state, and the third-largest percentage in-crease in the United States, just after Florida and New Mexico. Data on population growth by state is taken from en.wikipedia.org/wiki/List_of_U.S._states_by_his torical_population, with the original data derived from the U.S. Census Bureau. The District of Columbia actually grew faster than any state in this period, likely reflecting the growth of the New Deal bureaucracy.

18. Data from https://en.wikipedia.org/wiki/List_of_U.S._states_by_his torical_population, originally from the U.S. Census.

19. Hersch, "Equitable Growth," 17.

20. Warren was the state's attorney general, and he defeated a Democratic in-cumbent. Part of his early popularity was attributable to a reputation as a fair but tough prosecutor, unfortunately reinforced by his early embrace of the internment of California's Japanese population; see Starr, *California*, 226. Many who change the world in positive ways come replete with contradictions; the same Warren who defended internment—a policy he later regretted—would go on to lead a Supreme Court that struck down racial segregation in schools in the famous *Brown v. Board of Education* ruling in 1954.

21. He actually swept the Republican, Democratic, and Progressive primaries in his reelection campaign in 1946, in which he secured more than 90 percent of the eventual popular vote. See Starr, *Embattled Dreams*, 261; Kevin Starr, *Golden Dreams: California in an Age of Abundance, 1950–1963, Americans and the Cali-fornia Dream* (New York: Oxford University Press, 2009), 193.

22. Starr, *Golden Dreams*, 219.

23. Hersch, "Equitable Growth"; Stephanie Sabine Pincetl, *Transforming California: A Political History of Land Use and Development* (Baltimore, MD: Johns Hopkins University Press, 1999); Starr, *Golden Dreams*.

24. Becky M. Nicolaides, *My Blue Heaven: Life and Politics in the Working-Class Suburbs of Los Angeles, 1920–1965* (Chicago: University of Chicago Press, 2002); Robert O. Self, *American Babylon: Race and the Struggle for Postwar Oakland* (Princeton, NJ: Princeton University Press, 2003).

25. Nicolaides, *My Blue Heaven*.

26. Starr, *Embattled Dreams*, 242–43.

27. Ethan Rarick, *California Rising: The Life and Times of Pat Brown* (Berkeley: University of California Press, 2005), 115.

28. Ibid., 133.

29. Ibid., 153.

30. Peter Schrag, *Paradise Lost: California's Experience, America's Future*, updated with a new preface (Berkeley: University of California Press, 2004), 41.

31. The figures come from author calculations using the IPUMS online Survey Documentation and Analysis (SDA) system for the 1970 census, with the calculations constrained to adults between the ages of twenty-five and sixty-four; California is the second-highest-ranked state, but it is surpassed slightly by a non-state, the District of Columbia. Not all states' data are available, but the states whose data are not available are generally smaller and were less educated by this benchmark in 1960, a year in which data for all states were available. California also ranks fourth in terms of increase in that percentage of the working-age population between 1950 and 1970.

32. Again, this calculation is from the Bureau of Labor Statistics, www.bls .gov/data.

33. Ira Katznelson, *When Affirmative Action Was White: An Untold History of Racial Inequality in Twentieth-Century America* (New York: W.W. Norton, 2005).

34. Samuel Bowles, David M. Gordon, and Thomas E. Weisskopf, *Beyond the Wasteland: A Democratic Alternative to Economic Decline* (New York: Verso, 1984); Stephen A. Marglin and Juliet B. Schor, *The Golden Age of Capitalism: Reinterpreting the Postwar Experience* (Oxford: Clarendon Press, 1990).

35. Pincetl, *Transforming California*, 136. Another part of the exclusion was displacement: in Los Angeles, Latino families in both Bunker Hill and Chavez Ravine near downtown were removed to make room for skyscrapers and a ballpark. Meanwhile, spurred by the 1956 National Interstate and Defense Highways Act, the city's Mexican American east side was cut up by a series of freeways that made suburban commuting (the original "drive-by") easier even as it separated

long-standing neighborhoods. Decades later, this lattice of highways and the traffic they induced would stir into being environmental justice movements working to tackle the inequities of the built environment. See Eric Avila, *Popular Culture in the Age of White Flight: Fear and Fantasy in Suburban Los Angeles* (Berkeley: University of California Press, 2006).

36. Starr, *Golden Dreams*, 25.

37. Daniel Martinez HoSang, *Racial Propositions: Ballot Initiatives and the Making of Postwar California* (Berkeley: University of California Press, 2010), 56.

38. David Callahan, "How the GI Bill Left Out African Americans," *Demos*, November 11, 2013, www.demos.org/blog/11/11/13/how-gi-bill-left-out-african -americans; Josh Sides, *L.A. City Limits: African American Los Angeles from the Great Depression to the Present* (Berkeley: University of California Press, 2006), 106.

39. Sides, *L.A. City Limits*, 105.

40. HoSang, *Racial Propositions*, 56.

41. Self, *American Babylon*, 105.

42. Ibid., 111.

43. Starting in 1952, Democrats in the state sought to create a strengthened Democratic organization, forging the California Democratic Council. This built on earlier moves: in 1950, cross-filing practices were reformed so that voters could see party affiliation on both ballots and thus avoid unintentional support of candidates from other parties; see Rarick, *California Rising*, 72–73. By 1959, a closed primary was the order of the day; see Public Policy Institute of California, "Just the Facts: Primary Elections in California" (Public Policy Institute of California, San Francisco, May 2010).

44. Data for the demographic change are accessed using the IPUMS SDA system, U.S. Sample, 1850–2015; see Steven J. Ruggles, Katie Genadek, Ronald Goeken, Josiah Grover, and Matthew Sobek, *Integrated Public Use Microdata Series: Version 6.0 [Machine-Readable Database]* (Minneapolis: University of Minnesota, 2015).

45. Rarick, *California Rising*, 266–67.

46. HoSang, *Racial Propositions*, 54.

47. Kurt Schuparra, *Triumph of the Right: The Rise of the California Conservative Movement, 1945–1966*, The Right Wing in America (Armonk, NY: M.E. Sharpe, 1998), 105.

48. Rarick, *California Rising*, 356.

49. Ian Haney-López, *Dog Whistle Politics: How Coded Racial Appeals Have Reinvented Racism and Wrecked the Middle Class* (New York: Oxford University Press, 2014); Eugene Scott, "Donald Trump: I'm 'the Least Racist Person,'" CNN, September 15, 2016.

50. Robert Cohen and Reginald Zelnik, *The Free Speech Movement: Reflections on Berkeley in the 1960s* (Berkeley: University of California Press, 2002).

51. Robert M. Fogelson, "White on Black: A Critique of the McCone Commission Report on the Los Angeles Riots," *Political Science Quarterly* 82, no. 3 (September 1967): 337–38.

52. Ibid., 337.

53. Ibid.

54. This was not just occurring in the East Bay. "Many redevelopment zones selected in San Francisco were working-class areas, often home to people of color, including the old produce market near the Embarcadero (now developed as the Golden Gateway), the South of Market (which was home to working-class single room occupancy hotel [SRO] dwellers and gay leather bars), the old war housing out in Bayview-Hunter's Point, and two massive portions of the Fillmore/Western Addition, which by then was largely (but not entirely) African-American and Japanese"; quote from Rachel Brahinsky, "The Making and Unmaking of Southeast San Francisco" (PhD diss., Geography Department, Graduate Division, University of California, Berkeley, Fall 2012), 14, digitalassets.lib.berkeley.edu/etd/ucb/text/Brahinsky_berkeley_0028E_12679.pdf.

55. Self, *American Babylon*, 143–48.

56. Ibid.

57. Josh Sides, "Straight into Compton: American Dreams, Urban Nightmares, and the Metamorphosis of a Black Suburb," *American Quarterly* 56, no. 3 (2004): 125.

58. William Fulton, *The Reluctant Metropolis: The Politics of Urban Growth in Los Angeles* (Baltimore, MD: Johns Hopkins University Press, 1997).

59. Lisa McGirr, *Suburban Warriors: The Origins of the New American Right*, 2nd ed., Politics and Society in Twentieth-Century America (Princeton, NJ: Princeton University Press, 2015), 78.

60. Schuparra, *Triumph of the Right*, 45.

61. Donna Jean Murch, *Living for the City: Migration, Education, and the Rise of the Black Panther Party in Oakland, California* (Chapel Hill: University of North Carolina Press, 2010), 147.

62. Adam Winkler, "The Secret History of Guns," *The Atlantic*, September 2011.

63. "So Much News, So Little Time—NRA Silence on Philando Castile & Canceling Cuba," *The Daily Show with Trevor Noah*, aired June 19, 2017, on Comedy Central, www.cc.com/video-clips/iqhbhi/the-daily-show-with-trevor-noah-so-much-news—so-little-time—canceling-cuba—a-possible-trump-investigation—nra-silence.

64. Murch, *Living for the City*, 128–29.

65. Winkler, "The Secret History of Guns."

66. Thompson, *America's Social Arsonist*.

67. Juan Gómez-Quiñones, *Chicano Politics: Reality and Promise, 1940–1990* (Albuquerque: University of New Mexico Press, 1990), 53.

68. Mark M. Dodge and Martin Schiesl, *City of Promise: Race & Historical Change in Los Angeles* (Claremont, CA: Regina Books, 2006).

69. Gómez-Quiñones, *Chicano Politics*, 56.

70. Walter Nicholls, *The DREAMers: How the Undocumented Youth Movement Transformed the Immigrant Rights Debate* (Palo Alto, CA: Stanford University Press, 2013).

71. Ian Haney-López, *Racism on Trial: The Chicano Fight for Justice* (Cambridge, MA: Belknap Press, 2004), 20–27.

72. Gómez-Quiñones, *Chicano Politics*, 126.

73. Ibid., 128.

74. The share of Mexican-origin individuals in Los Angeles County as a share of all Mexican-origin individuals in the United States is now down to about 10 percent. Data for figures accessed using the SDA system, utilizing the 1970s census and the 2014 American Community Survey; see Ruggles et al., *Integrated Public Use Microdata Series*.

75. Laura Pulido, *Black, Brown, Yellow, and Left: Radical Activism in Los Angeles* (Berkeley: University of California Press, 2006), 112, 133–40.

76. Schuparra, *Triumph of the Right*, 146; Pulido, *Black, Brown, Yellow, and Left*, 112, 133–40.

77. See Schrag, *Paradise Lost*, 49. The initial proposal also included a measure to eliminate 3,700 jobs in the Department of Mental Hygiene, a number that was eventually reduced to 2,600 by the legislature, but the decision likely factored into the subsequent increase in the homeless mentally ill in the state. See Lou Cannon, *Governor Reagan: His Rise to Power* (New York: PublicAffairs, 2009), 189–93.

78. Cannon, *Governor Reagan*, 296.

79. Aaron Bady and Mike Konczal, "From Master Plan to No Plan: The Slow Death of Public Higher Education," *Dissent*, Fall 2012, www.dissentmaga zine.org/article/from-master-plan-to-no-plan-the-slow-death-of-public-higher-edu cation.

80. Rebecca J. Rosen, "Video: Ronald Reagan's Press Conference After 'Bloody Thursday,'" *The Atlantic*, February 24, 2014.

81. Cannon, *Governor Reagan*, 204–5.

82. Schrag, *Paradise Lost*, 137.

83. HoSang, *Racial Propositions*, 107.

84. Nineteen sixty-two is the first year for which we have California data available from the March Supplement of the Current Population Survey. Because these data are taken from the March Supplement, the figures may not square perfectly with the national annual BLS statistics for those years, but the patterns are similar and using the March Supplement allows us to do the comparison of state and nation.

85. Paul Webb Rhode, *The Evolution of California Manufacturing* (San Francisco: Public Policy Institute of California, 2001), www.ppic.org/content/pubs/re port/R_1001PRR.pdf.

86. Data on inflation are from the *Economic Report of the President, 2016*, Table B-10, www.gpo.gov/fdsys/pkg/ERP-2016/pdf/ERP-2016.pdf.

87. Steve Swatt with Susie Swatt, Jeff Raimundo, and Rebecca LaVally, *Game Changers: Twelve Elections That Transformed California* (Berkeley: Heyday and the California Historical Society, 2015), 196.

88. Data calculations by authors using historical data from the U.S. Census, www.census.gov/hhes/www/housing/census/histcensushsg.html.

89. Schrag, *Paradise Lost*, 136.

90. Cannon, *Governor Reagan*, 141.

91. Ibid., 366.

92. Narda Zacchino, *California Comeback: How a "Failed State" Became a Model for the Nation* (New York: Thomas Dunne Books, 2016), 43.

93. Ibid., 73.

94. Schrag, *Paradise Lost*, 143.

95. See State of California, Department of Finance, "Summary Schedules and Historical Charts," Chart A: Historical Data, General Fund Budget Summary, www.dof.ca.gov/budget/summary_schedules_charts/index.html.

96. Schrag, *Paradise Lost*; Swatt et al., *Game Changers*.

97. Another factor some say prompted Proposition 13 was sticker shock when properties began to be properly assessed. In the 1960s, San Francisco had a county assessor scandal wherein widespread corruption was found in how both business and residential property values were being assessed, with the former done directly for bribes and the latter likely as favors for voters. This was resolved by professionalizing and standardizing operations—which effectively raised property taxes for homeowners and produced the sticker shock that triggered voters into the tax revolt. See Swatt et al., *Game Changers*, 195.

98. Schrag, *Paradise Lost*, 149.

99. Ange-Marie Hancock, *Solidarity Politics for Millennials: A Guide to Ending the Oppression Olympics* (New York: Palgrave Macmillan, 2011); Paul Taylor and Pew Research Center, *The Next America: Boomers, Millennials, and the Looming Generational Showdown* (New York: PublicAffairs, 2014).

100. For this long-term historical series, I draw on data accessed with the IPUMS SDA system, U.S. Sample, 1850–2015; see Ruggles et al., *Integrated Public Use Microdata Series*.

101. Schrag, *Paradise Lost*, 139.

102. John Mollenkopf and Manuel Pastor, eds., *Unsettled Americans: Metropolitan Context and Civic Leadership for Immigrant Integration* (Ithaca, NY: Cornell University Press, 2016).

103. Calculated from census data accessed with the IPUMS SDA system, U.S. Sample, 1850–2015; see Ruggles et al., *Integrated Public Use Microdata Series*. The 1960 figure comes from the nativity series, whereas the 1980 and 1990 figures are from the citizen series (which was unavailable in 1960); since I am calculating as a share of U.S. residents of the foreign-born category, this reduces any issues that might be introduced by splicing the series.

104. Data from the U.S. Census as reported at www.census.gov/population /www/documentation/twps0029/tab13.html.

105. Swatt et al., *Game Changers*, 204.

106. Michael Stewart Foley, *Front Porch Politics: The Forgotten Heyday of American Activism in the 1970s and 1980s*, reprint ed. (New York: Hill and Wang, 2014), 238.

107. Frank Levy, "On Understanding Proposition 13," *Public Interest*, no. 56 (Summer 1979): 67.

108. Joe Mathews and Mark Paul, *California Crackup: How Reform Broke the Golden State and How We Can Fix It* (Berkeley: University of California Press, 2010), 47.

109. Schrag, *Paradise Lost*, 145.

110. Mathews and Paul, *California Crackup*, 39.

111. Pincetl, *Transforming California*, 227; Schrag, *Paradise Lost*, 151–52.

112. Mac Taylor, "Common Claims about Proposition 13" (Legislative Analyst's Office, Sacramento, CA, September 2016), lao.ca.gov/Publications/Report /3497.

113. Levy, "On Understanding Proposition 13," 87.

114. Mathews and Paul, *California Crackup*, 44–45.

115. Self, *American Babylon*, 326.

116. Mathews and Paul, *California Crackup*, 47.

117. Martin, *Permanent Tax Revolt*, 2.

118. Thomas Frank, *What's the Matter with Kansas? How Conservatives Won the Heart of America*, reprint ed. (New York: Holt Paperbacks, 2005); Vanessa Williamson, Theda Skocpol, and John Coggin, "The Tea Party and the Remaking of Republican Conservatism," *Perspectives on Politics* 9, no. 1 (March 2011): 25–43.

119. Martin notes that part of the revolt was spurred by professionalization of the tax system, including automatic updating of property values by neutral assessors; see Martin, *Permanent Tax Revolt*. So, in this sense, the rebellion was not against government in general, but rather, against well-functioning government that was not meeting the interests of particular groups.

120. Melissa J. Morrow, "Twenty-Five Years of Debate: Is Acquisition-Value Property Taxation Constitutional? Is It Fair? Is It Good Policy?" *Emory Law Journal* 53 (2004): 587–626.

121. Scott Wong, "Trump Medicare Promise Causes Heartburn for GOP," *The Hill*, January 11, 2017, sec. Policy, thehill.com/policy/healthcare/313677 -trump-medicare-promise-causes-heartburn-for-gop.

122. Self, *American Babylon*, 325.

123. As Self notes, this led Clayborne Carson, a then assistant professor of history at Stanford University with a history of activism in the Civil Rights Movement, to argue that suburban supporters of Prop 13 were "less interested in tax and government reform than in declaring their unwillingness to pay for public facilities and services that are needed for central cities." Ibid., 316–17.

124. Nico Calavita and Kenneth Grimes, "Inclusionary Housing in California: The Experience of Two Decades," *Journal of the American Planning Association* 64, no. 2 (1998): 39–40.

125. Jason Felch and Jack Dolan, "Corporations Get Big Edge in Prop. 13 Quirk," *Los Angeles Times*, May 5, 2013; Lenny Goldberg and David Kersten, "System Failure: California's Loophole-Ridden Commercial Property Tax" (California Tax Reform Association, Sacramento, May 2010); Mark Haveman and Terri Sexton, "Property Tax Assessment Limits: Lessons from Thirty Years of Experience" (Lincoln Institute of Land Policy, Cambridge, MA, 2008).

126. John Logan Palmer and Isabel Sawhill, *The Reagan Experiment: An Examination of Economic and Social Policies under the Reagan Administration* (Washington, D.C.: Urban Institute Press, 1982), 118.

127. One governor, Frank Merriam, lasted a bit over one term, but only because he was lieutenant governor and inherited the governorship when his predecessor passed away. Just a few months later, Merriam had the good fortune to run against Upton Sinclair, a declared socialist whose politics scared virtually every traditional business leader into supporting Merriam—who still managed to only barely win, with a plurality but not a majority.

128. Chip Jacobs and William J Kelly, *Smogtown: The Lung-Burning History of Pollution in Los Angeles* (Woodstock, NY: Overlook Press, 2008).

129. McGirr, *Suburban Warriors*; Schuparra, *Triumph of the Right*.

3. Things Fall Apart

1. This was more than twice the growth rate for the state prison population in the rest of the country. Trends calculated from data available from the Corrections Statistical Analysis Tool, from the Bureau of Justice Statistics, www.bjs.gov. Following the convention of the Prison Policy Initiative (www.prisonpolicy.org), the data are for state prisons and for individuals with a sentence of one year or more.

2. Data calculations by the author using data from the Bureau of Labor Statistics at www.bls.gov/data.

3. Joe Mathews and Mark Paul, *California Crackup: How Reform Broke the Golden State and How We Can Fix It* (Berkeley: University of California Press, 2010).

4. Anthony Thigpenn, interview with Michele Prichard of Liberty Hill Foundation, July 13, 2011.

5. Of note, California has a long history of immigrants that has included, among others, dependence on Mexican braceros to support the agricultural industry despite the lack of reciprocity with regard to their own economic security. Similarly, immigrants from Asia played an important role in the early development of the state's infrastructure in the form of railroads. The wave of immigrants in the 1990s was new for many residents but routine for the state.

6. J.I. Chapman, "The Fiscalization of Land Use," *Public Works Management and Policy* 12, no. 4 (2008): 55; Jonathan Schwartz, "Prisoners of Proposition 13: Sales Taxes, Property Taxes, and the Fiscalization of Municipal Land Use Decisions," *Southern California Law Review* 71 (1997): 183–218.

7. One fascinating symbol of this "fiscalization of land use" is the Uniroyal Tire factory in the city of Commerce, a plant that lay right along the major highway connecting Los Angeles with Orange County. Abandoned in 1978, it stood empty for a decade before developers came in, saved the "Assyrian Palace" frontage that looked borrowed from a bad Hollywood movie, and created a mall with a small hotel and a wide range of factory-to-retail outlets. Leon Whiteson, "An Assyrian Palace Is Reborn as a Discount Outlet in a Fusion of Style and Savvy," *Los Angeles Times*, February 3, 1991. The job levels likely exceeded the former factory employment—but low wages, limited benefits, and a healthy dose of part-time employment made jobs in the very same location less suited to maintaining families.

8. Barry Bluestone and Bennett Harrison, *The Deindustrialization of America: Plant Closings, Community Abandonment, and the Dismantling of Basic Industry* (New York: Basic Books, 1982).

9. That GM plant soon became a symbol of the fight to preserve decent employment, with fierce battles erupting between the company and labor and its community allies over whether it would be shuttered—which it eventually was, in 1992. Fred Glass, *From Mission to Microchip: A History of the California Labor Movement* (Oakland: University of California Press, 2016), 391.

10. According to Josh Sides, for example, "the proportion of the Black male workforce employed as operatives in manufacturing firms began to fall in the 1960s, and the absolute employment of Black men in manufacturing dropped in the early 1970s." Josh Sides, *L.A. City Limits: African American Los Angeles from the Great Depression to the Present* (Berkeley: University of California Press, 2006), 180.

11. According to an exhaustive study by the Public Policy Institute of California (PPIC), the state's employment of production workers actually increased

by nearly 6 percent between 1977 and 1982, even as national employment of such workers fell by nearly 10 percent. Over the longer 1972 to 1987 period, "the number of manufacturing establishments in the state increased about 42 percent compared to 12 percent nationally." Paul Webb Rhode, *The Evolution of California Manufacturing* (San Francisco: Public Policy Institute of California, 2001), 14, www.ppic.org/content/pubs/report/R_1001PRR.pdf.

12. Ibid., 23.

13. According to a report by the Economic Roundtable, between 1987 and 1990, defense funds flowing into Los Angeles County declined by about 20 percent and the number of contracts declined by 22 percent. Economic Roundtable, "Los Angeles County Economic Adjustment Strategy for Defense Reductions," March 17, 1992, economicrt.org/publication/los-angeles-county-economic-adjustment-stategy-for-defense-reductions.

14. This is calculated using data from the March Current Population Survey for that year; while it may not square perfectly with series from the Bureau of Labor Statistics, it allows us to essentially drop California from the national series and compare it to the rest of the country.

15. Latinos actually suffered a much smaller 6 percent decline in manufacturing, partly due to the general increase in Latinos in the California labor force and also because of relative stability in lower-paid nondurables, in which Latinos experienced a decline of less than 3 percent. Data on the shifts in employment were calculated using the IPUMS SDA system on the U.S. Sample, 1850–2015; see Steven J. Ruggles, Katie Genadek, Ronald Goeken, Josiah Grover, and Matthew Sobek, *Integrated Public Use Microdata Series: Version 6.0 [Machine-Readable Database]* (Minneapolis: University of Minnesota, 2015).

16. Data on California are taken from Union Membership and Coverage Database, www.unionstats.com. See also Megan Dunn and James Walker, "Union Membership in the United States," Spotlight on Statistics, U.S. Bureau of Labor Statistics, September 2016, www.bls.gov/spotlight/2016/union-membership-in-the-united-states/pdf/union-membership-in-the-united-states.pdf.

17. Mathews and Paul, *California Crackup*.

18. Brian C. Anderson, *The Beholden State: California's Lost Promise and How to Recapture It* (Lanham, MD: Rowman & Littlefield, 2013), 21–29.

19. Mark Baldassare, *When Government Fails: The Orange County Bankruptcy* (San Francisco: Public Policy Institute of California, 1998).

20. Floyd Norris, "Orange County's Bankruptcy: The Overview; Orange County Crisis Jolts Bond Market," *New York Times*, December 8, 1994, sec. Business.

21. Joint Venture Silicon Valley, "An Economy at Risk," Joint Venture Silicon Valley, June 1992, 26, www.jointventure.org/publications/institute-publications /286-an-economy-at-risk.

22. The rankings are done by the Gini coefficient, a standard measure of income inequality available from the U.S. Census, with data for this particular comparison taken from https://www.census.gov/data/tables/time-series/dec/his torical-income-states.html. For 1969, the Gini data are reported only for family income; I convert to a household-income-based Gini using the ratio of the 1979 household Gini to the 1979 family Gini because the contemporary Gini data are given only for households and this conversion affords for better comparison with the data in the post-2005 American Community Survey. If I were to report the ranks for this earlier period using just the family-income-based Gini coefficients, the shift is even more dramatic: California was the twenty-third-most unequal state in the nation in 1969 and the second-most unequal in the nation in 1999. In all state rankings, I exclude the District of Columbia, as it is not a state.

23. Daniel Martinez HoSang, *Racial Propositions: Ballot Initiatives and the Making of Postwar California* (Berkeley: University of California Press, 2010), 165.

24. Calculations from the U.S. Census historical data on the foreign born (see www.census.gov/population/www/documentation/twps0029/twps0029.html) and author calculations utilizing the IPUMS SDA system for the U.S. Sample, 1850–2015; see Ruggles et al., *Integrated Public Use Microdata Series*.

25. Calculations from the U.S. Census historical data on the foreign born (see www.census.gov/population/www/documentation/twps0029/twps0029.html) and author calculations utilizing the IPUMS SDA system of the U.S. Sample, 1850–2015; see Ruggles et al., *Integrated Public Use Microdata Series*. The 1990s gains are calculated by comparing those historical figures to the 2000 census figures taken from Table P021 of Summary File 3, accessed through American Fact-Finder, factfinder.census.gov/faces/nav/jsf/pages/index.xhtml.

26. Wallace Turner, "Man in the News; A New Chief in California: George Deukmejian Jr.," *New York Times*, January 5, 1983, sec. U.S.

27. Robert Lindsey, "Bradley Loses Close Contest on Coast," *New York Times*, November 4, 1982, sec. U.S.

28. Patt Morrison, "The 'Bradley Effect' in 2008," *Los Angeles Times*, October 2, 2008; J.G. Payne, "The Bradley Effect: Mediated Reality of Race and Politics in the 2008 U.S. Presidential Election," *American Behavioral Scientist* 54, no. 4 (2010): 417–35.

29. In the 1980s, the New Majority Task Force formed in Los Angeles, headed by now Los Angeles County supervisor Mark Ridley-Thomas, founding president and executive director of Asian Americans Advancing Justice Stewart Kwoh, and myself. The name reflected our reality: the city of Los Angeles was majority minority, before the state as a whole. While the task force came to a close, the concept of "new majority" has long outlasted it.

30. Peter Schrag, *Paradise Lost: California's Experience, America's Future*, updated with a new preface (Berkeley: University of California Press, 2004), 188.

31. Ibid., 194.

32. Ian Haney-López, *Dog Whistle Politics: How Coded Racial Appeals Have Reinvented Racism and Wrecked the Middle Class* (New York: Oxford University Press, 2014).

33. Steve Swatt with Susie Swatt, Jeff Raimundo, and Rebecca LaVally, *Game Changers: Twelve Elections That Transformed California* (Berkeley: Heyday and the California Historical Society, 2015), 255–56.

34. HoSang, *Racial Propositions*, 172.

35. Schrag, *Paradise Lost*, 231.

36. HoSang, *Racial Propositions*, 170–71.

37. See the discussion in Virginia Ellis and Paul Jacobs, "California Elections: 'Tax-the-Rich' Plan Put Hex on Welfare Cutbacks: Initiatives: Both Measures Failed, but Millions of Dollars Were Diverted from Backing Wilson's Proposed Benefits Overhaul," *Los Angeles Times*, November 5, 1992.

38. Schrag, *Paradise Lost*, 234; Swatt et al., *Game Changers*, 257.

39. "Pete Wilson 1994 campaign ad on illegal immigration," YouTube video, posted by "PeteWilsonCA," February 15, 2010, www.youtube.com/watch?v=lLIzzs2HHgY.

40. "Initiatives Voted into Law," California Secretary of State, www.sos.ca.gov/elections/ballot-measures/resources-and-historical-information/history-california-initiatives. See also Kevin Starr, *Coast of Dreams: California on the Edge, 1990–2003* (New York: Alfred A. Knopf, 2004), 198, 202.

41. Swatt et al., *Game Changers*, 258; Starr, *Coast of Dreams*, 202.

42. The demographic breakdown for the population in 1994 is derived from author calculations of data from the California Department of Finance, http://www.dof.ca.gov/Forecasting/Demographics. On the composition of the electorate, see Swatt et al., *Game Changers*, 258.

43. For example, in 1982, the U.S. Supreme Court in *Plyler v. Doe* in a 5–4 decision had established that by the Equal Protection Clause of the Fourteenth Amendment, all K–12 children, no matter their immigration status, should have access to the same state-funded education. For more on the problems with implementation, see Starr, *Coast of Dreams*, 202.

44. Maria Elena Durazo, interview with Michele Prichard from Liberty Hill Foundation, July 15, 2011. An interesting indicator of the new mobilization: between 1990 and 2010, there were an estimated eleven immigrant-rights-related protests per year—with notable spikes in 1994 and 2006. See Marcel Paret and Guadalupe Aguilera, "Golden State Uprising: Migrant Protest in California, 1990–2010," *Citizenship Studies* 20, nos. 3–4 (2016): 359–78.

45. HoSang, *Racial Propositions*, 180–81.

46. Ibid., 180.

47. In this case, "recently arrived" refers to immigrants who had entered the United States in 1970 or after, with all data from the 5 percent sample from the 1990 census; see Ruggles et al., *Integrated Public Use Microdata Series*. The geographic distribution is nearly identical if the cutoff is drawn at 1975 or 1990.

48. HoSang, *Racial Propositions*, 185–86.

49. I recall the divide vividly: I was in a room where a major Mexican American political figure was denouncing the display of Mexican flags while younger activists tried to make their case about the long haul. I was in the middle in terms of generation but not in terms of the debate at hand; I had participated in the march on city hall, something I sheepishly kept quiet about as I sought to reinforce the argument of the young organizers. For an argument that the demonstration probably did alienate undecided voters, see Jewelle Taylor Gibbs and Teiahsha Bankhead, *Preserving Privilege: California Politics, Propositions, and People of Color* (Westport, CT: Greenwood, 2001), 86.

50. Kevin de León and Anthony Rendon, "Joint Statement from California Legislative Leaders on Result of Presidential Election," California State Senate Majority Caucus, November 9, 2016, sd24.senate.ca.gov/news/2016-11-09-joint-statement-california-legislative-leaders-result-presidential-election; John Myers,

"California's Legislative Leaders on Trump's Win: 'We Woke Up Feeling Like Strangers in a Foreign Land,'" *Los Angeles Times*, November 9, 2016.

51. HoSang, *Racial Propositions*, 200.

52. Activists noted that while the general liberal leanings of San Francisco may have played a role, the voters were not as opposed to the three-strikes initiative put on the ballot the same year; see ibid. Hence the interest in the more grassroots organizing that had taken place in the San Francisco context.

53. HoSang, *Racial Propositions*.

54. Ruth Wilson Gilmore, *Golden Gulag: Prisons, Surplus, Crisis, and Opposition in Globalizing California* (Berkeley: University of California Press, 2007), 95–96; Schrag, *Paradise Lost*, 227.

55. Franklin E. Zimring, Gordon Hawkins, and Sam Kamin, *Punishment and Democracy: Three Strikes and You're Out in California* (New York: Oxford University Press, 2001), 4.

56. The quote is from Gibbs and Bankhead, *Preserving Privilege*, 56. The information on Democratic political figures also draws from Elihu Rosenblatt, *Criminal Injustice: Confronting the Prison Crisis* (Boston: South End Press, 1996), 75.

57. On the crime trends, see Magnus Lofstrom and Brandon Martin, "Crime Trends in California," Just the Facts (Public Policy Institute of California, San Francisco, August 2016), www.ppic.org/publication/crime-trends-in-california.

58. Data are from the Bureau of Justice Statistics, Corrections Statistical Analysis Tool for state-held prisoners with sentences of over one year, available at: www.bjs.gov.

59. On the infamous case of the "pizza thief," see Jack Leonard, "'Pizza Thief' Walks the Line," *Los Angeles Times*, February 10, 2010.

60. Calculated by the author using data available from the state's Department of Finance (Chart C), www.dof.ca.gov/budget/summary_schedules_charts/index .html.

61. Robin Respaut, "California Prison Reforms Have Reduced Inmate Numbers, Not Costs," Reuters, January 6, 2016. On the long set of legal struggles that finally forced California to address the prison overcrowding that was threatening the mental and physical health of inmates, see Amanda Lopez, "Coleman/Plata: Highlighting the Need to Establish an Independent Corrections Commission in California," *Berkeley Journal of Criminal Law* 15, no. 1 (2010): 97–126; Alicia Bower, "Unconstitutionally Crowded: *Brown v. Plata* and How the Supreme Court Pushed Back to Keep Prison Reform Litigation Alive," *Loyola of Los Angeles*

Law Review 45, no. 555 (2012): 555–68; Morgan MacDonald, "Reducing California's Overcrowded Prison Population," *Themis: Research Journal of Justice Studies and Forensic Science* 1, no. 1 (2013).

62. The prison demographics are from Gilmore, *Golden Gulag*, 111. Demographic data for the state calculated by the author using information from the California Department of Finance at www.dof.ca.gov.

63. Evelyn Nieves, "The 2000 Campaign: The Initiative; California Proposal Toughens Penalties for Young Criminals," *New York Times*, March 6, 2000, sec. U.S.

64. Kelly M. Angell, "The Regressive Movement: When Juvenile Offenders Are Treated as Adults, Nobody Wins," *Southern California Interdisciplinary Law Journal* 14, no. 1 (2004): 135–36; Nicholas Espiritu, "(E)Racing Youth: The Racialized Construction of California's Proposition 21 and the Development of Alternate Contestations," *Cleveland State Law Review* 52, nos. 1–2 (2005): 199; Jennifer Taylor, "California's Proposition 21: A Case of Juvenile Injustice," *Southern California Law Review* 74, no. 4 (2002): 983–84.

65. The first tried as adults under Prop 21 were eight suburban teens accused of racially motivated attacks on an elderly Mexican nursery worker in the northern part of San Diego; clearly, this was not who was intended, and their lawyers, with full parental support, launched a vigorous if unsuccessful attack on Prop 21. See Thomas Larson, "The Adult Boys of Rancho Penasquitos," *San Diego Reader*, December 7, 2000, www.thomaslarson.com/publications/san-diego-reader/129 -adult-boys.html.

66. Yuki Kidokoro, focus group interview with the author and Jennifer Ito from USC PERE, October 14, 2010.

67. Gibbs and Bankhead, *Preserving Privilege*, 95–119.

68. On the Democratic Leadership Conference, see HoSang, *Racial Propositions*, 205. On Wilson's gambit to secure conservative support, see B. Drummond Ayres Jr., "On Affirmative Action, Wilson's Moderate Path Veered Quickly to Right," *New York Times*, August 8, 1995, sec. U.S.

69. Schrag, *Paradise Lost*, 235.

70. HoSang, *Racial Propositions*, 211; Schrag, *Paradise Lost*, 235–36.

71. HoSang, *Racial Propositions*, 211–13.

72. The quote and the information on the implications for school desegregation programs comes from ibid., 207.

73. Ibid., 208–9.

74. Ibid., 218.

75. Thigpenn, interview.

76. "Initiatives Voted into Law," California Secretary of State, www.sos .ca.gov/elections/ballot-measures/resources-and-historical-information/history -california-initiatives.

77. Gibbs and Bankhead, *Preserving Privilege*, 104.

78. Karthick Ramakrishnan, "How Asian Americans Became Democrats," *The American Prospect*, Summer 2016, prospect.org/article/how-asian-americans -became-democrats-0.

79. Starr, *Coast of Dreams*, 217.

80. It was a frustrating time to argue in favor of bilingual education. My wife was a bilingual educator at the time who acknowledged that the evidence was incredibly nuanced about when it worked and under what circumstances. That did not stop new acquaintances with no knowledge of the issues pronouncing to me after I noted that my wife was such an educator that such education did not work.

81. Ken Grossinger, "How Labor Defeated California's Proposition 226," *WorkingUSA* 2, no. 3 (1998): 84–90.

82. HoSang, *Racial Propositions*, 239; Starr, *Coast of Dreams*, 220.

83. "1998 Election Los Angeles Exit Poll," *Los Angeles Times*, 1998, www.az bilingualed.org/AZ%20Hist-ALEC/exit_poll__los_angeles_times.htm.

84. Indeed, according to RAND Corporation researchers, "Part of the mo- tivation for federal welfare reform was the rapid increase in the welfare caseload in the late 1980s and early 1990s. That increase was especially large in California, which experienced a deep recession"; see Jacob Alex Klerman, V. Joseph Hotz, Elaine Reardon, Amy G. Cox, Donna O. Farley, Steven J. Haider, Guido Imbens, and Robert Schoeni, *Welfare Reform in California: Early Results from the Impact Analysis*, RAND Statewide CalWORKs Evaluation (Santa Monica, CA: RAND Corporation, 2002), xiii, www.rand.org/content/dam/rand/pubs/monograph _reports/MR1358/MR1358.pref.pdf. Other researchers found that between 1993 and 1994, nearly one in four California families participated in Aid to Fami- lies with Dependent Children, Supplemental Security Income, food stamps, or Medi-Cal—or a combination of those major welfare programs; see Thomas Mc- Curdy and Margaret O'Brien-Strain, *Who Will Be Affected by Welfare Reform in California?* (San Francisco: Public Policy Institute of California, 1997), www.ppic

.org/content/pubs/report/R_297TMR.pdf. On the cuts to legal immigrants, see Michael Fix, ed., *Immigrants and Welfare: The Impact of Welfare Reform on America's Newcomers* (New York: Russell Sage Foundation, 2009).

85. Terry Schwadron and Paul R. Richter, *California and the American Tax Revolt: Proposition 13 Five Years Later* (Berkeley: University of California Press, 1984), 180.

86. Isaac William Martin, *The Permanent Tax Revolt: How the Property Tax Transformed American Politics* (Stanford, CA: Stanford University Press, 2008).

87. Schwadron and Richter, *California and the American Tax Revolt*, 183–85.

88. Martin, *The Permanent Tax Revolt*, 126.

89. Bruce Bartlett, "Reagan's Forgotten Tax Record," *Stan Collender's Capital Gains and Games*, February 22, 2011, capitalgainsandgames.com/blog/bruce -bartlett/2154/reagans-forgotten-tax-record.

90. Martin, *The Permanent Tax Revolt*, 131.

91. Data on the fiscal balance and subsequently on the national debt is from the *Economic Report of the President* (Washington, D.C.: U.S. GPO, 2017), Table 18, www.gpo.gov/fdsys/pkg/ERP-2017. The fiscal balance is for the "on-budget" side and does not include, for example, the Social Security Trust Fund. In considering each president's fiscal history, I start from the first full year in office and continue one year past the term, since they essentially hand off a budget to the incoming presidents; hence, for Reagan, it's fiscal year 1981 to fiscal year 1989, and for George W. Bush, it's 2001 to 2009.

92. Naomi Jagoda, "Trump's Tax Outline Would Cost Trillions, Benefit Wealthy: Analysis," *The Hill*, July 12, 2017.

93. The latest attempt to try tax cutting as an economic growth strategy for a state was by Republican governor Sam Brownback in Kansas in 2012; it, too, ended with slow growth, fiscal imbalance, and eventually a bipartisan consensus to raise taxes and end the economic misery. See Justin Miller, "Kansas, Sam Brownback, and the Trickle-Down Implosion," *The American Prospect*, June 28, 2017, prospect .org/article/kansas-sam-brownback-and-trickle-down-implosion-0.

94. Rebecca Trounson and Stuart Silverstein, "Bid to Export Prop. 209," *Los Angeles Times*, July 8, 2003.

95. Lee Cokorinos, *The Assault on Diversity: An Organized Challenge to Racial and Gender Justice* (Lanham, MD: Rowman & Littlefield, 2003), 33–35;

Bradley Jones and Roopali Mukherjee, "From California to Michigan: Race, Rationality, and Neoliberal Governmentality," *Communication and Critical/Cultural Studies* 7, no. 4 (December 2010): 417.

96. Jones and Mukherjee, "From California to Michigan," 404.

97. Kathy Escamilla, S. Shannon, S. Carlos, and J. García, "Breaking the Code: Colorado's Defeat of the Anti-Bilingual Education Initiative (Amendment 31)," *Bilingual Research Journal* 27, no. 3 (2003): 357–82; William Ryan, "The Unz Initiatives and the Abolition of Bilingual Education," *Boston College Law Review* 43, no. 2 (2002): 34.

98. Walter J. Dickey and Pam Hollenhorst, "Three-Strikes Laws: Five Years Later," *Corrections Management Quarterly* 3, no. 3 (Summer 1999): 1.

99. Daniel C. Vock, "With Feds Stuck, States Take on Immigration," December 13, 2007, www.pewtrusts.org/en/research-and-analysis/blogs/stateline/2007 /12/13/with-feds-stuck-states-take-on-immigration; Alfonso Serrano, "Why Undocumented Workers Are Good for the Economy," *Time*, 2012.

100. For example, in 2012, the Georgia Agribusiness Council estimated that with stringent immigration enforcement laws and without adequate paths to citizenship, migrant labor shortages could cost state farmers between $300 million and $1 billion. See Serrano, "Why Undocumented Workers."

101. Lydia Seabol Avant, "Elois Zeanah, Active in Tuscaloosa County and Alabama GOP Politics, Dies at 73," *Tuscaloosa News*, January 26, 2015, www.tusca loosanews.com/article/20150126/News/605147099; Julie M. Weise, "Trump's Anti-Immigration Policy Rooted in '90s California," *San Francisco Chronicle*, May 12, 2016.

102. Weise, "Trump's Anti-Immigration."

103. The "ideological soul mate" comment comes from Dan Balz, "Calif. Gov.'s Race Heads into Great Divide," *Washington Post*, July 7, 1998. On the proposals to try teens as adults, see Virginia Ellis, "Lungren to Seek Lower Age for Trial as Adult: Law: Attorney General Will Propose Legislation Giving Judges Discretion in Cases of 14- and 15-Year-Olds Accused of Murder," *Los Angeles Times*, January 15, 1993; Dave Lesher, "Davis, Lungren Bicker Over 3-Strikes Law," *Los Angeles Times*, October 1, 1998.

104. Vincent J. Schodolski, "California Democrat Throws Wide Net to Snag Governor's Office," *Chicago Tribune*, November 5, 1998.

105. Narda Zacchino, *California Comeback: How a "Failed State" Became a Model for the Nation* (New York: Thomas Dunne Books, 2016), 87.

106. Paul L. Joskow and Edward Kahn, "A Quantitative Analysis of Pricing Behavior in California's Wholesale Electricity Market during Summer 2000," *Energy Journal* 23, no. 4 (2002): 1.

107. Christopher Weare, *The California Electricity Crisis: Causes and Policy Options* (San Francisco: Public Policy Institute of California, 2003).

108. One favorite trick was selling other states their own electricity rather than moving it to California and then claiming congestion relief in California for having not used that electricity; see ibid., 48. See also Starr, *Coast of Dreams*, 594–95; Zacchino, *California Comeback*, 105.

109. Ben Geier, "What Did We Learn from the Dotcom Stock Bubble of 2000?" *Time*, March 12, 2015; Amar Mann and Tony Nunes, "After the Dot-Com Bubble: Silicon Valley High-Tech Employment and Wages in 2001 and 2008," U.S. Department of Labor, August 2009, www.bls.gov/opub/regional_reports /200908_silicon_valley_high_tech.htm; "From Dot.Com to Dot.Bomb," *The Economist*, June 29, 2000.

110. Tara Clarke, "The Dot-Com Crash of 2000–2002," *Money Morning*, June 12, 2015, moneymorning.com/2015/06/12/the-dot-com-crash-of-2000-2002 /?utm_source=feedburner&utm_medium=feed&utm_campaign=Feed%3A+US MoneyMorning+%28Money+Morning%29.

111. Manuel Pastor and Carol Zabin, "Recession and Reaction: The Impact of the Economic Downturn on California Labor" (University of California Institute for Labor and Employment, 2002), 50, escholarship.org/uc/item/79j2w7q0.

112. Ibid., 41.

113. Jeffrey L. Rabin, "State Spent Its Way into Budget Crisis," *Los Angeles Times*, October 29, 2002.

114. "General Election—Statement of Vote, November 5, 2002," California Secretary of State, www.sos.ca.gov/elections/prior-elections/statewide-election-re sults/general-election-november-5-2002/statement-vote.

115. "Special Statewide Election—Statement of Vote, October 7, 2003," California Secretary of State, www.sos.ca.gov/elections/prior-elections/statewide-elec tion-results/statewide-special-election-october-7-2003/statement-vote.

116. Josh Richman, "What Happened to the Top 10 Finishers in California's 2003 Recall Election?" *Los Angeles Daily News*, October 7, 2013, www.dailynews .com/article/LA/20131007/NEWS/131009592.

117. Dave Downey, "Schwarzenegger Repeals Car Tax," *San Diego Union Tribune*, November 18, 2003.

118. Mark Martin, Carla Marinucci, and Lynda Gledhill, "The Special Election / Californians Say No to Schwarzenegger / State Measures: Governor Reaches out, Doesn't Concede," *SFGate*, November 9, 2005.

119. Paul Harris, "Will California Become America's First Failed State?" *The Guardian*, October 3, 2009, sec. U.S. news.

120. Joel Kotkin, "The Golden State's War on Itself," *City Journal*, Summer 2010, www.city-journal.org/html/golden-state%E2%80%99s-war-itself-13304.html.

4. Setting the Stage

1. David H. Autor, David Dorn, and Gordon H. Hanson, "The China Shock: Learning from Labor-Market Adjustment to Large Changes in Trade," *Annual Review of Economics* 8, no. 1 (2016): 205–40; George J. Borjas, "The Labor Demand Curve Is Downward Sloping: Reexamining the Impact of Immigration on the Labor Market," *Quarterly Journal of Economics* 118, no. 4 (2003): 1335–74.

2. David H. Autor, Lawrence F. Katz, and Melissa S. Kearney, "The Polarization of the U.S. Labor Market," *American Economic Review* 96, no. 2 (May 2006): 189–94; Erik Brynjolfsson and Andrew McAfee, *Race against the Machine: How the Digital Revolution Is Accelerating Innovation, Driving Productivity, and Irreversibly Transforming Employment and the Economy* (Cambridge, MA: Digital Frontier Press, 2011).

3. Raj Chetty, Nathaniel Hendren, Patrick Kline, and Emmanuel Saez, "Where Is the Land of Opportunity? The Geography of Intergenerational Mobility in the United States," BNER Working Paper 19843 (National Bureau of Economic Research, Cambridge, MA, January 2014), www.nber.org/papers/w19843; Enrico Moretti, *The New Geography of Jobs* (Boston: Mariner Books, 2013).

4. Thomas Piketty, *Capital in the Twenty-First Century*, trans. Arthur Goldhammer (Cambridge, MA: Belknap Press, 2014); Joseph E. Stiglitz, *The Price of Inequality: How Today's Divided Society Endangers Our Future* (New York: W.W. Norton, 2012).

5. Data for the figure come from the Labor Market Information Division (LMID) of the Employment Development Department of the state of California; see data.edd.ca.gov. Data are monthly for California from 1990 on; data from earlier years are not necessarily consistent with this series because of shifts in the industrial classification system. High-tech services consist of software publishing, data processing and hosting, computer systems and scientific management,

business support services, and "all other information" (with more than 90 percent of that sector's employment being Internet content provision between 2010 and 2016). Temporary employment is employment services and likely understates the size of that sector.

6. As mentioned in a previous note, California employment data for the 1980s use a slightly different industrial classification system. However, broad aggregates like durables and nondurables are roughly similar; between January 1983 and January 1990, employment in durable manufacturing rose by 7 percent while employment in nondurables rose by 16 percent. The employment data are no longer on the LMID website but were kindly made available to the author by researchers in that department.

7. Manuel Pastor Jr., Peter Dreier, J. Eugene Grigsby III, and Marta López-Garza, *Regions That Work: How Cities and Suburbs Can Grow Together* (Minneapolis: University of Minnesota Press, 2000).

8. Chris Benner, *Work in the New Economy: Flexible Labor Markets in Silicon Valley* (Oxford: Blackwell Publishers, 2002); Chris Benner, "Shock Absorbers in the Flexible Economy," in *A Nation at Work: The Heldrich Guide to the American Workforce*, written and edited by Herbert A. Schaffner and Carl E. Van Horn (New Brunswick, NJ: Rutgers University Press, 2003), 221–26.

9. The most recently available data for 2015 have nearly the same pattern as those for 2008 although there was a moderate improvement for those with less than a high school diploma, perhaps because the state minimum wage ticked up by a dollar per hour in 2014. There was, however, a slight decline for those with some college or an associate's degree. Data are calculated from a multiyear version of the annual March Supplements of the Current Population Survey as assembled by IPUMS; see Sarah Flood, Miriam King, Steven Ruggles, and J. Robert Warren, *Integrated Public Use Microdata Series, Current Population Survey: Version 4.0. [Dataset]* (Minneapolis: University of Minnesota, 2015). The hourly wage is calculated by taking the reported wage income from the previous year and dividing by the reported hours and weeks worked for that year. Following Luke Reidenbach, "California's Sinking Center: How the Economic Recovery Is Leaving CA's Midwage Earners Behind," issue brief (California Budget and Policy Center, Sacramento, June 30, 2015), calbudgetcenter.org/resources/californias-sinking-center-how-the-economic-recovery-is-leaving-californias-midwage-earners-behind, I constrain the sample to those reporting an hourly wage in excess of 0.50 and, in this case, less than $175. (Reidenbach uses a lower threshold, but in high-earning

California, that can cut off more than 2 percent of those reporting positive earnings in some of the later years in the sample.) The educational attainment variable has slightly different meanings before 1992, as it is based on years of school; I tried to match the series as best I could to better show the long-run trends.

10. As with the wage pattern, data are from the Current Population Survey (CPS) assembled by IPUMS; here no age or other restrictions were applied. The top income patterns from the CPS are likely to be lower than gains shown from tax records since the CPS does not collect information on capital gains. As compared to the rest of the United States, California's gains at the top were slightly higher over the same period (by about 2 percent), while its falls at the bottom were much larger than those in the rest of the United States (California had a 14-percentage-point sharper decline for those at the tenth percentile and a 13-percentage-point sharper decline for those at the twentieth percentile than did the rest of the United States).

11. This is also a bit of a nod to the fact that housing costs are more expensive in California than elsewhere in the nation. The figures are calculated by the author from a pooled sample of the census and the American Community Survey; see Steven J. Ruggles, Katie Genadek, Ronald Goeken, Josiah Grover, and Matthew Sobek, *Integrated Public Use Microdata Series: Version 6.0 [Machine-Readable Database]* (Minneapolis: University of Minnesota, 2015). Poverty is defined in this exercise as living in a family below 185 percent of the poverty level and full-time work defined as being more than thirty-five weeks a year and more than forty-five hours a week. This is a fairly strict definition of working poverty and similar to one employed by USC's Program for Environmental and Regional Equity in the National Equity Atlas (nationalequityatlas.org); if I were to include significant part-time work, the figures would be higher. It should be noted that most of the swing from having a poverty level well below that of the rest of the nation to having one well above that of the rest of the nation occurred in the 1990s, a trend that suggests that the emergence of working poverty in the state was more connected to the economic shifts of that decade than to the arrival of immigrant labor per se, most of which occurred in the 1980s.

12. Patricia Cohen, "Aid to Needy Often Excludes the Poorest in America," *New York Times*, February 16, 2015; Robert A. Moffitt, "The Deserving Poor, the Family, and the U.S. Welfare System," *Demography* 52, no. 3 (2015): 729–49.

13. Robert Pollin and Stephanie Luce, *The Living Wage: Building a Fair Economy* (New York: The New Press, 2000).

14. J. Chamberlain and P. Spilberg, "Trends in the Distribution of Income and Personal Income Tax Burden for California Taxpayers," Periodic Publication on Franchise Tax Board Issues & Topics (California Franchise Tax Board, Sacramento, March 8, 1991), www.ftb.ca.gov/Archive/AboutFTB/Tax_Statistics/Trends_Distribution_PIT_Burden_91.pdf.

15. I utilize this 1994–2013 time period from Jim Miller, "The Tax Man Cometh, and California Rich—Getting Richer—Pay Most," *Sacramento Bee*, April 14, 2016, because the data reported also included what happened to the bottom fifth. The statewide change for the top 1 percent between 1989 and 2013, a period comparable to the geographic trends I explore in Figure 4.4, was around 75 percent; these data were kindly calculated by researchers at the California Budget and Policy Center and provided to the author as the statewide figure was not stated explicitly in their report explaining the geographic variation in the fortunes of the top 1 percent; see Luke Reidenbach, Mark Price, Estelle Sommeiller, and Ellis Wazeter, "The Growth of Top Incomes across California," issue brief (California Budget and Policy Center, Sacramento, February 2015), calbudgetcenter.org/wp-content/uploads/The-Growth-of-Top-Incomes-Across-California-0217 2016.pdf.

16. For example, manufacturing employment in the Los Angeles metropolitan area actually fell by 55 percent between 1990 and 2012; see Kevin Smith, "Southern California Manufacturing Industry Struggles in the Wake of Increasing Competition," *San Gabriel Valley Tribune*, February 22, 2014, www.sgvtribune.com/business/20140222/southern-california-manufacturing-industry-struggles-in-the-wake-of-increasing-competition.

17. The chart in Figure 4.4 starts in 1985 because that is the first year for which the Current Population Survey offers such a full range of geographic locations within California. The data have been carefully constructed for consistency; for example, the current L.A. metro includes both Los Angeles and Orange Counties so I use the separate metro data for the first data point and the county data for the second. The San Francisco / Bay Area metro is not entirely consistent—for example, the latter period includes Contra Costa County whereas the early period does not—but this is not likely to bias the overall picture presented. Yet another problem for this data presentation: in 2014, the Current Population Survey shifted its question on income and began to collect more data on cash transfers and retirement payouts. This strategy has tended to shift reported incomes up, a fact that improves accuracy but is challenging for comparisons over time. To better compare

the two time periods, I utilized the fact that 2014 has a split sample (for income reported in the previous year, 2013) in which income is reported for one part of the sample using one method and another part using the other; I applied the ratio of the statewide medians of the old and new methods to adjust down the 2015 data.

18. Reidenbach et al., "Growth of Top Incomes," 3.

19. A four-year moving average helps to "smooth" the data series; I do this to illustrate trends since for some groups, particularly Asian Americans/Pacific Islanders and African Americans, the sample sizes are relatively small and so variations between single years could be due to that rather than underlying economic trends. We start here with 1990 because 1987 is the first year in which the consumer price index separates out income data for Asian Americans/Pacific Islanders; if we look at earlier years, the main takeaway is a slip in Latino household income as immigration increases in the 1980s. As with the previous household income analysis, in later years we adjust for the ways in which the Current Population Survey included more sources of income from the 2014 survey forward.

20. Manuel Pastor, "Not So Golden? Latino Fortunes and Futures in California's Changing Economy," in *The New Latino Studies Reader: A Twenty-First-Century Perspective*, ed. Ramón A. Gutiérrez and Tomás Almaguer (Oakland: University of California Press, 2016), 288–312.

21. The analysis of the immigrant to U.S.-born difference is for a shorter time period because the Current Population Survey did not break out income by immigration experience until 1993.

22. Mark Lilla, "The End of Identity Liberalism," *New York Times*, November 18, 2016; Conor Lynch, "Identity Politics vs. Populist Economics? It's a False Choice—Liberals Need to Look in the Mirror," *Salon*, December 3, 2016.

23. Javier Panzar, "It's Official: Latinos Now Outnumber Whites in California," *Los Angeles Times*, July 8, 2015.

24. Michael Storper, Thomas Kemeny, Naji Makarem, and Taner Osman, *The Rise and Fall of Urban Economies: Lessons from San Francisco and Los Angeles* (Stanford, CA: Stanford University Press, 2015), 3.

25. AnnaLee Saxenian, *Regional Advantage: Culture and Competition in Silicon Valley and Route 128* (Cambridge, MA: Harvard University Press, 1994).

26. Chris Benner and Manuel Pastor, *Equity, Growth, and Community: What the Nation Can Learn from America's Metro Areas* (Oakland: University of California Press, 2015), 163–70; Douglas Henton, John Melville, and Kim Walesh,

"The Rise of the New Civic Revolutionaries: Answering the Call to Stewardship in Our Times," *National Civic Review* 93, no. 1 (2004): 43–49.

27. Richard L. Florida, *The Rise of the Creative Class: And How It's Transforming Work, Leisure, Community and Everyday Life* (New York: Basic Books, 2002).

28. Scott Andres, Jesus Leal Trujillo, and Nico Marchio, "Rise of the Rest? The Bay Area Still Dominates Venture Capital," Brookings Institution, January 28, 2016, www.brookings.edu/blog/the-avenue/2016/01/28/rise-of-the-rest -the-bay-area-still-dominates-venture-capital.

29. Robert Gottlieb, *The Next Los Angeles: The Struggle for a Livable City*, updated with a new preface (Berkeley: University of California Press, 2006), 137–38.

30. Storper and colleagues note the rise of "Silicon Beach" in Los Angeles but essentially call it a drop in the bucket (Storper et al., *Rise and Fall of Urban Economies*, 92–93). However, the story has continued since their account ended and both the Westside and downtown areas are beginning to hum with activity.

31. Edna Bonacich and Jake B. Wilson, *Getting the Goods: Ports, Labor, and the Logistics Revolution* (Ithaca, NY: Cornell University Press, 2008); Storper et al., *Rise and Fall of Urban Economies*, 108–9.

32. Douglas Henton and John Melville, *Grassroots Leaders for a New Economy: How Civic Entrepreneurs Are Building Prosperous Communities* (San Francisco: Jossey-Bass, 1997).

33. Judith E. Innes and Jane Rongerude, "Collaborative Regional Initiatives: Civic Entrepreneurs Work to Fill the Governance Gap," *Insight* (James Irvine Foundation, San Francisco, CA, November 2005), folio.iupui.edu/handle /10244/46; Andrew E.G. Jonas and Stephanie Pincetl, "Rescaling Regions in the State: The New Regionalism in California," *Political Geography* 25, no. 5 (June 2006): 482–505.

34. Innes and Rongerude, "Collaborative Regional Initiatives."

35. Urban Habitat Program, "What If We Shared? Findings from Myron Orfield's San Francisco Bay Area Metropolitics: A Regional Agenda for Community and Stability" (Urban Habitat Program, San Francisco, CA, 1998).

36. Angela Glover Blackwell and Radhika K. Fox, "Regional Equity and Smart Growth: Opportunities for Advancing Social and Economic Justice in America" (PolicyLink, Oakland, CA, 2004).

37. Brett Martin, "America's Next Great City Is Inside L.A.," *GQ*, January 7, 2014.

38. See Manuel Pastor and John Mollenkopf, *Unsettled Americans: Metropolitan Context and Civic Leadership for Immigrant Integration* (Ithaca, NY: Cornell University Press, 2016), 30–31; Brookings Institution, "State of Metropolitan America: On the Front Lines of Demographic Transformation" (Brookings Institution, Washington, D.C., 2010), www.brookings.edu/multi-chapter-report/the -state-of-metropolitan-america. Prime cities are defined following the definitions offered in Pastor and Mollenkopf, *Unsettled Americans*, following a slight modification of the definition offered in Brookings Institution, "State of Metropolitan America"; the effort is to include only the largest cities in a metro given the U.S. Census shift to the use of "principal" cities, many of which are actually generally considered suburbs. Watsonville, Santa Cruz, and San Luis Obispo are "prime" cities for their metros but are dropped from the calculations throughout because 2015 population data were not available for them due to their smaller size. As noted in the text, for the 2010s, I took the growth rates over 2010–15 and assumed that would continue till 2020. The data for 1940 to 2010 are taken from the California Department of Finance, www.dof.ca.gov/Reports/Demographic_Reports/index .html#reports; the 2015 data are taken from the one-year version of the American Community Survey, available from American Factfinder, factfinder.census.gov /faces/nav/jsf/pages/index.xhtml.

39. Another measure of the change is increasing population density in general. To look at this, I took data on tract-level population and area from the National Historical Geographic Information System from 1980 on (the state was not fully tracted before this period). Calculating population density as the ratio of the number of people in a tract to the area of the tract in square miles, 52 percent of California residents in 1980 lived in a tract above the median population density in California. Using that same density benchmark, but applying it to the most recent 2011–15 pooled sample, 60 percent were living in tracts above the 1980 median.

40. See Innes and Rongerude, "Collaborative Regional Initiatives"; Joël Thibert, *Governing Urban Regions through Collaboration: A View from North America*, Global Urban Studies (Farnham, Surrey, UK: Ashgate, 2015). These sorts of dialogues eventually opened the space for the "Six Wins" campaign launched in 2010 by a series of social justice, faith, public health, and environmental organizations to create an alternative Equity, Environment, and Jobs scenario and have it influence the planning decisions of the Association of Bay Area Governments and the Metropolitan Transportation Commission; see Vanessa Carter, Manuel Pastor, and Madeline Wander, "Agenda for Equity: A Framework for Building a

Just Transportation System in Los Angeles County" (Program for Environmental and Regional Equity, University of Southern California, Los Angeles, November 2013), dornsife.usc.edu/pere/transportationequity; Public Advocates, "6 Big Wins for Social Equity Network," 2013, www.publicadvocates.org/6-big-wins-for-so cial-equity-network; Urban Habitat, "6 Wins for Social Equity Network," 2014, urbanhabitat.org/campaigns/6-wins-social-equity-network.

41. Full disclosure: I was part of that team. See Southern California Studies Center and Brookings Institution Center on Urban and Metropolitan Policy, *Sprawl Hits the Wall: Confronting the Realities of Metropolitan Los Angeles* (Los Angeles: University of Southern California; Washington, D.C.: Brookings Institution, March 2001), www.brookings.edu/research/sprawl-hits-the-wall-confront ing-the-realities-of-metropolitan-los-angeles.

42. Benner and Pastor, *Equity, Growth, and Community*, 141–42.

43. Alan Berube and Bruce Katz, "Katrina's Window: Confronting Concentrated Poverty across America" (Brookings Institution, Washington, D.C., 2005).

44. Carl Nolte, "Sprawl, Clutter Define Fresno / Civic Corruption Has Splotched the City's Image," *San Francisco Chronicle*, September 1, 1999; Manuel Pastor, Jennifer Ito, and Anthony Perez, "There's Something Happening Here . . . a Look at The California Endowment's Building Healthy Communities Initiative" (Program for Environmental and Regional Equity, University of Southern California, Los Angeles, February 2014), dornsife.usc.edu/assets/sites/242/docs/TCE -BHC-Narrative-PERE.pdf.

45. Miguel Bustillo, "Gov. Vows Attack on Global Warming," *Los Angeles Times*, June 2, 2005.

46. Ian Carlton, "Histories of Transit-Oriented Development: Perspectives on the Development of the TOD Concept," working paper (Institute for Urban and Regional Development, UC Berkeley, Fall 2007), http:/iurd.berkeley.edu/wp /2009-02.pdf.

47. Full disclosure: I sit on that council.

48. There was a slightly different story when Sacramento's metropolitan planning organization (known as SACOG) sought to promote smart growth through the Blueprint process—a public sector–led planning initiative that facilitated conversations among urban core residents, smaller rural town residents, environmentalists, nonprofit organizations, and developers; see Benner and Pastor, *Equity, Growth, and Community*, 92–94. A major critique of that plan was that it did too little to lift up equity—but into that gap stepped a group of affordable housing

developers and community advocates who pulled together a Coalition on Regional Equity to push SACOG and others to pay more attention to inclusion in its next round of revisions.

49. Christopher Thornberg, Hoyu Chong, and Adam Fowler, *California Green Innovation Index*, 8th ed. (Palo Alto, CA: Next 10, 2016), next10.org/2016 -gii.

50. Joe Mathews and Mark Paul, *California Crackup: How Reform Broke the Golden State and How We Can Fix It* (Berkeley: University of California Press, 2010), 46.

51. John Myers, "Remember When California's Budget Was Always Late? Here's Why Fiscal Gridlock Is a Thing of the Past," *Los Angeles Times*, June 18, 2016.

52. Mathews and Paul, *California Crackup*, 73.

53. Bruce E. Cain and Thad Kousser, *Adapting to Term Limits: Recent Experiences and New Directions* (San Francisco: Public Policy Institute of California, 2004), 38.

54. Mathews and Paul, *California Crackup*, 115.

55. Eric McGhee, "California's Political Reforms: A Brief History" (Public Policy Institute of California, San Francisco, April 2015), www.ppic.org/content /pubs/report/R_415EMR.pdf.

56. Steve Swatt with Susie Swatt, Jeff Raimundo, and Rebecca LaVally, *Game Changers: Twelve Elections That Transformed California* (Berkeley: Heyday and the California Historical Society, 2015), 283–86.

57. Todd Donovan and Joseph R. Snipp, "Support for Legislative Term Limitations in California: Group Representation, Partisanship, and Campaign Information," *Journal of Politics* 56, no. 2 (1994): 492–501.

58. Cain and Kousser, *Adapting to Term Limits*.

59. Mark Baldassare, Dean Bonner, Jennifer Paluch, and Sonja Petek, "Californians and Their Government" (Public Policy Institute of California, San Francisco, October 2008), www.ppic.org/publication/ppic-statewide-survey-cali fornians-and-their-government-october-2008.

60. Maura Dolan and Anthony York, "California High Court Rejects Challenges to Redistricting," *Los Angeles Times*, October 27, 2011.

61. "General Election—Statement of Vote, November 6, 2012," California Secretary of State, www.sos.ca.gov/elections/prior-elections/statewide-election-re sults/general-election-november-6-2012/statement-vote.

62. Los Angeles Chamber of Commerce, "Los Angeles Area Chamber of Commerce—L.A. Area Chamber Joins Gov. Schwarzenegger, Mayor Bloomberg to Urge Californians to Change Sacramento by Supporting Prop. 11," 2008, www.lachamber.com/news/2008/10/15/press-release/l.a.-area-chamber-joins-gov.-schwarzenegger-mayor-bloomberg-to-urge-californians-to-change-sacramento-by-supporting-prop.-11.

63. Benjamin Highton, Robert Huckfeldt, and Isaac Hale, "Some General Consequences of California's Top-Two Primary System," *California Journal of Politics and Policy* 8, no. 2 (2016); John Myers, "Unusual Election Outcomes Are the New Normal with California's Top-Two Primary Rules," *Los Angeles Times*, June 8, 2016.

64. Figure data through 2012 from "Historical Voter Registration and Participation in Statewide General Elections, 1910–2012," California Secretary of State, elections.cdn.sos.ca.gov/sov/2012-general/04-historical-voter-reg-participation.pdf; figure data for 2014 and 2016 from "Voter Registration Statistics," California Secretary of State, http://www.sos.ca.gov/elections/voter-registration/voter-registration-statistics.

65. For example, in the 2016 state senate primary, five of the races resulted in two Democratic candidates whereas none of them led to two Republican candidates; see Lily Mihalik, Anthony Pesce, and Ben Welsh, "California Primary 2016 Election Results and Map," *Los Angeles Times*, 2016.

66. Wyatt Buchanan and Justin Berton, "Prop. 25, Which Eases Budget Process, Passes," *SF Gate*, November 3, 2010.

67. Legislative Analyst's Office, "California's Fiscal Outlook: 2008–09 through 2013–14" (California Legislative Analyst's Office, Sacramento, November 2008), 2.

68. Legislative Analyst's Office, "The Budget Package: 2009–10 California Spending Plan" (California Legislative Analyst's Office, Sacramento, October 2009), 11.

69. Jesse McKinley, "Denied Tax Revenues, Local Officials in California Are Fuming," *New York Times*, July 21, 2009; Jennifer Steinhauer, "California Reaches Budget Deal, with Billions Cut," *New York Times*, July 20, 2009.

5. Making Change

1. Narda Zacchino, *California Comeback: How a "Failed State" Became a Model for the Nation* (New York: Thomas Dunne Books, 2016), 11.

2. California Federation of Teachers, "Talking Taxes 2.0 Case Study: How We Won, A Short History of Proposition 30, and Its Lessons," 2016, cft.org/gover nance/198-article/785-talking-taxes-2-0-case-study.html.

3. Dan Walters, "GOP's Southern California 'Fishhook' Just Not Catching Victories Nowadays," *Los Angeles Daily News*, November 26, 2012, www.daily news.com/article/ZZ/20121126/NEWS/121129574.

4. Laura Pulido, *Black, Brown, Yellow, and Left: Radical Activism in Los Angeles* (Berkeley: University of California Press, 2006).

5. Marshall Ganz, *Why David Sometimes Wins: Leadership, Organization, and Strategy in the California Farm Worker* Movement (New York: Oxford University Press, 2010), 248.

6. Fred Glass, *From Mission to Microchip: A History of the California Labor Movement* (Oakland: University of California Press, 2016), 398.

7. Ibid., 402–3.

8. Bob Baker, "Police Use Force to Block Strike March: Labor: About Two Dozen Demonstrators Are Injured During Protest by Janitors in Century City," *Los Angeles Times*, June 16, 1990, sec. Metro, part B, Metro Desk.

9. Glass, *From Mission to Microchip*; Ruth Milkman, *L.A. Story: Immigrant Workers and the Future of the U.S. Labor Movement* (New York: Russell Sage Foundation, 2006), 158.

10. Glass, *From Mission to Microchip*, 410.

11. On the economic determinants of the unrest, see Manuel Pastor, *Latinos and the Los Angeles Uprising: The Economic Context* (Claremont, CA: Tomas Rivera Center, 1993); Manuel Pastor, "Economic Inequality, Latino Poverty, and the Civil Unrest in Los Angeles," *Economic Development Quarterly* 9, no. 3 (1995): 238–58. On the post-unrest discussions and their roots in earlier interethnic efforts, see Jaime Regalado, "Community Coalition-Building," in *The Los Angeles Riots: Lessons for the Urban Future*, ed. Mark Baldassare (Boulder, CO: Westview Press, 1994). The role of the economy does not mean that there was a neglect of issues of police brutality. In Los Angeles, a 2000 consent decree with the Department of Justice opened the ground for major reform of that city's police department; this partly reflected the pressure of community organizers, followed up with a sophisticated inside-outside game in which advocates like Connie Rice of the Advancement Project were able to work with the police to shift their approach in a more community-oriented direction. See Connie Rice, *Power Concedes Nothing:*

One Woman's Quest for Social Justice in America, from the Courtroom to the Kill Zones (New York: Scribner, 2012).

12. See Manuel Pastor and Michele Prichard, "LA Rising: The 1992 Civil Unrest, the Arc of Social Justice Organizing, and the Lessons for Today's Movement Building" (Program for Environmental and Regional Equity, University of Southern California, Los Angeles, April 2012), dornsife.usc.edu/pere/larising. The unrest also led key immigrant groups, like Central Americans and Koreans, to see their fates as communities of color in America; for example, the Central American Refugee Center soon became the Central American Resource Center, reflecting an understanding of the permanence of the Central American diaspora and the way in which the community's fate was bound up in the future of Los Angeles. The Korean story was particularly complex since many Korean shop owners suffered from the looting, but younger organizers stressed the need for unity and pointed out that one reason the damage was so severe was that the police had withdrawn from protecting those business assets. See Edward J.W. Park, "Friends or Enemies? Generational Politics in the Korean American Community in Los Angeles," *Qualitative Sociology* 22, no. 2 (1999): 161–75; Jong Bum Kwon, "The Koreatown Immigrant Workers Alliance: Spatializing Justice in an Ethnic 'Enclave,'" in *Working for Justice: The L.A. Model of Organizing and Advocacy*, ed. Ruth Milkman, Joshua Bloom, and Victor Narro (Ithaca, NY: Cornell University Press, 2010), 23–48.

13. Anthony Thigpenn, interview with Michele Prichard from Liberty Hill Foundation, July 13, 2011.

14. Pastor and Prichard, "LA Rising."

15. Amy Dean, David B. Reynolds, and Harold Meyerson, *A New New Deal: How Regional Activism Will Reshape the American Labor Movement* (Ithaca, NY: ILR Press, 2009).

16. Harold Meyerson, "No Justice, No Growth: A New Labor-Left Alliance Scrambles L.A.'s Growth Politics—and Creates Middle-Income Jobs in a City Where They're Vanishing," *LA Weekly*, July 23, 1998, www.laweekly.com/1998-07-23/news/no-justice-no-growth.

17. Annette Bernhardt and Sarah Thomason, "What Do We Know about Gig Work in California? An Analysis of Independent Contracting" (UC Berkeley Center for Labor Research and Education, Berkeley, CA, June 2017), laborcenter.berkeley.edu/what-do-we-know-about-gig-work-in-california.

18. Dean, Reynolds, and Meyerson, *A New New Deal.*

19. See Partnership for Working Families, "Policy & Tools: Community Benefits Agreements and Policies in Effect," www.forworkingfamilies.org/page /policy-tools-community-benefits-agreements-and-policies-effect.

20. Larry Frank and Kent Wong, "Dynamic Political Mobilization: The Los Angeles County Federation of Labor," *WorkingUSA* 8, no. 2 (2004): 155–81; George Ramos, "Cedillo Beats Castro in 46th District," *Los Angeles Times*, November 20, 1997.

21. E.J. Dionne, "Lean Labor's Big Win," *Washington Post*, March 14, 2000; Hilda Solis and Immanuel Ness, "Labor Keeps the Democratic Party Accountable," *WorkingUSA* 4, no. 1 (2000): 127–35.

22. Data on the demographic composition of the janitorial industry is based on author analysis of the 1970 census and the 2005 American Community Survey, using the IPUMS SDA system, U.S. Sample, 1850–2015.

23. An account of this is available in Manuel Pastor, "Keeping It Real: Demographic Change, Economic Conflict, and Inter-Ethnic Organizing for Social Justice in Los Angeles," in *Black and Brown in Los Angeles: Beyond Conflict and Coalition*, ed. Laura Pulido and Josh Kun (Berkeley: University of California Press, 2014). A modern-day manifestation of the effort to keep Black workers at the center of labor and economic concerns is the Los Angeles Black Worker Center (LABWC), which, among other things, has looked for opportunities to leverage public sector investments to create apprenticeships and long-term employment for African Americans in construction. See Ryan Reft, "L.A. Black Worker Center Pushes for Inclusion," *KCET*, March 2, 2016, www.kcet.org/shows/departures/los -angeles-black-worker-center-pushes-for-inclusion.

24. The term "intersectionality" was coined by legal scholar Kimberlé Crenshaw, who sought to show how the experiences of systems of oppression, such as racism and sexism, could not be viewed in singular fashion; for example, *both* race and gender shape Black women's experience of labor markets and domestic violence. See Kimberlé Crenshaw, "Demarginalizing the Intersection of Race and Sex: A Black Feminist Critique of Antidiscrimination Doctrine, Feminist Theory and Antiracist Politics," *University of Chicago Legal Forum* (1989): 139–67; Kimberlé Crenshaw, "Mapping the Margins: Intersectionality, Identity Politics, and Violence against Women of Color," *Stanford Law Review* 43, no. 6 (1991): 1241. The concept has since been expanded and the literature is vast and rich; my use of the term here is more akin to the use of Ange-Marie Hancock, who links the

understanding of interlocking systems to the development of a new form of solidarity. See Ange-Marie Hancock, *Solidarity Politics for Millennials: A Guide to Ending the Oppression Olympics* (New York: Palgrave Macmillan, 2011).

25. Ruth Milkman, "Labor and the New Immigrant Rights Movement: Lessons from California," Social Science Research Council, July 28, 2006, sec. Border Battles: The U.S. Immigration Debate, borderbattles.ssrc.org/Milkman/index.html.

26. Glass, *From Mission to Microchip*, 412.

27. As longtime community-labor leader Victor Narro put it, "When I first came to LA, there was no connection at all between immigrant rights and the labor movement; they were like two totally separate movements. But . . . Miguel Contreras as secretary-treasurer of the county fed started reaching out to immigrant workers, both union and nonunion, day laborers, and domestic workers." Victor Narro, interview with Michele Prichard from Liberty Hill Foundation, June 24, 2011.

28. Victor Narro, "¡Sí Se Puede! Immigrant Workers and the Transformation of the Los Angeles Labor and Worker Center Movements," *Los Angeles Public Interest Law Journal* 1 (2009): 65–106.

29. Christopher Trenholm, Embry M. Howell, Dana Hughes, and Sean Orzol, "The Santa Clara County Healthy Kids Program: Impacts on Children's Medical, Dental, and Vision Care" (Mathematica Policy Research, Princeton, NJ, July 2005), 38.

30. State of California, Department of Finance, Race/Ethnic Population with Age and Sex Detail, 1990–1999, Sacramento, CA, revised May 2009, www .dof.ca.gov/Forecasting/Demographics/Estimates/Race-Ethnic/1990-99/index .html.

31. Steve Phillips, interview with the author, December 28, 2015.

32. Nate Cohn, "How the Obama Coalition Crumbled, Leaving an Opening for Trump," *New York Times*, December 23, 2016, sec. The Upshot.

33. Toni Broaddus, "Vote No If You Believe in Marriage: Lessons from the No on Knight / No on Proposition 22 Campaign," *Berkeley Journal of Gender, Law and Justice* 15, no. 1 (2000).

34. Dan Berger, *Captive Nation: Black Prison Organizing in the Civil Rights Era* (Chapel Hill: University of North Carolina Press, 2016).

35. Ruth Wilson Gilmore, *Golden Gulag: Prisons, Surplus, Crisis, and Opposition in Globalizing California* (Berkeley: University of California Press, 2007), 89–92.

36. Ryan Lindsay, "Community Members Celebrate the Ella Baker Center's 20th Anniversary," Oakland North, September 21, 2016, oaklandnorth.net /2016/09/21/community-members-celebrate-the-ella-baker-centers-20th-an niversary-of-providing-advocacy-and-restorative-justice; Zaineb Mohammed, "Looking Back on Our Revolutionary Roots with Van Jones—#Roots2Liberation," Ella Baker Center, September 7, 2016, ellabakercenter.org/blog/2016/09/looking -back-on-our-revolutionary-roots-with-van-jones%E2%80%94roots2liberation.

37. Lindsay, "Community Members Celebrate"; Robin Templeton, "California Youth Take Initiative: Four Hundred Teenagers Converged Outside the Four-Star Hilton Hotel in San Francisco, Then Pushed Inside the Plush Lobby with Whoops and Chants," *The Nation*, February 23, 2000; Karla Solheim and Vince Beiser, "Juvenile Injustice," *LA Weekly*, February 9, 2000, www.laweekly .com/news/juvenile-injustice-2131613.

38. Manuel Pastor and Enrico A. Marcelli, "What's at Stake for the State: Undocumented Californians, Immigration Reform, and Our Future Together" (USC Center for the Study of Immigrant Integration, Los Angeles, CA, May 2013), csii.usc.edu/undocumentedCA.html.

39. Matt A. Barreto, Ricardo Ramirez, and Nathan D. Woods, "Are Naturalized Voters Driving the California Latino Electorate? Measuring the Effect of IRCA Citizens on Latino Voting," *Social Science Quarterly* 86, no. 4 (December 2005): 792–811; Adrian D. Pantoja, Ricardo Ramirez, and Gary M. Segura, "Citizens by Choice, Voters by Necessity: Patterns in Political Mobilization by Naturalized Latinos," *Political Research Quarterly* 54, no. 4 (2001): 729–50.

40. Manuel Pastor, "Migrating toward Justice: How the Immigrant Rights Movement Catalyzed Progressive Politics in Los Angeles," *Dissent*, 2015, www.dis sentmagazine.org/article/how-immigrant-activists-changed-los-angeles.

41. Caitlin Patler, "Alliance-Building and Organizing for Immigrant Rights: The Case of the Coalition for Humane Immigrant Rights of Los Angeles," in *Working for Justice: The L.A. Model of Organizing and Advocacy*, ed. Ruth Milkman, Joshua Bloom, and Victor Narro (Ithaca, NY: Cornell University Press, 2010), 73–74.

42. Michael Fix, ed., *Immigrants and Welfare: The Impact of Welfare Reform on America's Newcomers* (New York: Russell Sage Foundation, 2009).

43. S. Karthick Ramakrishnan and Allan Colbern, "The California Package: Immigrant Integration and the Evolving Nature of State Citizenship," *Policy Matters* 6, no. 3 (Spring 2015): 1–19.

44. Ibid., 2.

45. Cathy Cha, interview with Vanessa Carter from USC PERE, December 9, 2015.

46. Rachel Morello-Frosch, "Environmental Justice and California's 'Riskscape': The Distribution of Air Toxics and Associated Cancer and Non-Cancer Health Risks Among Diverse Communities" (PhD diss., Department of Health Sciences, University of California, Berkeley, 1997); Manuel Pastor, Rachel Morello-Frosch, and James Sadd, "The Air Is Always Cleaner on the Other Side: Race, Space, and Ambient Air Toxics Exposures in California," *Journal of Urban Affairs* 27, no. 2 (2005): 127–48.

47. Roger A. Bruns, *Cesar Chavez and the United Farm Workers Movement* (Santa Barbara, CA: Greenwood, 2011); Matt García, *From the Jaws of Victory: The Triumph and Tragedy of Cesar Chavez and the Farm Worker Movement* (Berkeley: University of California Press, 2012).

48. CalEPA, "CalEPA Environmental Justice Program Update 2014," 2014, www.calepa.ca.gov/publications/reports/2014/ejupdaterpt.pdf; Luke W. Cole and Sheila R. Foster, *From the Ground Up: Environmental Racism and the Rise of the Environmental Justice Movement* (New York: New York University Press, 2001).

49. Since then, a local community group called El Pueblo para el Aire y Agua Limpio / People for Clean Air and Water of Kettleman City, with support from EJ and legal advocates like Greenaction for Health and Environmental Justice, CRPE, California Rural Legal Assistance, and others, has been fighting against proposed expansions of the site. These groups and many others across California's Central Valley have also come together to make up the Central California Environmental Justice Network, which works on issues of environmental racism and economic justice at the regional scale. For more on the origins of CRPE, see Elaine Woo, "Luke Cole Dies at 46; Leading Practitioner of Environmental Law," *Los Angeles Times*, June 11, 2009.

50. Liberty Hill Foundation, "Building a Regional Voice for Environmental Justice" (Liberty Hill Foundation, Los Angeles, September 2004), cjtc.ucsc.edu /docs/ej_finalpub201.pdf.

51. Manuel Pastor, Rachel Morello-Frosch, and James L. Sadd, "LULUs of the Field: Research and Activism for Environmental Justice," in *Collaborations for Social Justice: Professionals, Publics, and Policy Change*, ed. Andrew L. Barlow (Lanham, MD: Rowman & Littlefield, 2007), 81–106.

52. Roger Kim, interview with Jennifer Ito from USC PERE, April 20, 2016.

53. Catherine Lerza, "California's New Environmental Movement," *Shelterforce*, Spring 2012, www.shelterforce.org/article/2766/californias_new_environmental_movement.

54. Mark Baldassare, Dean Bonner, David Kordus, and Lunna Lopes, "PPIC Statewide Survey: Californians and the Environment" (Public Policy Institute of California, San Francisco, July 2015), www.ppic.org/main/publication.asp?i=1159.

55. Space precludes a full telling of this complicated story, including the ways in which EJ voices were not fully considered in the implementation of AB 32 and the fact that their concerns about cap-and-trade potentially exacerbating localized pollution seem to have had some merit. See Lara Cushing, Madeline Wander, Rachel Morello-Frosch, Manuel Pastor, Allen Zhu, and James Sadd, "A Preliminary Environmental Equity Assessment of California's Cap-and-Trade Program" (Program for Environmental and Regional Equity, University of Southern California, Los Angeles, September 2016), dornsife.usc.edu/PERE/enviro-equity-CA-cap-trade; Jonathan London, Alex Karner, Julie Sze, Dana Rowan, Gerardo Gambirazzio, and Deb Niemeier, "Racing Climate Change: Collaboration and Conflict in California's Global Climate Change Policy Arena," *Global Environmental Change* 23, no. 4 (August 2013): 791–99. The point here is simply about the way in which organizers had learned to play the political game in a more sophisticated way.

56. Richard Brenneman, "Chevron Defeated in CEQA Lawsuit; Richmond Refinery Plans in Doubt," *Berkeley Daily Planet*, June 11, 2009, www.berkeleydailyplanet.com/issue/2009-06-11/article/33129?headline=Chevron-Defeated-in-CEQA-Lawsuit-Richmond-Refinery-Plans-in-Doubt—By-Richard-Brenneman-; Ellen Choy and Ana Orozco, "Chevron in Richmond," in "Climate Change: Catalyst or Catastrophe?" *Race, Poverty and the Environment* 16, no. 2 (Fall 2009).

57. The political imperative was reinforced when a 2012 refinery fire caused a startling fifteen thousand people from the neighboring community to seek treatment for breathing problems, chest pain, shortness of breath, sore throats, and headaches, with twenty people admitted as inpatients. See U.S. Chemical Safety Board, "Final Report: Chevron Regulatory Report," January 28, 2015, www.csb.gov/chevron-refinery-fire. On the broader political struggle in Richmond, see Alex Schafran and Lisa M. Feldstein, "Black, Brown, White, and Green: Race, Land Use, and Environmental Politics and a Changing Richmond," in *Social Justice in*

Diverse Suburbs: History, Politics, and Prospects, ed. Christopher Neidt (Philadelphia: Temple University Press, 2013), 162.

58. Richard Gonzales, "Chevron Spends Big, and Loses Big, in a City Council Race," *NPR*, 2014; Mike Parker, "A Social Policy Case Study and Follow-Up on Richmond Progressive Alliance Two Years Later: Richmond Progressive Alliance: Defeating Big Money in Politics," 2016, www.richmondprogressivealliance.net /docs/RPAHist2-mp.pdf.

59. Paige St. John, "Prop. 47 Would Cut Penalties for 1 in 5 Criminals in California," *Los Angeles Times*, October 11, 2014.

60. Lenore Anderson, interview with the author, July 10, 2017.

61. Paige St. John, "Prop. 47 Puts State at Center of a National Push for Sentencing Reform," *Los Angeles Times*, November 1, 2014; St. John, "Prop. 47 Would Cut Penalties."

62. Anderson, interview.

63. As Anderson notes, "Extreme overincarceration was supported by both Democrats and Republicans, and so working our way out of it this is not a partisan issue." Anderson, interview.

64. Michael Ash, James K. Boyce, Grace Chang, Manuel Pastor, Justin Scoggins, and Jennifer Tran, *Justice in the Air: Tracking Toxic Pollution from America's Industries and Companies to Our States, Cities, and Neighborhoods* (Amherst: Political Economy Research Institute [PERI] at the University of Massachusetts, Amherst; Los Angeles: Program for Environmental and Regional Equity [PERE] at the University of Southern California, 2009).

65. There quite literally was a "power analysis" tool, developed by SCOPE in South L.A., that was adopted by many grassroots organizations in California. It was used to chart constituency preferences and constituency strengths and informed multiple campaigns; see Deepak Pateriya and Patricia Castellanos, eds., *Power Tools: A Manual for Organizations Fighting for Justice* (Los Angeles: Strategic Concepts in Organizing and Policy Education, 2003). An extension of that early thinking is a recent national effort called Changing States. See Manuel Pastor, Jennifer Ito, and Madeline Wander, "Changing States: A Framework for Progressive Governance" (Program for Environmental and Regional Equity, University of Southern California, Los Angeles, June 2016), dornsife.usc.edu/pere /changing-states.

66. Walters, "GOP's Southern California 'Fishhook.'"

67. Taj James, interview with the author, July 16, 2017.

68. As one participant put it, "Through the 2000s, the movement was siloed and folks were doing what they could to defend their piece of the pie. It was really challenging to build a broad enough movement to push for larger reforms."

69. Manuel Pastor, Gihan Perera, and Madeline Wander, "Moments, Movements, and Momentum: Engaging Voters, Scaling Power, Making Change" (Program for Environmental and Regional Equity, University of Southern California, Los Angeles, March 2013), dornsife.usc.edu/pere/m3; Lee Winkelman and Jeff Malachowsky, "Integrated Voter Engagement: A Proven Model to Increase Civic Engagement" (Funders' Committee for Civic Participation, New York, 2009), funderscommittee.org/files/FCCP_Integrative_Voter_Engagement_Case_Studies_2009_FINAL_0.pdf.

70. Kurtis Lee, "Meet Indivisible, the Young Progressives Leading the Resistance to President Trump," *Los Angeles Times*, March 26, 2017.

71. Sabrina Smith, interview with Vanessa Carter, Jennifer Ito, and Víctor Sánchez Jr. from USC PERE, February 3, 2016.

72. For more on California Calls and its use of IVE, see Steve Phillips, *Brown Is the New White: How the Demographic Revolution Has Created a New American Majority* (New York: The New Press, 2016), 111–13. Earlier in 2012, voters also passed a reform of term limits: rather than facing limits of fourteen years overall, six in the assembly and eight in the senate, legislators were limited to a total of twelve years, but they could all be served in the same house. This was designed to allow for legislators to develop more experience and be less focused on their next move.

73. Cathy Cha, interview with Vanessa Carter and Víctor Sánchez Jr. from USC PERE, December 9, 2015.

74. Unfortunately, the mayor was found to have engaged in a pattern of sexual harassment and forced to resign from office before he had even completed his first year. This was a setback for local progressives, who had hoped that he would unleash a wave of more progressive policies but were obviously not counting on that being derailed by his personal behavior.

75. Matt Ford, "Californians Vote to Weaken Mass Incarceration," *The Atlantic*, November 5, 2014.

76. Jennifer Calefati, "Gov. Jerry Brown Signs Law Allowing Illegal Immigrants to Drive Legally," *Mercury News*, October 3, 2013, www.mercurynews.com/2013/10/03/gov-jerry-brown-signs-law-allowing-illegal-immigrants-to

-drive-legally; Michael Hiltzik, "California's Huge Blow against Stupidity about Immigrant Driver's Licenses," *Los Angeles Times*, January 2, 2015.

77. Nicolas C. Vaca, *The Presumed Alliance: The Unspoken Conflict between Latinos and Blacks and What It Means for America* (New York: Rayo, 2004).

78. The list of individual donors to the Trump campaign is at www.publicin tegrity.org/2016/12/09/20516/donald-trump-rewarding-million-dollar-donors -plum-postings. Trump himself was the largest donor; if we exclude him, Palmer would be eighth on the list.

79. Milk was assassinated by a fellow San Francisco County supervisor, Dan White, just weeks after helping to defeat the anti-gay initiative.

80. CNN, "Local Exit Polls—Election Center 2008—Elections & Politics from CNN.Com," 2008. Subsequent analysis suggested that the Black vote for Proposition 8 was overstated, but by that time, the political damage in terms of strains between these two strands of the human rights fight had been done.

81. See "Grow the Obama Phenomenon: This Weekend at Camp Courage," Liberty Hill Foundation, www.libertyhill.org/2009/04/16/grow-the-obama-phe nomenon-weekend-camp-courage.

82. Manya Brachear Pashman, "Groups Lose Nearly $300,000 from Catholic Charity over Gay Marriage Issue," *Chicago Tribune*, October 18, 2013; Dan Frosch, "Catholic Fund Heightens Scrutiny of Recipients' Ties," *New York Times*, April 5, 2012; Hunter Schwartz, "Immigrant Groups Lose Catholic Funding Over Gay Marriage Support," *BuzzFeed*, October 19, 2013; Joanne Zuhl, "Voz Loses Catholic Funding over Solidarity with Marriage Equality," *Street Roots News*, July 15, 2014, news.streetroots.org/2014/07/15/voz-loses-catholic-funding-over -solidarity-marriage-equality.

83. Prerna Lal, "How Queer Undocumented Youth Built the Immigrant Rights Movement," *Huffington Post*, March 28, 2013; Jorge Rodrigues-Jimenez, "UndocuQueer Activist Changing the Immigration Debate," May 7, 2015, www .wearemitu.com/mitu-world/undocumented-queer-activist; Veronica Terriquez, "Intersectional Mobilization, Social Movement Spillover, and Queer Youth Leadership in the Immigrant Rights Movement: Table 1," *Social Problems* 62, no. 3 (August 2015): 343–62.

84. Manuel Pastor, "How Immigrant Activists Changed L.A.," *Dissent*, 2015, www.dissentmagazine.org/article/how-immigrant-activists-changed-los-angeles.

85. Pastor and Prichard, "LA Rising"; James Sadd, Rachel Morello-Frosch, Manuel Pastor Jr., Martha Matsuoka, Michele Prichard, and Vanessa Carter, "The

Truth, the Whole Truth, and Nothing but the Ground-Truth: Methods to Advance Environmental Justice and Researcher–Community Partnerships," *Health Education & Behavior* 41, no. 3 (June 2014): 281–90.

86. See Kristina ("Yna") C. Moore, "Less Than One Quarter of California Foundation Grants Explicitly Target Underserved Communities," January 26, 2017, National Committee for Responsive Philanthropy, www.ncrp.org/2017/01/one-quarter-california-foundation-underserved.html; "Appendix H: Which Foundations Invested Most in Social Justice Strategies?" National Committee for Responsive Philanthropy, www.ncrp.org/chapter/appendix-h-foundations-invested-social-justice-strategies.

87. For a description of Engage San Diego including key partners, see the network's website: www.thecentersd.org/programs/engage-san-diego.

88. Cathy Cha and William H. Woodwell Jr., *Bolder Together 2: Building Grassroots Movements for Change* (San Francisco: California Civic Participation Funders, 2016), 22.

89. Ibid., 26.

90. Gabriel Thompson, *America's Social Arsonist: Fred Ross and Grassroots Organizing in the Twentieth Century* (Oakland: University of California Press, 2016), 237–38.

91. Irving Stone, *Men to Match My Mountains: The Opening of the Far West, 1840–1900*, ed. Lewis Gannett (Edison, NJ: Castle Books, 2001).

6. What Happens in California . . .

1. Mark Muro and Sifan Liu, "Another Clinton-Trump Divide: High-Output America vs Low-Output America," Brookings Institution, November 29, 2016, www.brookings.edu/blog/the-avenue/2016/11/29/another-clinton-trump-divide-high-output-america-vs-low-output-america.

2. The celebrated growth in Texas has come at the cost of the other forty-nine states: one report by University of California Center for Labor Research and Education quantified the cost of poverty to the federal government. Texas was consistently at the top of states with the highest share of federal anti-poverty funds going to working families. See Ken Jacobs, Ian Perry, and Jenifer MacGillvary, "The High Public Cost of Low Wages: Poverty-Level Wages Cost U.S. Taxpayers $152.8 Billion Each Year in Public Support for Working Families," research brief, UC Berkeley Center for Labor Research and Education, Berkeley, CA, April 2015), laborcenter.berkeley.edu/pdf/2015/the-high-public-cost-of-low-wages.pdf; Harold

Meyerson, "A Flawed 'Texas Miracle,'" *Washington Post*, June 10, 2015, sec. Op-Ed. The tension between the California and Texas models—and the ways in which Texas has moved dangerously to the right—are reviewed in Lawrence Wright, "America's Future Is Texas," *The New Yorker*, July 10, 2017.

3. See Adam Nagourney, "California Strikes a Bold Pose as Vanguard of the Resistance," *New York Times*, January 18, 2017. One sign that California is serious: when the state's attorney general, Kamala Harris, was elected to the Senate in the same year as the Trump wave, the governor's chosen replacement was Xavier Becerra, a seasoned veteran of the Congress well versed in the sort of political and legal warfare that the position was soon to require.

4. Lisa Friedman, "Jerry Brown Announces a Climate Summit Meeting in California," *New York Times*, July 6, 2017, sec. Climate.

5. While one nuanced measure of sprawl (which looks at the balance of high-density and low-density neighborhoods in any given metro area) rose nationwide between 1970 and 2010, it has been on the decline in coastal California, including the main metros of San Francisco, San Jose, Los Angeles, and San Diego. See Russell Lopez, "Urban Sprawl in the United States: 1970–2010," *Cities and the Environment (CATE)* 7, no. 1 (2014), digitalcommons.lmu.edu/cate/vol7/iss1/7.

6. See Rent Jungle, "Average Rent in San Francisco, San Francisco Rent Trends and Rental Comps," January 2017, www.rentjungle.com/average-rent-in-san-francisco-rent-trends. This builds on a longer trend in which inflation-adjusted rents on the same-size units in that most pleasant of cities by the bay—pleasant enough and celebrated enough to simply be called "*the* city" in Northern California—more than doubled between 1990 and 2011, the start of the most recent run-up. See Chris McCann, "1979 to 2015—Average Rent in San Francisco," *Medium*, August 17, 2015, medium.com/@mccannatron/1979-to-2015-average-rent-in-san-francisco-33aaea22de0e#.hqlv9cnff.

7. Thomas Fuller, "San Francisco Asks: Where Have All the Children Gone?" *New York Times*, January 21, 2017.

8. For example, using the same definition of "prime" cities as deployed in the consideration of urban and suburban growth in Chapter 4, the share of renter households paying more than 40 percent of their income in rent barely budged between 2005 and 2015, while the share in the rest of the state actually rose by 2 percentage points. Calculated by the author using data from the American Community Survey for each of the two years in question.

9. California Department of Housing and Community Development, "California's Housing Future: Challenges and Opportunities, Public Draft," January 2017, 5–6, www.hcd.ca.gov/policy-research/plans-reports/docs/California's-Housing-Future-Full-Public-Draft.pdf.

10. James Pappas, "Confronting California's Rent and Poverty Crisis: A Call for State Reinvestment in Affordable Homes" (California Housing Partnership Corporation, April 2016), chpc.net/wp-content/uploads/2016/04/State-Housing-Need-2016.pdf.

11. Liam Dillon, "Gov. Brown Just Signed 15 Housing Bills. Here's How They're Supposed to Help the Affordability Crisis," *Los Angeles Times*, September 29, 2017.

12. Chris Benner, "Building a Real Sharing Economy: Socializing the Wealth Produced by Social Knowledge," in *Blueprint for Belonging: A Strategic Narrative for Our Future* (Berkeley, CA: Haas Institute for a Fair and Inclusive Society, 2016), 119.

13. The UBI concept has found support not just among those enamored of a European-style social safety net but also among Silicon Valley elites, including Netscape co-founder Marc Andreessen and fellow venture capitalist Sam Altman. See Jathan Sadowski, "Why Silicon Valley Is Embracing Universal Basic Income," *The Guardian*, June 22, 2016, sec. Technology. UBI appeals to their libertarian instincts—rather than the government mandating certain services or goods, people can purchase what they need—but the appeal to business leaders is partly because they realize that so many of their market ambitions will be under threat if more and more people are stranded with neither income nor work.

14. In 2016, the governor signed legislation that set up more ambitious targets for reducing greenhouse gas emissions. Among the allies making it happen were a set of clean tech businesses that did their own lobbying, often going up against traditional business groups and the oil industry. See Chris Megerian, "Clean Tech Leaders Try to Put a Business-Friendly Spin on Climate Change Policies," *Los Angeles Times*, August 19, 2016. Another fruitful avenue for collaboration: the development of advanced manufacturing enterprises that can generate well-paying and secure employment. One fascinating effort has been Jobs to Move America, initially founded by LAANE, which seeks to leverage public spending on mass transit to ensure that the manufacture of rail cars, electric buses, and related parts happens in the same metro regions where they will operate.

15. john a. powell, "Post-Racialism or Targeted Universalism," *Denver University Law Review* 86 (2009–8): 785.

16. A key forerunner to LCFF was the Williams case, filed in 2000 and settled in 2004, which alleged that California's educational system was providing inadequate education—insufficient textbooks, overcrowded classrooms, and less-qualified teachers—to low-income, immigrant, and minority children. The legal action was accompanied by organizing efforts, including by affected youths themselves, that have continued to help drive education reform in California. See Jeannie Oakes and John Rogers, *Learning Power: Organizing for Education and Justice* (New York: Teachers College Press, 2006); Veronica Terriquez, John Rogers, and May Lin, "Youth Voice in School Finance: The Building Healthy Communities Initiative and Young People's Involvement in Shaping Local Control Accountability Plans" (USC Program for Environmental and Regional Equity and UCLA Institute for Democracy, Education, and Access [IDEA], Los Angeles, CA, July 2016), idea.gseis.ucla.edu/projects/youth-voice-in-school-finance.

17. See Laura Hill and Iwonze Ugo, "Implementing California's School Funding Formula: Will High-Need Students Benefit?" (Public Policy Institute of California, San Francisco, March 2015), www.ppic.org/main/publication_quick .asp?i=1127. Californians Together, a statewide coalition focused on the needs of English learners, has offered initial reviews of LCFF and accountability plans: "Report on 2nd Year of LCAPs Calls for the State, Districts and County Offices of Education to Make the Remaining Years of LCFF about Closing Gaps and Raising Levels of Language and Academic Growth," Californians Together, April 6, 2016, www.californianstogether.org/study-of-year-2-local-control-accountability-plans -lcaps-reveals-a-weak-response-to-the-needs-of-english-learners-save-and-exitexit -without-saving. Their bottom line is that Local Control Accountability Plans fall short in terms of goals, programs, and services specific to accelerating the language and academic growth of English learners.

18. See Jonathan Kaplan, "California's Support for K–12 Education Ranks Low by Almost Any Measure," fact sheet (California Budget and Policy Center, Sacramento, November 2015), calbudgetcenter.org/wp-content/uploads/Californias-Support-for-K12-Education-Ranks-Low-by-Almost-Any-Measure_FactSheet _11.17.2015.pdf; Larry N. Gerston and Terry Christensen, *California Politics and Government: A Practical Approach*, 13th ed. (Boston: Cengage Learning, 2016), 114.

19. Mac Taylor, "Common Claims about Proposition 13" (Legislative Analyst's Office, Sacramento, CA, September 2016), 10, lao.ca.gov/Publications/Report/3497.

20. Jason Felch and Jack Dolan, "Corporations Get Big Edge in Prop. 13 Quirk," *Los Angeles Times*, May 5, 2013.

21. See Jennifer Ito, Justin Scoggins, and Manuel Pastor, "Getting Real about Reform" (Program for Environmental and Regional Equity, University of Southern California, Los Angeles, May 2015), dornsife.usc.edu/assets/sites/242/docs/Commercial_Property_Tax_Brief_PERE_web_updated2.pdf. For reference, the total proposed 2017–18 expenditure for the California state budget is $248.5 billion. California Budget and Policy Center, "California Budget Perspective, 2017–18," February 2017, calbudgetcenter.org/wp-content/uploads/Chartbook_California_Budget_Perspective_02.2017.pdf.

22. An early equity assessment of the cap-and-trade program showed facilities that emit large amounts of GHG and PM_{10} (particulate matter 10 micrometers or less in diameter) are located in neighborhoods with higher proportions of residents of color and those living in poverty. Moreover, the neighborhoods near top-emitting facilities that increased emissions were poorer and had a higher share of people of color than neighborhoods near top-emitting facilities that decreased their emissions. See Lara Cushing, Madeline Wander, Rachel Morello-Frosch, Manuel Pastor, Allen Zhu, and James Sadd, "A Preliminary Environmental Equity Assessment of California's Cap-and-Trade Program" (Program for Environmental and Regional Equity, University of Southern California, Los Angeles, September 2016), dornsife.usc.edu/PERE/enviro-equity-CA-cap-trade. The California Cap-and-Trade Program, which began in 2012, was extended in July 2017 through 2030 under AB 398. The legislation met mixed reactions from many EJ advocates (including members of the California Environmental Justice Alliance), who criticized it for being lax with regulations for polluters and not prioritizing direct emissions reductions in EJ communities. While the specific legislation fell short of EJ priorities, the impact of the advocates on many aspects of climate policy, including new restrictions on offsets, has been significant. See California Environmental Justice Alliance, "Justice Deferred: A Break Down of California's Cap & Trade Bill from the Environmental Justice Perspective," caleja.org/2017/07/justice-deferred-a-breakdown-of-californias-cap-trade-bill-from-the-environmental-justice-perspective.

23. Jazmine Ulloa, "California Becomes 'Sanctuary State' in Rebuke of Trump Immigration Policy," *Los Angeles Times*, October 5, 2017.

24. Kim Bobo, *Wage Theft in America: Why Millions of Working Americans Are Not Getting Paid—and What We Can Do About It* (New York: The New Press, 2011).

25. This is exactly the sort of intersectional framework being lifted up by groups like Silicon Valley Rising and Bay Rising, both multisectoral organizing efforts that bring together a wide range of labor, community, and faith groups to encourage civic engagement and work for a more inclusive economy in the red-hot—and disequalizing—markets of the Bay Area.

26. See Manuel Pastor and John Mollenkopf, "The Cases in Context: Data and Destinies in Seven Metropolitan Areas," in *Unsettled Americans: Metropolitan Context and Civic Leadership for Immigrant Integration*, ed. John Mollenkopf and Manuel Pastor (Ithaca, NY: Cornell University Press, 2016), 252. The Utah Compact included five principles including respect for local law enforcement decisions, the value of keeping families together, the need to welcome strangers, and the way in which immigration is consistent with free market economics. The head of one statewide Latino group noted that its adoption helped to turn the tide, remarking in 2015 that "in the last three sessions, I haven't had to go up to the Capitol at all because there haven't been any anti-immigration bills." See Lee Davidson, "How the Path of the Utah Immigration Debate Turned a Corner," *Salt Lake Tribune*, March 18, 2015.

27. The California generation gap uses the same data sources as used in Figure 1.3 in Chapter 1. To calculate the U.S. racial generation gap, I utilized the March Supplement of the Current Population Survey; because the samples are not as large as those in, say, the American Community Survey, I used a three-year moving average for the period 1990–2014. From 2015 on, I used census population projections by race and age, available at www.census.gov/population/projections/data/national/2014/downloadablefiles.html.

28. Jacob S. Hacker and Paul Pierson, *Winner-Take-All Politics: How Washington Made the Rich Richer—and Turned Its Back on the Middle Class* (New York: Simon and Schuster, 2011), 117.

29. Lyrics from "My Back Pages" by Bob Dylan.

30. Calculated from the 2016 National House Popular Vote Tracker available from the Cook Political Report (cookpolitical.com). Gerrymandering has become such a problem that it is a priority of former attorney general Eric Holder and president Barack Obama as they step away from their appointed and elected positions.

31. Brennan Center for Justice, "New Voting Restrictions in Place for 2016 Presidential Election," Brennan Center for Justice at New York University School of Law, September 12, 2016, www.brennancenter.org/voting-restrictions-first-time-2016.

32. Katie Sanders, "Have Democrats Lost 900 Seats in State Legislatures since Obama Has Been President?" PunditFact, 2015, www.politifact.com/punditfact/statements/2015/jan/25/cokie-roberts/have-democrats-lost-900-seats-state-legislatures-o.

33. Manuel Pastor, Jennifer Ito, and Madeline Wander, "Changing States: A Framework for Progressive Governance" (Program for Environmental and Regional Equity, University of Southern California, Los Angeles, June 2016), dornsife.usc.edu/pere/changing-states.

34. For example, see Chris Benner and Manuel Pastor, *Equity, Growth, and Community: What the Nation Can Learn from America's Metro Areas* (Oakland: University of California Press, 2015); Chris Benner and Manuel Pastor, "Embracing the Challenge: The Diversity, Equity, and Inclusion Imperative for Chambers of Commerce," *Chamber Executive*, Winter 2017.

35. David Streitfeld, "Tech Opposition to Trump Propelled by Employees, Not Executives," *New York Times*, February 6, 2017.

36. One effort to try to come up with an alternative statewide vision was the Fair Shake Commission on Inequality in California, created by businessman, environmentalist, and progressive Democrat Tom Steyer and his organization, NextGen California, in collaboration with the Center for American Progress and others. For its report, see fairshakeca.org.

37. Mark Lilla, "The End of Identity Liberalism," *New York Times*, November 18, 2016.

38. Alicia Garza, "Our Cynicism Will Not Build a Movement. Collaboration Will," *Mic*, January 26, 2017, mic.com/articles/166720/blm-co-founder-protesting-isnt-about-who-can-be-the-most-radical-its-about-winning.

39. Pastor, Ito, and Wander, "Changing States."

40. Taj James, interview with the author, July 16, 2017.

41. Javier C. Hernández and Adam Nagourney, "As Trump Steps Back, Jerry Brown Talks Climate Change in China," *New York Times*, June 6, 2017, sec. Asia Pacific.

INDEX

Note: Italic page numbers refer to figures.